Learn
Rust Programming

*Safe Code, Supports Low Level and Embedded
Systems Programming with a Strong Ecosystem*

Claus Matzinger

www.bpbonline.com

Group Product Manager: Marianne Conor
Publishing Product Manager: Eva Brawn
Senior Editor: Connell
Content Development Editor: Melissa Monroe
Technical Editor: Anne Stokes
Copy Editor: Joe Austin
Language Support Editor: Justin Baldwin
Project Coordinator: Tyler Horan
Proofreader: Khloe Styles
Indexer: V. Krishnamurthy
Production Designer: Malcolm D'Souza
Marketing Coordinator: Kristen Kramer

First published: August 2022

Published by BPB Online
WeWork, 119 Marylebone Road
London NW1 5PU

UK | UAE | INDIA | SINGAPORE

ISBN 978-93-55511-546

www.bpbonline.com

Dedicated to

My wife and my daughter.

About the Author

Claus Matzinger: In the last 10 years as a Software Engineer I have worked with many programming languages, but Rust stood out from the beginning. With its unique approaches to some of the most challenging issues when developing large-scale applications.

After getting to know the language in its infancy, I spoke at and hosted several Rust Meetups (in Munich, Berlin, Linz, ...), joined the official Community team, connected Microsoft's security engineers with the Rust core team, and wrote several books and courses on Rust.

Today, I am a senior engineer working on a major Rust code base in FinTech, covering everything from no_std code, to different CPU architectures, and soon WebAssembly. In the past, I have created games for improving mental health, helped build a distributed SQL database at a startup, maintained a Smalltalk application, and worked on customer's business critical enterprise systems at Microsoft.

As a quickly evolving language that is deeply technical in nature, Rust has a daunting learning curve, that I love to help new and experienced programmers overcome. For that, I also blog regularly about practical things to do with Rust at **https://blog.x5ff.xyz**.

Acknowledgement

Creating something as fundamental as a programming language is a major undertaking by many people and it would require another book to honor each contribution. However I'd like to thank all contributors to the Rust programming language for creating such a great language - it has become more than a tool for me and many others. With this book I want to pay it forward by instilling this passion in others.

In these early days of Rust, it's not common to work with my favorite programming language on a daily basis. Thanks to the team at DEX Labs I get to tinker and work in an exciting environment that takes Rust from the lowest levels of CPUs to WebAssembly - I truly enjoy every minute of that.

Preface

Rust is still a young language and throughout its "formative years" it has passed through many stages. Before Rust 1.0 was released, the language had already tried different paradigms for memory management and even types. However, leaving those initial ideas behind made the language what it is today: a really fast and safe language with a quirky memory management technique and an opinionated compiler.

While it comes with a steep learning curve, the ideas have spread and other programming languages (for example Apple's Swift) picked some parts up quickly, resulting in an overall improvement for programmers and software engineers. I am convinced that by learning Rust, you learn more about programming as well and become better for it.

In many ways, the system of borrowing and ownership of memory keeps the questions "Where does this come from?" and "Where does this go?" always at the forefront of your programming mind. Even while writing JavaScript, a much more permissible language, you will become aware of where your objects are and where they should be, as well as whether or not you should create a copy. Personally, I think that alone is worth learning more Rust.

To start your journey, this book provides 16 chapters in increasing difficulty. Starting with the basics, you will quickly advance towards fundamentals of the standard library, memory management, and end with highly advanced features such as Rust's unsafe features. Each chapter comes with a challenge in the end so you can experiment with what you learned.

After completing this book, you will have built your own LinkedList data structure and several other small programs from along the way. Before we start off, let's look at what each chapter contains:

Chapter 1 provides you with the basics of the Rust programming language. To set the stage appropriately, you'll learn about byte code, compilers and compilation, simple types, and variables.

Chapter 2 goes a little deeper into program flow and controlling it. This is where you see decision making with if, as well as while and for loops introduced.

Afterwards, reading short code examples in Rust won't pose much of a challenge for you any longer.

Chapter 3 covers the heart of how Rust stores data in memory. This chapter is all about creating data structures (structs), modules, and functions. For your programming journey, that means you can now store data and attach behavior (do stuff with it).

Chapter 4 ventures further into the depths of Rust's type system by exploring enumerations (enums), traits, and pattern matching. These constructs allow for more efficient decision making based on type variants and share behavior between types using traits.

Chapter 5 gets to the heart of Rust's memory management system: borrowing and ownership. The chapter details sharing data structures between functions, how to add mutability, and introduces the notion of scopes. This chapter concludes the fundamentals of the programming language, so afterwards you can solve basic and intermediate problems using Rust.

Chapter 6 introduces the Rust standard library collections, which will play an important role in any Rust programming career. This includes the Vector, HashMap, HashSet, their BTree counterparts, and the Iterator trait which allows to traverse these collections.

Chapter 7 covers working with input and output of various sorts, utilizing the Read and Write traits of the Rust standard library, as well as interacting with the outside world with command line arguments, Files and environment variables. Afterwards your programs can easily interact with the environment.

Chapter 8 gets into how to add third party dependencies from the crates.io package repository. Additionally, the chapter covers custom build processes and custom cargo commands.

Chapter 9 provides details on testing your Rust code, including unit tests, integration tests, and benchmarking. Once you know this, there is no excuse not to test your code!

Chapter 10 adds documentation to your Rust repository. This means that you can generate websites from your code comments and even test the examples. After testing, this is Rust's way of making documenting code convenient.

Chapter 11 starts the advanced part of the book by introducing macros. These code constructs allow to generate code and insert it right before the final steps of compilation. Next to using macros, you'll learn how to create the different kinds supported in Rust as well.

Chapter 12 dives deep into heap memory allocation and the types Rust provides for managing it. Together with borrowing and ownership concepts, this chapter explores reference counters, boxes, memory layouts, and the interior mutability pattern.

Chapter 13 is all about concurrency using threads, locks, and synchronization. Thanks to borrowing and ownership principles, this is significantly less error-prone than in other languages.

Chapter 14 expands on concurrency by explaining async, short for asynchronous programming. The chapter includes using the provided syntax elements async and await and how to use Futures to schedule tasks on an I/O loop.

Chapter 15 introduces the topic of generics. Generics are a way to provide implementations on functions without relying on specific types, instead using traits. This is complemented by a deeper dive on lifetimes, since those may differ between the generic types.

Chapter 16 concludes the book with an overview over unsafe and the foreign function interface (FFI). These language constructs allow you to integrate with other programs, the operating system, or other programming languages by linking libraries to Rust or creating linkable libraries from Rust. You'll also learn about the dark arts of writing unsafe code that the compiler is less strict about…

Coloured Images

Please follow the link to download the
Coloured Images of the book:

https://rebrand.ly/8r7c0wi

We have code bundles from our rich catalogue of books and videos available at **https://github.com/bpbpublications**. Check them out!

Errata

We take immense pride in our work at BPB Publications and follow best practices to ensure the accuracy of our content to provide with an indulging reading experience to our subscribers. Our readers are our mirrors, and we use their inputs to reflect and improve upon human errors, if any, that may have occurred during the publishing processes involved. To let us maintain the quality and help us reach out to any readers who might be having difficulties due to any unforeseen errors, please write to us at :

errata@bpbonline.com

Your support, suggestions and feedbacks are highly appreciated by the BPB Publications' Family.

Did you know that BPB offers eBook versions of every book published, with PDF and ePub files available? You can upgrade to the eBook version at www.bpbonline.com and as a print book customer, you are entitled to a discount on the eBook copy. Get in touch with us at :

business@bpbonline.com for more details.

At **www.bpbonline.com**, you can also read a collection of free technical articles, sign up for a range of free newsletters, and receive exclusive discounts and offers on BPB books and eBooks.

Piracy

If you come across any illegal copies of our works in any form on the internet, we would be grateful if you would provide us with the location address or website name. Please contact us at **business@bpbonline.com** with a link to the material.

If you are interested in becoming an author

If there is a topic that you have expertise in, and you are interested in either writing or contributing to a book, please visit **www.bpbonline.com**. We have worked with thousands of developers and tech professionals, just like you, to help them share their insights with the global tech community. You can make a general application, apply for a specific hot topic that we are recruiting an author for, or submit your own idea.

Reviews

Please leave a review. Once you have read and used this book, why not leave a review on the site that you purchased it from? Potential readers can then see and use your unbiased opinion to make purchase decisions. We at BPB can understand what you think about our products, and our authors can see your feedback on their book. Thank you!

For more information about BPB, please visit **www.bpbonline.com**.

Table of Contents

1. Building the Basics..1
   Structure..2
   Objectives...2
   Compiling Rust code...2
     What is compilation..2
     Memory management and dynamic versus static typing..............4
     Executing the code..5
   Programming in Rust...6
     Managing memory in Rust...6
     Writing Rust code..7
     Working with variable types..8
     Being literal..11
   Conclusion..11
   Challenge..12

2. Controlling the Program Flow..13
   Structure..13
   Objectives...14
   Making decisions with if...14
     Using conditions..14
     What if condition fails...16
     Using If/Else expressions...17
   Repetitions and repetitions with loop...19
     Continuing and breaking with values..19
     Enumerating with for..21
   Conclusion..24
   Challenge..26

3. Organizing for Reuse...27

    Structure...28

    Objectives..28

    Encapsulating behavior with functions.................................28

        Parameterizing functions 30

    Encapsulating data with structs 30

        Getting a deeper look..34

    Exporting and importing with modules 37

        Aliasing types and exporting imports 41

    Conclusion...43

    Challenge 44

4. Interfacing with Code and Errors..45

    Structure...46

    Objectives..46

    Using traits for fun and pleasure..46

        Implementing traits 48

        Using traits in functions 49

    Creating variations with enums 52

        Handling errors with enums 54

        Matching patterns to extract data 56

    Conclusion...59

    Challenge 61

    Further reading 62

5. Borrowing Ownership with Scopes..63

    Structure...63

    Objectives..64

    Taking ownership of memory..64

        Working with both kinds of memory 66

Borrowing memory *68*

Working in scopes *69*

Controlling mutability *72*

Introducing clones 75

Conclusion 77

Challenge 77

6. Working with Collections **81**

Structure 81

Objectives 82

Using sequential collections: slices and Vec<T> 82

Operating the Vec<T> *83*

Borrowing the Vec<T>: slices *85*

Deriving keys from values with sets and maps 87

Sorting keys: trees and hashes *88*

Using sets and maps *90*

Iterating over any collection... 92

Chaining iterators together *93*

Collecting the results *94*

Conclusion 95

Challenge 96

Further reading 99

7. Reading Input and Writing Output **101**

Structure 101

Objectives 102

Reading from and writing to I/O streams 102

Console, networking, and file systems *103*

Using formatted print *108*

Configuration options for programs...................................... 111

Using command-line arguments *111*

Using environment variables *112*

Conclusion 113

Challenge 113

8. Using Crates with Cargo **115**

Structure 115

Objectives 116

Creating crates with cargo 116

Writing the build manifest *119*

Adding third-party crates *121*

Going deeper into cargo 125

Customizing the build *126*

Using workspaces for large projects *127*

Conclusion 128

Challenge 129

Further reading 129

9. Testing What you Build **131**

Structure 131

Objectives 132

Testing Rust code 132

Testing units *133*

Testing integration *136*

Benchmarking Rust code 137

Conclusion 140

Challenge 141

10. Documenting What You Build **145**

Structure 145

Objectives 146

Documenting Rust code 146

    Using sections, links, and others 147

    Writing documentation tests 149

Publishing your documentation 152

Conclusion 153

Challenge 154

11. Generating Code with Macros **157**

Structure 157

Objectives 158

Declarative macros 158

    Using arguments with names and designators 159

    Adding complexity to arguments 160

    Exporting macros 162

Procedural macros 163

    Writing function-like macros 164

    Deriving stuff with macros 165

    Using attributes to extend code 167

Conclusion 169

Challenge 170

12. Using Heap Memory Effectively **173**

Structure 173

Objectives 174

Putting things in boxes 174

    Boxing data 175

    Boxing behavior 176

Counting references 177

    Counting references with multi-threading 179

Creating mutability as required 181

Using locks for global mutability... *183*

Conclusion 185

Challenge 186

Further reading 187

13. Running Concurrent Code **189**

Structure.. 190

Objectives.. 190

Threading with Rust.. 190

Using Send and Sync 193

Using alternatives... *195*

Bridging threads with channels.. 196

Conclusion 198

Challenge 199

14. Writing Async Code **201**

Structure.. 201

Objectives.. 202

Scheduling tasks in a loop 202

Polling futures *203*

Using futures-rs 205

Using async-std... 206

Working asynchronously *208*

Running blocking code *212*

Conclusion 214

Challenge 215

15. Working with Generics **217**

Structure.. 217

Objectives.. 218

Using Generics 218

Parameterizing functions 219

Parameterizing structs, traits, and enums 221

Going deeper 223

Using const Generics 224

Working with lifetimes 225

Conclusion 228

Challenge 228

16. Calling Unsafe and Foreign Functions 231

Structure 231

Objectives 232

Working with unsafe 232

Sharing native Rust code 235

Importing a shared library 237

Binding Rust code 237

Exporting as shared library 240

Conclusion 242

Further reading 243

Index **245-249**

CHAPTER 1
Building the Basics

Learning Rust is a daunting task for many. Although there is a wealth of free information available, this information is not always well structured and can be overwhelming with details and other sidetracks that are not always important. What is important, however, is to enjoy writing code and having fun with the outcome—and that is what the Rust programming language can provide.

Before we can dive into full-on application building, component architecture, or even just writing sorting algorithms, we should discuss the basics. In this chapter, we are exploring the foundations that make Rust what it is a compiled, statically typed systems programming language. If none of those words means anything to you, then this chapter is for you. Rust is among the most complex of languages with a steep learning curve and a compiler that can feel infuriatingly assumptive—this is normal and to be expected. These experiences become much more reasonable once you understand the basics of the programming language and what it is all about: knowing types and when to dispose of their instances.

If this chapter is your first adventure into programming, this chapter provides a few aspects of computer science that go much deeper than a single chapter of a book ever could. We encourage you to find more information on any of the topics that interest you here or simply play with the code samples and try out your own ideas. Think of this as the first step in your Rust journey (or programming as a whole), and as with any craft, and you will get better if you try things out—no matter how crazy, obvious, or ludicrous the thought. You are learning, after all.

Before we discuss the intricate details of the borrow checker, we should start at the beginning: what is computer code?

Structure

In this chapter, we will be covering the following topics:

- Compiling Rust code
    - What is compilation
    - Memory management and dynamic versus static typing
    - Executing the code

- Programming in Rust
    - Managing memory in Rust
    - Writing rust code
    - Working with variable types
        - Being literal

Objectives

After reading this chapter, you will be able to know some background about the Rust project and language, you will be able to identify different types of byte code and compilation, and you will be able to declare, define, and use Rust variables.

Compiling Rust code

Rust is a compiled, statically typed programming language. This means that the source code is not interpreted (like JavaScript) or dynamically typed (also JavaScript). In practice, this means that:

- You will have to tell the compiler what type a code construct is going to be.
- Code is "compiled" into a binary format that the operating system can execute natively.

Let us examine these two points closer.

What is compilation

Interpreting text is hard work for a computer because a word is essentially a list of characters that have to be compared as such. Humans appreciate that kind of clarity, but a computer works a lot better with bytes (that is, numbers). Consequently, a processing step is required to create a set of bytes from the text that is a programming language.

Note: There are programming languages that work without a visible intermediary "byte-code step"; however, the in-memory representation of a program is still based on tokens, not the actual text.

After this first compilation step, there are two decisions to be made (from a high level):

1. Go over the bytes, build an execution order, and run everything right away.

2. Go over the bytes, build a universal execution order, and save them to disk.

The former is typical for interpreted languages, such as Python, JavaScript, Lua, Perl, PHP, and so on. Those use something like an interpreter or virtual machine to execute the provided code, not the operating system directly. The major drawback to this is performance (because there are many layers involved), but they typically work well across CPU platforms or operating systems. The underlying virtual machine or interpreter can also dynamically manage memory, so these languages often skip static typing altogether. A purist might also not speak of compilation in this case but rather translation (do not be a purist).

The latter difference is the universality—that is, it works on the operating system natively (C, C++, Haskell, and so on). This has implications for the binary layout of the file (so that the operating system knows where to start execution—more on that later) and how to acquire memory. Primarily, if instructions are saved to disk, the sizes of individual parts become important. Think of a recipe where it says salt to taste versus 10 grams of salt—in some way, that is why you often have to provide the type for compiled languages (versus interpreted ones as previously). In the file, there will be an instruction saying, allocate 10 bytes of memory for the type Salt (and free said memory after the usage).

To make matters worse, these two major types of language compilation can be endlessly combined and stacked endlessly. Java uses a hotspot virtual machine that compiles code to native code if code parts are called often enough. C#'s Common Language Runtime does the same thing with a different strategy.

Rust uses the LLVM (https://llvm.org/) compiler infrastructure, which has a byte-code frontend and outputs native code for each platform. This provides great benefits since it makes the language instantly available for many operating systems and platforms (ARM, ×86, and RISC) without much work on the Rust team's side. Instead, they can focus on creating efficient and fast byte-code for LLVM to process (translate?) further.

Memory management and dynamic versus static typing

If allocating and freeing memory is done automatically, it presents a fundamental problem for the programming language. How does the compiler or runtime know how much memory to allocate, where, and until when?

Note: Memory is actually organized in stack and heap memory, which we will get into in *Chapter 5—Borrowing Ownership with Scopes*. For now, let us treat them equally.

Most recent programming languages use references (addresses pointing to the real object in memory) for most in-memory data because references have the same size regardless of their target. Cleaning up then becomes a matter of counting the number of active references and freeing the associated memory once the counter hits zero. The latter part is what a garbage collector does. When observing the memory required by a Java program (because Java uses a garbage collector), a typical pattern emerges that you can see in *figure 1.1*.

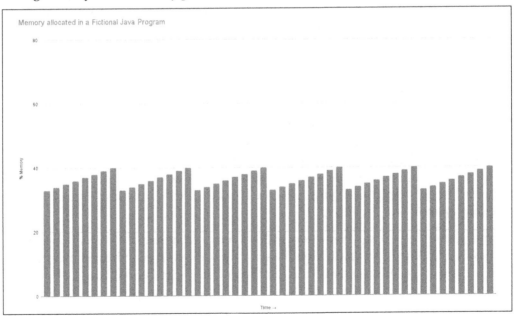

Figure 1.1: *Garbage collection at work: memory is acquired and released periodically as the variables become obsolete*

C and C++ do not provide an automated way of managing memory, and the developer has to actively call malloc() and free() to reserve and release the required amounts. As a consequence, the developer has to know the size of the data so the reserved amount fits the object.

Knowing the size of an object beforehand makes a large difference in how safe a language can be. Dynamic typing refers to a very lenient approach to specifying types, and it is often entirely optional, which leads to the compiler/runtime picking a common type that it knows the size of. If the developer then uses that type, the runtime uses an elaborate lookup mechanism to find out whether an action is permissible (or crash if not).

Although dynamic typing is more comfortable to write as a developer, static typing avoids the problem of runtime lookups by knowing the type at compile time (that is, the developer specifies the type or the compiler infers it). Consequently, there is almost no uncertainty of whether an action is permissible—the compiler would have refused to compile if it was not. Most languages are hybrids in that respect; however, Rust—owed by the memory management model—has to know a variable's type all the time to guarantee safety.

The Rust compiler is famously strict with that and will check the types thoroughly—and fail to compile if something is amiss (something that will come up in *Chapter 15—Working With Generics*).

Executing the code

Once code is written, the compiler creates machine code (through multiple steps) that a CPU can execute. Before everything is 100% binary, the last human-readable machine code is famously called Assembly, which has only a few instructions and directly works with memory addresses and numbers of all kinds.

Popular executable layouts for these compiled instruction files are *nix's ELF (now named executable and linkable format—https://refspecs.linuxbase.org/elf/elf.pdf) and Microsoft's PE (portable executable—https://docs.microsoft.com/en-us/previous-versions/ms809762(v=msdn.10)).

Leaving the actual binary layout aside, the underlying assembler is pretty much the same, and you can use a disassembler on any binary to get something like the following:

```
adosseg
.model small
.stack 100h

.data
hello_mesage db 'Hello, World!',0dh,0ah,'$'

.code
main  proc
      mov    ax,@data
      mov    ds,ax
```

```
        mov     ah,9
        mov     dx,offset hello_message
        int     21h

        mov     ax,4C00h
        int     21h
main    endp
end     main
```

As the operating system is running this binary, it feeds each of the instructions (mov, int, and so on in the preceding example) to the CPU, which uses the attached **Random Access Memory (RAM)** to store data and instructions as required. In later chapters in this book, we will touch on details of the compilation output again and again because it is an important factor in optimizing code or picking the right libraries. Especially Rust—as a systems programming language—is often used to write embedded software, drivers, and operating systems (for example, https:// www.redox-os.org/).

Programming in Rust

Now that we have established the foundations of what it means to program, let us look at Rust. Rust's past is full of changes and novel ideas: after its introduction in 2010, the language went through several changes—syntactically and otherwise—until 2015, the release of Rust v1.0. One noteworthy change was the addition and later removal of a garbage collector, which often framed the language as a Go competitor in the past. Rust's purpose, however, was different.

Up until the announcement of the Rust foundation in February 2021, Mozilla was the main sponsor for the language development in order to improve the—by then dated—Firefox's rendering engine. Through the Rust foundation, developers who previously worked at Mozilla could now officially dedicate their time to improving the language and surrounding frameworks.

Note: In order to run the code provided in the following sections, use the online editor and compiler at play.rust-lang.org so you can focus on the language elements and not the setup.

Managing memory in Rust

There is going to be an entire section dedicated to this novel way of memory management later in the book (*Chapters 5, Borrowing Ownership With Scopes*, and *Chapter 12, Using Heap Memory Effectively*). Until then, let us keep it brief.

In Rust, scopes (most notably { /* areas in curly braces */ } are scopes) play a decisive role: they determine when the compiler can (automatically) allocate and free the variables inside the scope (exceptions apply, but let us keep it simple for now). This means that scopes own that memory, and in some sense, the compiler inserts **malloc()** and **free()** calls at the start and end of a scope, respectively. The parent scope, therefore, defines a variable's lifetime, and within that lifetime, the variable can be borrowed from child scopes or returned to its parent scope.

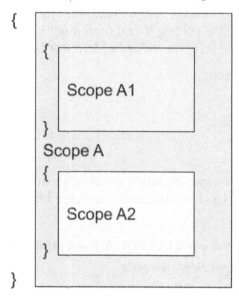

Figure 1.2: Rust uses scopes to allocate and free memory automatically

In order to borrow a variable from a child, the borrower has to conform to certain rules, which the borrow checker enforces at compile-time. Thus there should never be any variable that is freed before it is being read, or any unowned data, or even null values because the compiler knows everything.

As a consequence, Rust can achieve on-par performance with C while having none of the hassles that manual memory management introduces (for example, read after **free()**, writing outside of allocated memory, and so on—many of which cause crashes or security vulnerabilities). This comes at the cost of compilation times, which can be quite long.

Writing Rust code

With memory out of the way, let us write our first lines of Rust code. Rust looks a lot like C in some ways, especially with its use of {} for scopes and blocks. Other elements and keywords such as **let**, **fn**, **for**, and **loop**. will be introduced gradually in part one of this book.

The quintessential program is always the hello world code, which looks like that:

```rust
fn main() {
  println!("Hello, World"); // prints Hello, World
}
```

With these three lines of code, the compiler creates an executable unit with a designated entry point (the main function), which allocates a String Hello, World and prints the result on the console when executed. The String allocation is done implicitly, and we just used a String literal (note the "), which the compiler treats like an anonymous variable with the value Hello, World.

We can make that explicit too:

```rust
fn main() {
  let text = "Hello, World";
  println!("{}", text); // still prints Hello, World
}
```

Using the keyword **let**, you can declare a variable; by adding = to the right of that variable's identifier (here **text**), you define the value before ending the statement with a ;.

> **Note: Variable identifiers are not free text. Among other things, they:**
> - **Cannot contain spaces/whitespace**
> - **Cannot start with a number**
> - **Cannot use special characters such as !, ?, -, +, .,.**
> - **Cannot be a reserved keyword like** while
> - **Cannot use unicode characters**

Additionally, Rust has a convention for the underscore character _. When used as the sole variable name, the variable and its content is ignored right away. Starting a variable identifier with _ (so **_my_variable**) tells the compiler explicitly that it will remain unused. For an up-to-date style guide on how to name variables and other code constructs, visit https://doc.rust-lang.org/1.0.0/style/style/naming/README.html

This variable (or rather its contents) is then used in the macro **println!**, but more on that in *Chapter 11, Generating Code with Macros*. Until then, know that macros are designated by the ! and can require literals as arguments, which is a format string with a single placeholder in this case.

Working with variable types

If you thought that there cannot possibly be more to talk about variable declarations, prepare to be disappointed. Types of variables are a big deal in Rust, especially since its reliance on static typing allows all kinds of efficient copies and lookups that would not be possible in other languages.

In the previous code listing, the variable text was implicitly typed. However, which type did it have? We called it String, but is it actually a called that? Let us try it out on the Rust project's playground at play.rust-lang.org.

Change the predefined code to include a type for the variable. Unlike many other languages, Rust uses a notation where the type follows the variable identifier: let **<variable identifier>: <type> = <value>**. Hence, add a type String to the previous snippet:

```
fn main() {
  let text: String = "Hello, World!";
  println!("{}", text);
}
```

On compiling and running the snippet, you will see the compiler responding with a helpful error message:

```
   Compiling playground v0.1.0 (/private/tmp/playground)
error[E0308]: mismatched types
  --> src/main.rs:2:22
   |
 2 |    let text: String = "Hello, World!";
   |              ------   ^^^^^^^^^^^^^^^
   |              |        |
   |              |        expected struct `String`, found `&str`
   |              |        help: try using a conversion method: `"Hello, World!".to_string()`
   |              expected due to this

error: aborting due to previous error

For more information about this error, try `rustc --explain E0308`.
error: could not compile `playground`

To learn more, run the command again with --verbose.
```

Figure 1.3: *Error message*

The Rust compiler, **rustc**, is rather self-conscious and tries to be helpful. In this case, the suggestion is that it is not actually a String, but a **&str**. Here you see how tricky the types get: **&str** is a reference to a String, that is, something you had to get from borrowing a String variable. Since it is literal, it will not ever run out of scope either!

> **Note: &str is, confusingly, a borrowed String—similar to &String, which is also a borrowed string. However, the underlying types str and String have the same purpose (UTF-8 character sequences), so their differences are subtle and relate to the borrowing and ownership structure we will discuss in *Chapter 5— Borrowing Ownership With Scopes*. However, you have noticed that & in front of a type designates a reference—which technically is its own type.**

In order to fix the preceding example, follow the compiler's advice and call the **.to_string()** function on the literal:

```
fn main() {
    let text: String = "Hello, World!".to_string();
    println!("{}", text);
}
```

Now, like before the error, the output is as follows:

```
Hello, World!
```

Like any programming language, Rust has numeric types with various lengths and sizes. The integer types follow a naming pattern that is **u** (unsigned) or **i** (signed) together with the bit-width of the type—for example, u32 is a 32-bit unsigned number and stores values from 0 to 2^{32-1}. The type labels **isize** and **usize** refer to the compiled architecture's type size (for example, **usize** is **u64** on 64-bit systems).

The smallest types are **u8** and **i8,** together with bool, which requires a byte (or less) to store. In addition to integer types, there are also float types that have 32 or 64 bits at their disposal.

All numeric data types have their lower and upper bounds defined as a constant in the standard library. You can try it yourself over on the play.rust-lang.org and see what each type's boundaries are.

```
fn main() {
    println!("f64: from {} to {}", f64::MIN, f64::MAX);
    // prints (shortened for readability)
    // f64: from -17976931348623157000...0 to 17976931348623157000...0
}
```

Here is a table of all basic Rust data types. It includes some we already discussed (integers, floats) but also the bool and character types, along with two as of yet unknown types: tuples and arrays.

Type	Example	Name
u8, u16, u32, u64, u128	1, 10, 999999999	Unsigned integers
i8, i16, i32, i64, i128	-1, 0, -99999, 9999	Signed Integers
f32, f64	1.0, 10.123, 99999.9999	Floating point numbers
char	,a', ,B', ,🚀'	Character
bool	true, false	Boolean
()		Tuple/Unit if empty
[u8; 4]	[1,2,3,4]	Array

Table 1.1: Basic Rust data types and examples

Tuples and arrays are compound data types because it is your regular old type, just more of them. Tuples contain a defined number of specific data types and are denoted with parentheses: (**u8**, **u32**, char) is a valid type for a variable of this type. However, tuples have special use as well, the unit type, which is basically an empty tuple ( ) and represents the absence of data explicitly, something other programming languages express with the void.

Arrays, on the other hand, are simpler and very rigid in Rust. They can only be defined at compile-time, so they are not dynamically expanding or shrinking—just a number (*table 1.1* declares an array of length 4) of whichever data type (**u8** in table 1.1) the array's elements are. Each element can be accessed individually as well with a zero-based index (so 0 to length −1): **my_array[1]** returns the value of the second element in the array. Unless specifically required, using an array in Rust is very rare, but more on that in *Chapter 6, Working With Collections*. Check the *Conclusion* section for examples of tuples and arrays.

Being literal

The earlier example with a String literal **Hello, World!** already provided a tiny window into the world of literals. A literal is always known at compile-time and can already imply certain data types. The String literal has additional properties, and one of them is the use of a prefix to change allocation details; for example, b"hello" results in a collection of ASCII characters which are one byte each. Another is the raw string r#"I am a raw string"# which is a convenient way to skip escaping special characters.

Integer literals provide a way of explicitly appending the type to the number with (or without) an underscore, so **1_u32** will definitely be a u32. Underscores can also be used as a separator for long numbers **1_000_000_u32** is an example of that. Additionally, integer literals may also be written in hex with a **0x** prefix: **0x5ff_u16** is the same as **1535_u16**.

Conclusion

Congratulations, this was the first chapter in your Rust story. We looked at a lot of things, so let us briefly summarize:

Unlike the popular Python or JavaScript, Rust is a compiled, statically typed programming language that uses borrowing and ownership as a memory management model. During compilation, the compiler tries to figure out (infer) a variable's type so it can budget the required memory accordingly. Since this does not always work, and it can be handy to know a variable's type explicitly, you have to provide that type explicitly sometimes.

In doing so, we learned basic Rust syntax. The main function (called main) houses our first programming steps inside { }, and we use let to declare a variable identifier and its type after the :. Storing values in this variable (which can be done as part of the declaration), you use a = and the actual value after the type. Here are some examples:

```rust
fn main() {
    let text: String = "Hello, World!".to_string();
    let my_u32: u32 = 1234;
    let a_char = 'c';
    let byte_buffer = b"raw-byte-buffer";
    let (one, two): (u8, u8) = (1, 2);
    let my_array: [u8; 3] = [1, 2, 3];
    // Nothing is printed, so this just ends
}
```

Declaring and defining variables is among the most important basics in programming, and you will use them a lot. In later chapters, we will look into where variables are allocated (stack versus heap memory) and why that matters. Until then, remember the syntax and that a variable is a way of storing data in memory and accessing that data using the variable identifier.

Challenge

Let us put this chapter's learnings into practice. Since a program does more than just store literal, how about we do some math to warm up for the chapters ahead. Math operations such as +, -, or * are simple functions that can be applied to numeric data types. If you add two different data types, will it work? What will the result be?

Try to find the data types for the following code. Does this even compile?

```rust
fn main() {
    let x: ?? = 1.0 * 10.0;
    let y: ?? = 100 / 10;
    let z: ?? = 100000 * 100000;
}
```

As we progress with the language, the amount of code per chapter will increase significantly—starting with the upcoming chapter *Controlling the Program Flow*.

CHAPTER 2
Controlling the
Program Flow

In the previous chapter, we discussed how to store data in variables and that it is important to know the type of a variable. You probably also have an idea of what a type is: a number (u32 or i32, for example), a character ("◎"), or a collection of those ([1, 2, 3] or ['a', 'b', 'c']). A String, therefore, can be seen as an array of characters (we will discuss in a later chapter what it actually is).

However, we never did anything with a variable's content—so let us fix that. In this chapter, you will learn how to make decisions based on those values using if expressions as well as loops to iterate over any collection, although we will only look at arrays for now.

Structure

In this chapter, we will be covering the following topics:

- Making decisions with if
  - Using conditions
  - What If conditions Fail
  - Using If/Else expressions

- Repetitions and repetitions with loop
  - o Continuing and breaking with values
  - o Enumerating with for
  - o Breaking on conditions with *while*

Objectives

By the end of this chapter, you will be able to know about if and else, how to use loops and their variations, and understand expressions and return values.

Making decisions with if

Simply expressing a conditional sentence in the English language provides a view into the if expression:

"If the amount of rain becomes too big, I'll open my umbrella—else I'm just going to ignore it".

Someone, probably

Or in Rust code:

```
if amount_of_rain > MAX_BEARABLE_AMOUNT {
  umbrella.open(); // we'll look at functions and calling them in the
next chapter
} else {
  // do nothing
}
```

The else clause in this snippet is empty—so we could have (and in many cases should) skip it. The amount_of_rain is a variable that may have changed because of the first assigned, so we need to check whether it exceeds the MAX_BEARABLE_ AMOUNT, which is a constant.

Let us look closer at those conditions: what are those, and how do they work?

> Note: Constants use the const keyword instead of let, cannot change, live in the global scope, and you can use literals to initialize them. For example const MAX_BEARABLE_AMOUNT: u32 = 1_000_000_u32;

Using conditions

Conditions for an if the expression is expressions (more on following expressions) that return a bool variable as a result. Therefore, it could be anything that creates true or false results: equations, Boolean algebra, or range queries. However, the bool result is obtained, true leads to executing the if branch, false to executing the else branch (see next section).

The simplest few comparisons are probably known from the first or last math class:

- = equals
- > greater than
- < less than

Boolean algebra is a basic form of calculating things that have turned out to be fundamental for computer logic. In Rust, those Boolean operators are as follows:

Expression	Example	Name
&&	true && true == true, true && false == false	AND
||	true || true == true, true || false == true	OR
!	!false == true, !true == false	NOT
^	true ^ true == false, true ^ false == true	XOR

Table 2.1: Boolean algebra, a primer

If you want to get deeper into this type of logic, read more at Wolfram Mathworld (https://mathworld.wolfram.com/BooleanAlgebra.html) or the Rust language reference (https://doc.rust-lang.org/reference/types/boolean.html#operations-on-boolean-values). As a developer, you will face those types of comparisons a lot, and it pays to be able to do them in your head and doubly so as an embedded developer with some fancy bit-shifting going on.

Since the expression's head (that is, the part within the parentheses in the if) is evaluated first, you can place anything bool in there. Most expressions are evaluated left-to-right, but keep in mind the operator precedence which may result in unexpected behavior. Learn more in the docs at https://doc.rust-lang.org/reference/expressions.html#expression-precedence) and in the following example:

```rust
fn main() {
    let greater_than: bool = 5 < 10;
    let not_equals: bool = 1 != 0;
    let equals: bool = "0x5ff" == "0x5ff";
    // true and false are actually just 1 and 0 respectively
    let combined: bool = greater_than && not_equals || equals > true;
    println!("{}", combined); // prints "true"
}
```

Try running this snippet on the Rust playground (play.rust-lang.org) and experiment with different operators and see how the results change. You can use brackets to ensure a certain order of evaluation (precedence) as well. Meanwhile, we will look at the else clause.

What if condition fails

If is a binary decision, so it is either one branch or the other that the program runs. Thus, when the if the condition evaluates to false, code execution continues in the else branch of the if/else block. The following snippet illustrates this:

```rust
fn main() {
  let n = 8; // 8 is even, therefore ...
  if n % 2 == 0 { // ... this condition is true ...
    println!("n = {}, which is even", n); // ... so this will be printed
...
  } else {
    println!("n = {}, which is odd", n); // ... but not this
  }
}
```

In this tiny program, we create a variable n with some numeric value, and by using the modulo operator (which uses the % and returns a division's remainder), the program determines whether the number is even or odd in this if clause. If we change n to something odd (such as 9 or 7), a division by 2 will definitely lead to a remainder of 1, and consequently, the else branch is executed.

In many situations, this might not be enough. Instead of accepting that the condition evaluated to false (for example, if $x > 10$ is false, we still do not know if $x > 3$), you might need additional qualifications to react properly. In this case, cascading if statements are helpful, and in Rust, they do not require much special syntax:

```rust
fn main() {
  let n = 1; // 1 is odd, therefore ...
  if n % 2 == 0 { // ... this condition is false ...
    println!("n = {}, which is even", n); // ... so this won't be
printed ...
  } else if n == 1 { // this else clause contains another if, which is
true ...
    println!("n = 1, which is a special case");
  } else { // this else belongs to if n == 1 and executes when n is odd
and not 1
```

```
    println!("n = {}, which is odd and not 1", n);
  }
}
```

In this snippet, we see a bunch of paths that the code can take based on the value in *n*. Specifically, the else block { } can be fully replaced with another if block in order to produce cascading if evaluations, which is typically useful for creating data flows or rule-based processes. Additionally, Rust relies a lot on cascading ifs to work with extracting data from enum variants (*Chapter 4, Interfacing with Code*).

> **Note: If you know your Boolean logic, you may have recognized that some cascading ifs can be included in the original if conditional by using AND, OR, or XOR operators. This is certainly true and, when possible, follows a short-circuit evaluation that is more efficient. "Short-circuit evaluation" refers to using boolean logic to skip evaluating parts of the equation.**
>
> **For example, if the expression is 1 != 1 || 1 != 0, the compiler already knows the outcome of the OR (||) because the first part (1 != 1) is false; thus, the entire expression will evaluate to false, no matter what the second part yields. It can therefore skip evaluating the second part of the OR and jump to the else clause right away.**

After using the expression expression so many times, let us explore what it actually means.

Using If/Else expressions

According to the Rust language reference, expressions are everything that generates some kind of value after being invoked or has effects on the program (https://doc. rust-lang.org/reference/expressions.html, note that expressions that do not return a value or have effects on the program are called statements). It sounds vague—and it is, intentionally so. The reason for this is that, as a programming language, things become much easier to handle and use if they are grouped together. In practical terms, you can use any expression to return a value and assign this value to a variable—including if, loop, and match (*Chapter 4, Interfacing with Code*). Here is an example snippet:

```
fn main() {
  let n = 10;
  let number = if n == 1 { "one" } else { "not one" };
  println!("number = {}", number); // this prints "number = one"
}
```

Similarly, a regular block { } is an expression, written as follows:

```
fn main() {
  let number = { // this starts a new block
    let n = 10;
    if n == 1 { "one" } else { "not one" } // this is an implicit return
  };
  println!("number = {}", number); // this prints the same as above:
"number = one"
}
```

Using the if/else block as an expression requires two additional things:

1. Both if and else blocks.

2. Both blocks have to return the same type.

We will touch on return values in the upcoming chapter as they are highly relevant to functions. Since if/else blocks are expressions just like functions, they too can return values. Rust, being very statically typed, wants those values to be of the same type, which means that each arm has to return the same type.

Syntactically, return values can be explicitly stated using the return keyword or implicitly by leaving out the ";" after the last expression in the block. The latter is idiomatic Rust because return statements can be confusing as to what to return from. In fact, return is typically used to exit functions early.

Recall the preceding example, and you will find no ";" after the if and not inside the if/else blocks either:

```
fn main() {
  let number = { // this starts a new block
    let n = 10;
    if n == 1 { "one" } else { "not one" } // No semicolons anywhere
  };
  println!("number = {}", number); // "number = one"
}
```

We will have more to explore for if in a later chapter (*Chapter 4, Interfacing with Code*) when we go into de-structuring and pattern matching. Until then, let us look at loops.

Repetitions and repetitions with loop

`loop` is a pretty self-explanatory expression: it repeats (loops) indefinitely. The thing it repeats is the block it takes. Let us look at the following code snippet:

```
fn main() {
  let mut i = 0; // we'll talk more about mutability in chapter 5
  // a basic loop
  loop {
    i += 1; // increment the variable by 1
  }
  // ... this never exits
}
```

This `loop` statement repeats the provided block (`{ i += 1; }`) and thereby increments the variable i by one forever. Although this is not the most useful of loops in ordinary circumstances, infinite loops are great for server and daemon processes. However, Rust provides control statements to make loops less infinite.

Continuing and breaking with values

Since infinite loops are not as common in regular algorithms, every language has some control instructions to break a loop, continue with the next iteration from a certain point and even return a value.

In order to get out of an infinite loop statement, you can use a break, a keyword in Rust. Here is what that looks like:

```
fn main() {
  let mut i = 0;
  loop {
    i += 1; // increment the variable by 1
    if i > 10 { // test if it has reached 11
      break; // exit the loop if true
    }
  }
}
```

Alternatively, it sometimes makes sense to skip the remainder of the loop's body and start with the next iteration. This is where you can use continue. This example shows how this works, the `println!` is never actually executed:

```
fn main() {
```

```
let mut i = 0; // we'll talk more about mutability in chapter 5
// a basic loop
loop {
  i += 1; // increment the variable by 1
  continue;
  printnln!("This is never printed");
}
// ... this never exits
}
```

Since a loop just repeatedly executes a given block, loops can easily be nested. In this case, how can you break the outer loop from the inner loop? In fact, how do you know which loop is being continued or stopped? Rust provides a great solution to this problem: loop labels.

Let us consider the following example:

```
fn main() {
  let mut i = 0; // we'll talk more about mutability in chapter 5
  // a basic loop
  'outer: loop {
    'inner: loop {
      i += 1; // increment the variable by 1
      break 'inner;
    }
    break 'outer;
  }
  // i == 1
}
```

This snippet increments the variable once because both loops break right away. Using Rust's label syntax labelname: right in front of the loop statement creates this reference point that breaks and continues can use.

Since loops are expressions just like conditionals, they can return values. However, the semantics do not allow a simple return as the last expression as with if/else. Instead, the loop has to break to return a value:

```
fn main() {
  let a_number = 10;
  let mut i = 0;
  let outcome = loop {
```

```
  if i + a_number > 100 {
    break i + a_number;
  } else if i + a_number < 50 {
    i += 10;
  }
  else {
    i += 1;
  }
}; // assignments are ended with a ;
println!("outcome = {}", outcome); // outcome = 101
}
```

This syntax allows to write compact statements and algorithms but is not necessarily useful for every use case. Specifically, the requirement for a mutable variable in the parent scope (the main function in this case) is not always satisfied.

For these situations, most developers prefer a for a loop.

Enumerating with for

The kind of loop that goes through a range of numbers or elements is called a for loop (or sometimes for each when it is about more than numbers). In this loop type, the loop declaration contains a variable assignment {declaration and definition} that contains the current element for each (ha!) element in the collection—and a range of numbers is nothing more than an ordered collection of all the numbers in between, right?

This style is called iteration, with the iterator providing always the next element. Rust has a few actual collections, which we will explore in *Chapter 6, Working with Collections,* and when writing your own collections, you can implement the `IntoIter` trait (*Chapter 4, Interfacing with Code*) to use. For now, know that an iterator simply provides the next element in a range when called.

Until you have mastered that, you can rely on built-in iterators as well. The most useful for numbers is using the range expression *m...n* or *m..=n* to generate numbers from *m* to *n* or *m* to and including *n*, respectively. So, let us look at a code snippet to find out how everything fits together for:

```
fn main() {
  for i in 0..10 {
    // this block gets called 10 times
  }
  for i in 0..=10 {
```

```
      // this block gets called 11 times
  }
}
```

Each of these loops repeatedly calls the block and provides a variable *i* that contains the current element from the iteration. In this case, these are the numbers from 0 to 9 and 0 to 10, respectively.

Now, we should turn our attention to collections as well. Since we are going to explore those a lot deeper in *Chapter 6, Working with Collections*, we can start with a simple array (reference) first:

```
fn main() {
  for e in &[6, 7, 8, 0, 4, 5, 3, 1, 2, 9] {
    // this block gets called 10 times
    // e's value each round: 6, 7, 8, 0, ..., 9
  }
}
```

We will encounter this `for` each variant a lot more in *Chapter 6, Working with Collections* and we will look at implementing the required trait (called `IntoIter`) in *Chapter 4, Interfacing with Code*. This trait is what tells the for loop what type the iteration variable's type is going to be (*e* and *i* above).

In order to really see how useful the for loop is, let us look at a sorting algorithm called "bubble sort". Although it is neither the best implementation nor the best algorithm to sort collections, it will be the first one we discuss in this book. Do not worry if this goes over your head—we are only in the second chapter! See it as a puzzle and try to figure it out (maybe even use play.rust-lang.org).

```
fn main() {
  let mut haystack = [4, 6, 3, 2, 8];
  println!("unsorted haystack: {:?}", haystack);

  // bubble sort algorithm
  for _ in 0..haystack.len() {
      let mut swaps = 0;
      for i in 1..haystack.len() {
          if haystack[i - 1] > haystack[i] {
              let tmp = haystack[i];
              haystack[i] = haystack[i - 1];
              haystack[i - 1] = tmp;
              swaps += 1;
```

```
            }
        }
    }
    println!(" sorted haystack: {:?}", haystack);
}
```

In this snippet, you will find mutability (*Chapter 5, Borrowing Ownership with Scopes* and another syntactical thing that we did not use a lot yet: indexing collections using [], where `haystack[i]` returns the *i*th element of the haystack collection, starting with 0. The outer loop's variable is a _, thus, explicitly not being used.

Let us walk through bubble sort and what it does: essentially, the algorithm requires a mutable collection of i32 numbers for iterating over the indices (the outer loop) from 0 to haystack's length (`.len()` returns a collection's length). Inside of this loop, a nested loop compares each element to its neighboring element (`haystack[i-1]` > `haystack[i]`) and swaps them if the order is not ascending. In this fashion, each element is swapped one by one into its correct place.

Note: Bubble sort has its name because each element "bubbles up" into the appropriate place by swapping with its neighbor. As much as bubble sort is quick to implement, bubble sort is very inefficient, unfortunately.

If that felt confusing, it is highly recommended to play and experiment with the code a little. Maybe print out the various comparisons or swap the > with a <=? Alternatively, you can postpone the experimentation until the challenge at the end of this chapter and move on to learn about while.

Breaking on conditions with while

The `while` loop is exactly what the English word suggests: a loop that runs while a provided condition is true—equivalent to what we have created in an earlier section where a condition broke the infinite loop. Since this construct is very common across algorithms and other implementations, Rust (as in many other languages) provides a while loop that simplifies that conditional exit.

As a consequence, the syntax is similar to the loop statement from earlier in this chapter, and we can now easily build an equivalent to the for loop as well:

```
fn main() {
    let mut i = 0;
    while i <= 10 {
        i += 1; // increment the variable by 1
    }
}
```

In many cases, this type of iteration is viewed as a more powerful alternative to the for a loop. Specifically, the idea that while something has not happened is a very versatile condition that enables things such as tree walks *Chapter 6, Working with Collections,* something that a for loop with its predefined ending cannot do.

In particular, the ability to connect multiple expressions using short-circuit evaluation (explained earlier in this chapter) adds to the versatility of while. One example is early stopping when trying to find a spot in an ordered collection to insert data in a sorted fashion:

```rust
fn main() {
  let needle = 3;
  let haystack = [1, 2, 4, 5, 6];
  let mut i = 1;
  while i < &haystack.len() && &haystack[i] <= needle {
    i += 1; // increment the variable by 1
  }
}
```

In fact, the preceding snippet can be turned into a simple search algorithm—can you think of a way how?

Conclusion

Within this chapter of Rust, you learned about conditionals, loops, and how to stop them. Especially the latter parts are crucial for beginner programmers because many algorithms can result in infinite loops from tiny mistakes.

In addition to that, we explored a bit what an "expression" is in the world of programming languages. An expression is the code part that returns a value and can be anything from a block ({ }) to a conditional **(if {} else {})**, any kind of loop or … a function (we will learn about those in the next chapter). Whatever the actual expression, loops, if/else, or while return values that can be assigned to variables and used accordingly—as long as their types match.

In terms of syntax, this snippet has it all:

```rust
fn main() {
  let a_number = 10; // we'll get to user input in chapter 7. Until then just modify this number
  let parity: String = if a_number % 2 == 0 { "even".to_string() } else { "odd".to_string() };

  println!("{} is {}", a_number, parity); // prints 10 is even
```

```
// prints a sequence from 10 - 19
for i in 0..10 {
  println!("{}", a_number + i);
};

let mut i = 0;
'myloop: loop {
    if i + a_number > 100 {
       break 'myloop;
    } else if i + a_number < 50 {
       i += 10;
    }
    else {
       i += 1;
       continue 'myloop;  // skips the println!
    }
    println!("+10"); // prints 4 times
}

// reset
i = 0;

// the same loop as above, although a little more compact with while
while i + a_number <= 100 {
    if i + a_number < 50 {
       i += 10;
    }
    else {
       i += 1;
       continue;  // skips the println!
    }
    println!("+10"); // prints 4 times
  }
}
```

In the snippet, you will find: the if/else expression, which assigns a string even or odd to the variable—feel free to experiment with changing **a_number** on the Rust playground. Next, there is a for loop that simply adds an incrementing number (typically i) to **a_number** and prints that. Note the range expression **0..10**, which is an iterator *Chapter 6, Working with Collections* over the numbers 0 to 10 (excl.)

Afterward, the snippet contains the most relevant loop constructions and control operators. Particularly, the first loop has a label **myloop** that can be used to directly target the break and continue operators. This loop also will only exist if the condition applies—which the while loop in the lower parts of the snippet does as well. However, while it has the breaking condition built-in, and therefore, reverses the condition—it is a condition to keep running, not to break!

In the upcoming chapter, we are going to look into organizing code in functions, structs, and modules. Let us conclude this chapter with a challenge to solidify the concepts and your first real Rust program to tinker with. It is a puzzle; can you figure it out?

Challenge

For this challenge, try to optimize the sorting algorithm (bubble sort) we covered in the section about for loops. Can you improve it by stopping early (and why are we counting swaps)? As a reminder, here is the code:

```rust
fn main() {
    let mut haystack = [4, 6, 3, 2, 8];
    println!("unsorted haystack: {:?}", haystack);

    // bubble sort algorithm
    for _ in 0..haystack.len() {
        let mut swaps = 0;
        for i in 1..haystack.len() {
            if haystack[i - 1] > haystack[i] {
                let tmp = haystack[i];
                haystack[i] = haystack[i - 1];
                haystack[i - 1] = tmp;
                swaps += 1;
            }
        }
    }

    println!("  sorted haystack: {:?}", haystack);
}
```

Hint: Sorting algorithms are all about reducing the number of comparisons between elements. What happens if there are 0 swaps?

CHAPTER 3
Organizing for Reuse

After discussing loops, variables, if/else, and expressions in the previous chapters, we have now finally arrived at one of the core disciplines of software development: reuse. Reuse is mostly a question of abstraction, so the more abstract something is, the easier it is to find a new purpose—although that comes at a cost. This trade-off between building something very generic and broadly applicable versus something that only serves a single purpose is often determined by other factors like time constraints or simply the complexity of using something too generic.

Regardless, software engineers like to engage in this kind of debate—and we love to rebuild things that already exist because of variations of "this is not how I would have built it". So let us get that out of the way: typically, other people spend the same amount or more hours on creating something, so your code will not be better in most cases.

Now, let us talk about reuse. Software generally consists of units, which are called modules in Rust. Those modules contain the actual code and have to be imported from other modules in order to use them. Consequently, if you have a good set of modules that solve your everyday problems, you can use it across projects, which speeds up development considerably.

Modules are not the only thing that you can share. There are also structs, functions, and traits (*Chapter 4—Interfacing with Code*) that are the actual contents that can be used from those modules. Multiple modules are also collected in crates (*Chapter 8—Using Crates with Cargo*), which would be called libraries/frameworks (depending on how much they offer) in other languages.

In this chapter, we will dive into functions and structs, their purpose, declarations, implementations, and other things.

Structure

In this chapter, we will be covering the following topics:

- Encapsulating behavior with functions
  - o Parameterizing functions
- Encapsulating data with structs
  - o Combining functions and structs
  - o Getting a deeper look
- Exporting and importing with modules
  - o Aliasing types and exporting imports

Objectives

After reading this chapter, you will have learned to declare and call Rust functions and lambdas, create data structures using structs, and implement structures and functions in that context.

Encapsulating behavior with functions

A function in its simplest form is a relatively independent code construct that can be called from different places and uses parameters and returns values to transfer data back and forth. If you remember the previous chapter, functions are definitely expressions.

> **Note: In a strictly object-oriented fashion, a function is not a method—which is a function associated with a particular class object (learn more at https://www.win.tue.nl/~wstomv/edu/2ip30/year-2005/slides-4up/lloseng2.pdf). However, Rust does not have classes (structs, although similar, are not classes), so, therefore, all functions are … functions—although they can be associated with a struct.**

First, let us look at the overall syntax:

```
fn four() -> i32 {
    4
}
```

This example is a function (**fn**) with the name four but without any input parameters (**()**) and a return value of type i32 (**-> i32**). The entire line is called a function signature, and it generally should tell you most of what you need to know about it (if the naming is good). In its body, it simply allocates and returns the literal 4, just like anyone would expect from the function name.

Calling the function is as simple as invoking let nr = four(); to assign the return value to a variable. Going back to the assembler language from *Chapter 1*, *Building the Basics*, the function call compiles to a jump to the function's address in memory, runs through the function—top to bottom—and then jumps back to one instruction past the original location, potentially with return values. Calling a function, therefore, pauses the current execution, executes the function code, and returns with the result (if any).

Note: You have already used the function main several times in the previous chapters. This is a special pattern that provides the binary with an entry point. Consequentially, the function signature looks almost always the same.

Especially when following the functional and imperative programming paradigms, functions take center stage. Rust supports either of these, and contrary to object-oriented languages such as Python, standalone functions (that is, those that are not attached to a struct/object) are much more common in Rust, especially for convenience.

We will explore more of that difference in the next chapter (*Chapter 4*, *Interfacing with Code*), but let us look at what should go into functions:

```rust
// This code won't compile since the functions and struct aren't
implemented
// Use this as an illustration of how to think about functions
fn main() {
    let mut door = Door {}; // create a new Door struct instance
    let mut player = Player {};

    // imperative style programming
    open(&mut door);
    walk_in(&mut player, &door);
    close(&mut door);

    // object orient style
    door.open();
    player.walk_through(&door);
    door.close();
}
```

These functions have roughly the same implementations, and it is mainly where their code lives that is different.

Parameterizing functions

If the point of functions is to make them universally usable, then the input parameters have to be carefully designed. When you think about a function, you could also think about a set of actions that transforms the input into the output.

In principle, those parameters are somewhat like variables that are available when the function executes and are filled with values from the outside. Those values are passed into the function from the calling scope in a wide variety of ways. Let us walk through a few parameter types now, and the rest will be discussed in throughout the book (you may not even need that anymore). Note the following exemplary function headers with each point:

- &-prefix signals an (immutable) reference (a borrow, see *Chapter 5, Borrowing Ownership with Scopes*) to the function. For example: `fn f(a: &str)`.

- `mut` makes an input variable mutable (refer to *Chapter 5, Borrowing Ownership with Scopes*), for example, `fn f(mut a: String)`.

- `no` prefix, which is a simple transfer of ownership into the function. `fn f(a: i32)`.

- `impl` prefix is handy for allowing structs/enums that implement a trait dynamically `fn f(a: impl std::io::Write)`.

- `T` or other generic types are represented through letters (see *Chapter 15, Working with Generics*), for example, `fn f<T>(a: T)`.

Obviously, there are also a lot of ways to combine types, lifetimes (*Chapters 5* and *15*), mutable structures, references, closures, enums, and so on. However, most of them can be treated like any other type (for example, a `&std::fs::File` is a different type from `std::fs::File` for the compiler).

> **Note: Closures are anonymous functions that have a shorthand syntax, are typically short, and can access variables from their parent scope in addition to declared parameters. Their upside is usually brevity when dealing with extracting data from a collection of complex structs or checking whether a condition applies (those are called predicates). Read more here: doc.rust-lang. org/rust-by-example/fn/closures.html or in chapter 6 (Working With Collections) together with collections.**

Encapsulating data with structs

If functions encapsulate behavior, then structs do the same for data. In *Chapter 1, Building the Basics*, we were looking at simple types which can only store a limited amount of information. Imagine the preceding door example; any program that wants to store information about a door would need to create individual variables for each piece of information:

```rust
fn main() {
  let door_width = 100;
  let door_height = 200;
  let door_is_open = false;
}
```

This can even work when there is a single door in the program—which is unlikely. Instead, you had to use a complex type—that is, a struct—to ensure uniformity and reusability:

```rust
struct Door {
  width: u32,
  height: u32,
  is_open: bool
}

fn main() {
  let living_room_door = Door {
    width: 100,
    height: 200,
    is_open: false,
  };
}
```

Looking at this example, you will find the struct declaration on top, with its name right before the {. Similar to variable names, you can only use a limited set of characters (no numbers, only underscores as special characters, but all ASCII letters) to name your structs. Convention also dictates using CamelCase capitalization for naming structs.

After the name in the struct declaration (**Door**), you will find the member declarations inside of the { }, which follow the same pattern as the variable declarations from *Chapter 1, Building the Basics*. These declarations use name: type notations followed by commas, whereas the name conforms to the **snake_case** that variables use. Additionally, type members can have access modifiers preceding them, which tell the compiler whether code is allowed to access the member.

Rust does not have a lot of those modifiers, and typically the usage of the pub is enough, but it can go much more fine-grained (check the reference docs for a complete list). Let us see how we can add this modifier and see if we can access these members:

```rust
pub struct Door { // This makes the struct accessible from outside
  width: u32,   // When using Door from a different module, this ...
  height: u32, // ... and this member aren't accessible
  pub is_open: bool // only this one is
}
```

We will explore the pub modifier deeper in the section about modules. Know that the preceding snippet is not very handy without a constructor function.

Combining functions and structs

Because we now have a place to store data and a way to store behavior, how about combining them? Let us recall the **Door** struct from previously:

```rust
struct Door {
  width: u32,
  height: u32,
  is_open: bool
}


fn main() {
  let living_room_door = Door {
    width: 100,
    height: 200,
    is_open: false,
  };
}
```

When allocating a struct, you will have to provide values for the members; otherwise, the compiler may not know how much memory to allocate—which is only added to the fact that an empty struct may not be useful anyways

What you see when assigning the **living_room_door** variable is that each member is individually assigned a value, which uses several lines of precious screen estate. So let us add an **impl** block to define functions that are then associated with our struct:

```rust
struct Door {
  width: u32,
  height: u32,
  is_open: bool
}
```

```
impl Door {
  pub fn new(width: u32, height: u32, is_open: bool) -> Self {
    Door {
      width, // shorthand for width: width
      height,
      is_open,
    }
  }
}


fn main() {
  let living_room_door = Door::new(100, 200, false);
}
```

The **impl** block provides function implementations for a specified struct (or enum—*Chapter 4, Interfacing with Code*. It is fine to have several **impl** blocks too! In this block, we added a new function with three parameters: **width**, **height**, and **is_open**, just like in the struct definition. In fact, we also used the same names, which allows the compiler to shorten the assignment when creating the struct instance. The new function has a few additional aspects that are … new. Let us see a list:

- **pub** modifier to make the function accessible from outside the struct.

- A return type self that refers to the current type, so it is equivalent to writing -> Door without the search/replace maintenance.

- Shorthand initialization thanks to matching variable names and members.

This **new** function is bound to the struct generally and will not have any instance data available—for that, we had needed the current object as an input parameter (we will explore this next). Thus, when calling the function, the caller has to specify the struct first and separate the function with :: (see **Door::new(...)** preceding). Recall that a regular function in the same module would be called with **new(...)** without having additional qualifications.

Let us add some more functions that are attached to a **Door** instance, such as **open()** and **close()**:

```
struct Door {
  width: u32,
  height: u32,
  is_open: bool
}
```

```rust
impl Door {
  pub fn new(width: u32, height: u32, is_open: bool) -> Self {
    Door {
      width, // shorthand for width: width
      height,
      is_open,
    }
  }

  pub fn open(&mut self) {
    self.is_open = true;
  }

  pub fn close(&mut self) {
    self.is_open = false;
  }

}

fn main() {
  let mut living_room_door = Door::new(100, 200, false);
  living_room_door.open();
  assert!(living_room_door.is_open); // crashes when false
}
```

These two additional functions are real instance-bound functions (you could say methods), as signaled by the first parameter named **self**. In this particular case, it is even a mutable reference to the object, so the variable calling the function has to be mutable as well.

Getting a deeper look

Structs are types because they govern the interpretation of a few bytes in memory. Given that we want to work as efficiently as possible, it is particularly important to minimize administrative overhead for such data structures. This overhead typically consists of meta information in other languages and technologies, and therefore, uses extra space and CPU time that makes their use in some environments (for example, embedded systems) more difficult.

The Rust teams, however, tried to remain as close to no overhead as possible— and they succeeded. Let us take a look at a struct and its members. Ideally, a struct comprising five u32 members is going to be as large as 32 bits * five members = 160 bits (or 20 bytes), and anything beyond that can be considered overhead. Luckily, Rust comes with a memory sizing function that tells us the size of a particular type. Let us try a few structs and see how much Rust adds:

```rust
use std::mem;

struct Door {
  width: u32,
  height: u32,
  is_open: bool
}

struct DoorDoor {
    sub_door: Door
}

fn main() {
  println!("Size of a Door: {} bytes", mem::size_of::<Door>());
  println!("Size of the members: {} bytes", mem::size_of::<(u32, u32, bool)>());
  println!("Size of a DoorDoor: {} bytes", mem::size_of::<DoorDoor>());
}
```

Here is the output of the preceding snippet, which confirms that Rust adds no overhead to manage structs:

```
Size of a Door: 12 bytes
Size of the members: 12 bytes
Size of a DoorDoor: 12 bytes
```

Because all of the structs, even the nested ones, are 12 bytes in size (4 bytes for each u32, 4 bytes for a bool), we can rule out any overhead for structs of that nature. To show this in another way, let us take this hex representation of a few bytes in memory (32 bit*3): 5FF000005FF000005FF00000 (it is three times 5FF00000). For a program, there are an unlimited number of ways to interpret these bytes: they could be six u16 or three i32 values or one weird string. Using a struct can provide a blueprint for guiding the program as to how to interpret those bytes; for example, such a struct works:

```rust
struct MyData {
  first: u32,
```

```
    second: i32,
    third: u32
}
```

If you remember the previous chapter, you will also know that tuples can be aligned in a similar way. In a way, they are like structs in that sense, just without the named members, you can also make the tuple into a struct:

```
struct MyData(u32, i32, u32); // a semicolon is required here
// This is basically a named tuple. Access "members" with .0, .1.
```

So for many types, it is pretty much no overhead—if the type is not a reference type. As we will see in the following chapter, references are—almost like pointers—**usize** types that, in some cases, also store additional information. One example is a String-type member. Let us expand on the previous example and see what changed:

```
use std::mem;

struct Door {
  name: String,
  width: u32,
  height: u32,
  is_open: bool
}

struct DoorDoor {
    sub_door: Door
}

fn main() {
  println!("Size of a Door: {} bytes", mem::size_of::<Door>());
  println!("Size of the members: {} bytes", mem::size_of::<(u32, u32,
bool)>());
  println!("Size of a DoorDoor: {} bytes", mem::size_of::<DoorDoor>());
}
```

This leads to a significant change in the size in bytes for the structs:

```
Size of a Door: 40 bytes
Size of the members: 12 bytes
Size of a DoorDoor: 40 bytes
```

So why the massive increase? Internally a String is a collection of bytes that is allocated in one continuous area of memory and referenced by a 64bit pointer (on a

64bit OS and CPU). Additionally, the collection (a `Vec<u8>` to be precise) stores its own length and capacity (both u64 on a 64bit platform); thus, 8 bytes per each of those items yields 24 bytes in total. As a 64bit platform, Rust playground will add the remaining 4 bytes (40–12–24) to the struct because since they cannot be addressed individually there (if you add another u32 there, the total size will remain the same).

These zero-overhead structs can be used extensively to interpret data structures from all kinds of sources: any digital device output can suddenly be used without any major bit-shifting magic, file formats can be parsed quickly if the memory layout is known, and interoperability with other languages is much simpler with raw bytes. If that does not make sense to you just yet, do not worry—just remember that Rust's memory management model allows for having zero-overhead structs. For the next section, however, we want to move further up in the abstraction layers to modules.

Exporting and importing with modules

Like any good language, Rust provides a mechanism for encapsulating major components in your code, including a unified mechanism to use them from anywhere. This mechanism is typically referred to as modules and went through a simplification in Rust 2018. Its basic premise is to allow sub-modules (and sub-sub-modules, and so on.) with multiple files that abstract code components for easy reuse.

There are many ways in Rust to create modules, and the simplest one is to use the **mod** keyword—no extra file required!

```rust
mod PhysicalAccessControl {
  pub struct Door {
      pub width: u32,
      pub height: u32,
      pub is_open: bool
  }

  impl Door {
    pub fn new(width: u32, height: u32, is_open: bool) -> Self {
      Door {
        width, // shorthand for width: width
        height,
        is_open,
      }
    }
  }
}
```

```
fn main() {
    let my_door = PhysicalAccessControl::Door::new(100, 200, false);
}
```

This is the easiest way of creating modules, and it is frequently used in unit testing (*Chapter 9, Testing What You Build*. Alternatively, the content of the mod block can move into a dedicated file:

```
// PhysicalAccessControl.rs
pub struct Door {
    pub width: u32,
    pub height: u32,
    pub is_open: bool
}

impl Door {
    pub fn new(width: u32, height: u32, is_open: bool) -> Self {
        Door {
            width, // shorthand for width: width
            height,
            is_open,
        }
    }
}
```

This situation still requires the main file of the project to declare the module in a **mod** statement. Afterward, a use statement enables the simple inclusion of the new thing in your code:

```
// main.rs
mod PhysicalAccessControl;
use PhysicalAccessControl::Door;

fn main() {
    let my_door = Door::new(100, 200, false);
}
```

However, modules do not always fit into a single file that is why Rust's module system also supports using directories that contain a file called mod.rs to create submodules. Within the directory, the same pattern repeats: each new file has to be declared in **mod.rs** (mod **mysubmodule**; to declare **mysubmodule.rs**).

Note: Rust has keywords to clarify from where to use which function/type: —crate imports from the root level—super imports from one level up—self refers to something that is defined within this module but shadowed otherwise

Whenever any ambiguity between types or functions exists, these qualifiers can be helpful in being precise with imports and calls.

As an example of a more complex module system, let us look at an open-source project called MiniFaaS (**https://github.com/celaus/minifaas, License MIT/by the author**); specifically inside the MiniFaaS-common project, which contains several modules:

```
.
|-- Cargo.toml
`-- src
    |-- datastore
    |   |-- config.rs
    |   |-- json_file.rs
    |   |-- mod.rs
    |   `-- record.rs
    |-- environment
    |   |-- environment.rs
    |   |-- environments.rs
    |   `-- mod.rs
    |-- errors.rs
    |-- lib.rs
    |-- runtime
    |   |-- functions.rs
    |   |-- mod.rs
    |   `-- ops.rs
    |-- triggers
    |   |-- http.rs
    |   |-- mod.rs
    |   `-- timer.rs
    `-- types.rs

5 directories, 17 files
```

In this print (produced by the "tree" program), we see that there are directories that act as modules, with mod.rs as their root. The entire project, however, has a **lib.rs** as root and declares all of the other modules: datastore, environment, errors, runtime, triggers, and types. Each of them has to be imported (if they are public) just like this: use **minifaas_common::errors::ExecutionError**.

Now that we know how to work with modules, what are these use statements, and what do they do? Their primary purpose is to import code from wherever (a defined location) into the current module. Because this has major implications on how developers use libraries and such things, it is not good practice to let everyone import everything from a particular module. Instead, it should be specific and provide maximum flexibility with respect to changing internal workings (also called implementation details) so updates are painless.

Let us consider the previous example where we declared a Door type to be pub—so it could be exported. It was split into two files:

```rust
// PhysicalAccessControl.rs
pub struct Door {
    pub width: u32,
    pub height: u32,
    pub is_open: bool
}

impl Door {
  pub fn new(width: u32, height: u32, is_open: bool) -> Self {
    Door {
      width, // shorthand for width: width
      height,
      is_open,
    }
  }
}

// this struct is private to this module
struct Window {
  width: u32,
  height: u32
}
```

This situation still requires the main file of the project to declare the module in a **mod** statement. Afterward, a **use** statement enables the simple inclusion of the new thing in your code:

```rust
// main.rs
mod PhysicalAccessControl;
use PhysicalAccessControl::Door;
use PhysicalAccessControl::Window; // <- this will fail
```

```
fn main() {
  let my_door = Door::new(100, 200, false);
}
```

However, that is only part of the story; let us look at how we can export imports and even use aliases to create a nice and consistent type/module structure for the crate's users.

Aliasing types and exporting imports

Using **mod.rs** in a directory creates a problem: how to access the sub-modules? As we noted earlier, Rust requires to specify access to a particular type or function via the pub modifier—and the same is true for sub-modules.

Recall the previously shown directory tree for the MiniFaaS-common crate:

```
.
|-- Cargo.toml
`-- src
    |-- datastore
    |   |-- config.rs
    |   |-- json_file.rs
    |   |-- mod.rs
    |   `-- record.rs
    |-- environment
    |   |-- environment.rs
    |   |-- environments.rs
    |   `-- mod.rs
    |-- errors.rs
    |-- lib.rs
    |-- runtime
    |   |-- functions.rs
    |   |-- mod.rs
    |   `-- ops.rs
    |-- triggers
    |   |-- http.rs
    |   |-- mod.rs
    |   `-- timer.rs
    `-- types.rs

5 directories, 17 files
```

If you want to access the types and functions in **triggers/http.rs** from **lib.rs**, you will have to expose the contents (or the entire module) via **triggers/mod.rs**. Depending on what should be exposed, you can then use **pub mod http.rs** inside of **mod.rs**:

```
// triggers/mod.rs
pub mod http;
mod timer;


// or if only a specific type should be exposed:
pub use timer::TimerTrigger;
```

The preceding module can then be declared and used from the **lib.rs** file:

```
// lib.rs
mod triggers;


use triggers::http;
use triggers::timer; // this won't work, timer was not made pub(lic)
use triggers::TimerTrigger; // note the lack of the timer sub-module
here
```

These two examples show how to hide implementation details (for example, where the **TimerTrigger** type is truly coming from) and how to expose an entire sub-module with **pub** mod.

Furthermore, types (and functions) can be renamed for export and import—which can be useful for hiding implementation details as well. One way is to rename imports using the use ... as ...; construct: use **triggers::http::HttpMethod** as **TriggersHttpMethod;**. Another way is a type alias using the type keyword (or **pub** type if you want to expose it to others):

```
// errors.rs
pub type EmptyResult = Result<(), MyError>;


pub struct MyError {}
```

lib.rs declares and uses the preceding module like so:

```
// lib.rs
mod errors;


use errors::EmptyResult;
```

Using a type alias for a custom **Result** type is a common thing to do—but the type keyword allows for naming previously anonymous types as well, for example, type **TwoNumbers = (u64, u64);**. With these aliases, your code can be much more readable and easier to manipulate or use imports from different crates that have the same names.

Conclusion

This chapter detours into hypothetical construction with doors that are 100 by 200 cm with instant opening and closing and explores a few areas around functions, structs, and modules. Here is a quick recap:

- Structs in Rust are zero-overhead.

- Functions can be standalone or part of a struct's **impl** block.

- Modules are sub-sections of code with defined imports and exports.

In essence, this chapter was all about encapsulating code and reusing it. The first part focused on the behavioral aspects that go into functions, whereas the second part with structs (also known as types) keeps data separated from that code. A struct in Rust behaves somewhat like a blueprint for the in-memory bytes that allows defining bytes and interacts with their values. Since there is no metadata stored with these types, the overhead is very low, and they can be nested and composed in different ways—as we will see in the remainder of the book.

In order to attach behavior to these data points, Rust allows adding **impl** blocks which contain the function implementations. These can be instance related by requiring a special **self** parameter or generally related to the struct just like a regular function with a prefix—by convention, this is how you build constructors.

Another way of grouping together functions are modules. Modules can exist either on disk as files and folders or in a single file using the **mod** keyword. These modules are made for exposing their wares selectively so as to be able to change implementation details without having to rework half of the program. This is where the use keyword comes into play that can import whatever is exported (**pub**) by the module (or library / crate). Let us get the most important things together in a single snippet:

```rust
mod PhysicalAccessControl {
  pub struct Door {
      pub width: u32,
      pub height: u32,
      pub is_open: bool
  }

  impl Door {
    pub fn new(width: u32, height: u32, is_open: bool) -> Self {
      Door {
        width, // shorthand for width: width
```

```
        height,
        is_open,
      }
    }
  }
}

fn main() {
  let my_door = PhysicalAccessControl::Door::new(100, 200, false);
}
```

The upcoming chapter will be more about interfacing with other code, so there will be more traits, more **impl** blocks, and a revival of if. Before we get there, let us figure out the challenge of this chapter to solidify what we learned.

Challenge

Do you remember the challenge from the previous chapter? Let us improve bubble sort by putting the code into a module and a function for easy import. Then call the function with the appropriate arguments!

```
mod sorting_algorithms {
  fn bubble_sort(haystack: &mut [i32]) {
    /* code goes here */
  }
}

fn main() {
  let mut haystack = [4, 6, 3, 2, 8];
  println!("unsorted haystack: {:?}", haystack);
  /* add any necessary qualifiers here */ bubble_sort(/* your args here
*/);
  println!("  sorted haystack: {:?}", haystack);
}
```

Hint: Follow the compiler's directions about the input parameter.

Next, we will continue with code abstractions in the shape of traits, enums, and pattern matching!

CHAPTER 4
Interfacing with Code and Errors

After exploring data storage in the structs and defining behavior in functions, let us see how they can be combined using component interfaces. These things allow to make the behavior of a struct abstract, so another component can just use the behavior without having to worry about the actual struct. Over the long term, this makes all components replaceable and thereby a lot easier to maintain.

Rust's flavor of interfaces is called traits, and it is built to encapsulate a group of functions with a semantic relationship between them. The standard library's `std::io::Write`, for example, provides several generic ways to write data onto itself, which is why files, network streams, and the simple `Vec<T>` (a collection of elements with type T, see *Chapter 6, Working with Collections* and *Chapter 15, Working with Generics* can be treated the same. As a user, you do not need to worry about where the actual writing takes place, and you can rely on the function to provide the best possible implementation (or at least reasonably good).

In this chapter, we will explore how you can do that for your own codebase along with two other great aspects of Rust: enums and pattern matching.

Enums and pattern matching are related concepts that allow a developer to express variants of something together with additional data and values. Pattern matching is a syntactical construct that allows to get that data out again (you will see) and does other type-matching tasks.

Structure

In this chapter, we will be covering the following topics:

- Using traits for fun and pleasure
  - o Implementing traits
  - o Using traits in functions
- Creating variations with enums
  - o Handling errors with enums
  - o Matching patterns to extract data

Objectives

By the end of the chapter, you can look forward to learning how to use and implement traits to semantically group functions, enums, error handling, and using pattern matching to extract data.

Using traits for fun and pleasure

As mentioned in the introduction, traits are typically grouping together functions that semantically belong together and can be implemented by multiple structs. This allows the compiler to treat those structs interchangeably when it comes to function parameters or even properties—because the compiler only needs to know that the trait's functions exist and are implemented.

However, before we dive deeper into this topic, let us look at the syntax:

```rust
trait MyTrait {
  fn function_a();
}
```

As the trait **MyTrait** shows, you can provide the signature of each function, with or without a default implementation that a struct can override if required. The syntax should be familiar from struct **impl** blocks:

```rust
trait MyTrait {
  type Associate;

  fn function_a();

  fn function_b() {
    // do stuff here
  }
}
```

function_a and **function_b** are both lacking the crucial self parameter that makes them instance-specific. Thus, these functions can only be called with the struct prefix—in the same way that you cannot always provide a default implementation if the **self** parameter's type is not known.

Developers can constrain the **self** type (referred to as **Self**, with an upper case **S**) and require it to implement certain other traits, thereby making functions available to the self (but more on that in the next section and in *Chapter 15, Working with Generics.* Additionally, traits can have associated types (those too can be constrained) that an implementor has to specify. This makes a trait flexible without using actual generics (*Chapter 15, Working with Generics*).

One such example is the **IntoIterator** trait that the standard library provides. Iterators are (as we already mentioned in *Chapter 2, Controlling the Program Flow,* but really will be discussed in *Chapter 6, Working with Collections* ways to loop over collections or other series of elements of the same type. This is easy to generalize with a trait (**std::iter::Iterator** in the standard library) but requires the developer to specify the return type for the function that produces the **next** element. This is where the **Iterator** trait uses an associated type so a developer can integrate seamlessly into anything with an iterator because the element type is associated with the Iterator's implementation.

Iterators are great, and we will talk more about them throughout the book. However, it is equally important—and much simpler—to talk about how to turn a struct into an iterator for use in a for a loop. Another upside is that the trait is much simpler than the **Iterator** itself:

```
pub trait IntoIterator {
    type Item;
    type IntoIter: Iterator<Item = Self::Item>;
    fn into_iter(self) -> Self::IntoIter;
}
```

This trait exists just like that in the standard library (doc.rust-lang.org/std/iter/trait. IntoIterator.html) and features two associated types: **Item** and **IntoIter**. The **Item** type is the element type that the Iterator is going to return. The **IntoIter** type has the type constraint Iterator (that is, the type has to implement Iterator), including the trait's own associated type, which has to match the **Item** type (also, both associated types are called Item).

If that was confusing, do not worry. Actually, implementing a trait brings a lot of clarity.

Implementing traits

Once a trait is defined, structs have to provide an implementation for it to make sense, and this is done using an **impl** block:

```
impl MyTrait for MyStruct {
  fn function_a() {
    // do stuff here
  }

  fn function_b() {
    // do stuff here
  }
}
```

Similarly, associated types are simply declared within the **impl** block:

```
impl MyTrait for MyStruct {
  type Associate = usize;

  fn function_a() {
    // do stuff here
  }

  fn function_b() {
    // do stuff here
  }
}
```

These **impl** blocks use a slightly different syntax than the regular **impl** block by adding the for to declare the struct the trait is implemented … for. Inside the block, any associated types along with only the functions declared in the trait can be implemented; anything else has to go in a regular **impl** block.

Traits can also depend on other traits to require their implementation as well. As an example, the preceding trait could look like that:

```
trait MyTrait : std::fmt::Debug {
  // ...
}
```

The addition of the **: std::fmt::Debug** (note the **:**) requires all implementors to also implement the **std::fmt::Debug** trait (a trait that allows printing debug information about a type instance), or the compiler will throw an error. However, it also allows using whichever functions the super trait offers! Additionally, some traits can be implemented using a derive macro *Chapter 11, Code Generation with Macros*, and Debug is one of them.

Implementing traits enables seamless integration with the standard library (including common operators!). The previously mentioned **IntoIterator** trait is only necessary for custom collection data structures, but the trait Default (doc.rust-lang.org/std/default/trait.Default.html) is a handy and quick way to add a default instance to your struct.

Imagine having a configuration type like this:

```
// Automatically impl std::fmt::Debug if all members implement it
#[derive(Debug)]
struct SimpleConfiguration {
  no_threads: usize,
  verbosity: u8,
}
```

The default is **0** for both numeric types, which will not make a lot of sense for the number of threads (concurrent CPU execution paths), or your app will not do a lot of processing. Therefore we should tell the compiler and all standard library types that if they need a default instance for this type, they can call the **Default** trait implementation:

```
impl Default for SimpleConfiguration {
  fn default() -> Self {
    SimpleConfiguration {
      no_threads: 2,
      verbosity: 1,
    }
  }
}
```

Implementing this trait allows the standard library to work with this trait as well and simply call **Default::default()** to call the default() function for the appropriate type. This does not only work for default or iterators but also regular operators, such as +, −, and so on. For that, the library holds traits in **std::ops**, and they follow this exact same pattern as well. Because many of these aspects rely on traits to find the functions you are calling, you will sometimes have to import the trait for the compiler to find those trait-bound functions.

Using traits in functions

Initially, we mentioned that traits are great since they let you define a set of functions. This means that whenever another function requires exactly this set of functions, it can simply use the trait as a parameter (or return) type. There are several ways to achieve this:

- **impl trait**: A signal for the compiler to infer the actual type under the hood.
- **Trait objects**: that is, heap-allocated structs that implement said trait (*Chapter 12, Using Heap Memory Effectively.*
- Generics by using type constraints (*Chapter 15, Working with Generics*).

So far, we have seen **impl** only as a block that contains the functions to be implemented by a struct, but its use was extended in Rust 1.26 with the **impl** trait feature (blog. rust-lang.org/2018/05/10/Rust-1.26.html#impl-trait). Here is an example:

```rust
/// A simple trait with getters
trait Configuration {
    /// Returns the number of threads
    fn no_threads(&self) -> usize;

    /// Returns verbosity settings 0 = none, >3 = high
    fn verbosity(&self) -> u8;
}


impl Configuration for SimpleConfiguration {

    fn no_threads(&self) -> usize {
        self.no_threads
    }

    fn verbosity(&self) -> u8 {
        self.verbosity
    }
}


pub fn run_app(config: &impl Configuration) {
    // this statement creates a list of thread::Builder instances using a
    range (0..n) and the map function
    // .collect() executes the iteration (otherwise nothing happens) and
    returns the result as a Vec<Builder>
    let threads: Vec<_> = (0..config.no_threads()).map(|_|
    std::thread::Builder::new()).collect::<Vec<std::thread::Builder>>();
    // Verbosity levels
    match config.verbosity() {
```

```
    1 => println!("Threadpool set up"),
    2 => println!("Threadpool set up with {} threads", config.no_
threads()),
    3 => println!("Threadpool set up with {} threads: {:?}", config.no_
threads(), threads),
    _ => {}
  }
  run(threads); // Run the actual app
}
```

This example adds another trait **Configuration** that is implemented by our previously defined **SimpleConfiguration**. Because any application requires some configuration parameters, they have to be retrieved and stored in a somewhat organized manner. Because modern service applications usually have command line parameters, config files (in various formats), as well as environment variables as configuration options, their result has to be uniformly addressable. One option for doing that is by using a trait that can be passed into a function using an **impl** Trait parameter like in the preceding snippet. Inside the **run_app()** function, only the functions specified in the trait are available, so they can be used without having to know where and how those values came into being.

Note: In terms of software architecture, specifying only the trait allows to program to an interface [trait], not to implementation (as computer science professors instill in their students); that is, remove the actual struct from the function interface to allow other implementations to take its place without major code changes. In fact, this allows using the tried and true patterns in software engineering as recommended by the Gang of Four (Erich Gamma, Richard Helm, Ralph Johnson, and John Vlissides) in their '94 classic: Design Patterns.

Using simple generics provides a (more verbose) alternative to using **&impl** trait. For this, let us see change the preceding **run_app** function to accept any type that implements **Configuration** as a generic parameter. It looks like this:

```
pub fn run_app<T: Configuration>(config: &T) {
  //...
}
```

Another alternative is using the where clause to constrain the generic type (**T** in the preceding snippet) even further:

```
pub fn run_app<T>(config: &T) where T: Configuration {
  //...
}
```

All three snippets are functionally identical but differ in their notation (that is, how much code you have to write). The **impl** trait notation is quicker, but once multiple traits or multiple parameters come in, it is quicker and easier to change the trait bounds of a single parameter.

Creating variations with enums

In many languages, enums are synonymous with named numbers—basically, instead of writing 1, 2, 3, 4, and so on, you had to use an enum that represents their actual meaning, for example, months: January, February, and so on. This allows adding semantic meaning to the expression while retaining its efficient numeric form, which is especially important for storing data. Let us see what the most basic syntax is as follows:

```
enum Weekdays {
    Monday,
    Tuesday,
    Wednesday,
    Thursday,
    Friday,
    Saturday,
    Sunday
}
```

This is a straightforward way of mapping days to numbers (starting with 0), which can be stored as such (use **Weekdays::Monday as u8** in your code to cast). Obviously, you can also assign specific numbers to your enum variant:

```
enum Weekdays {
    Monday = 1,
    Tuesday = 2,
    Wednesday = 3,
    Thursday = 4,
    Friday = 5,
    Saturday = 6,
    Sunday = 7
}
```

However, we wanted to store more than just the number—for example, a name for displaying the weekday on a user interface (most people do not know what weekday 0 is supposed to mean). Paradoxically—printing enums has always involved mapping the enum variants to a string. So let us improve on that and store a display name with the variant:

```
enum Weekdays {
  Monday(String),
  Tuesday(String),
  Wednesday(String),
  Thursday(String),
  Friday(String),
  Saturday { display_name: String },
  Sunday { display_name: String }
}
```

If you feel reminded of structs for each variant, you have the right intuition. Just like a struct, an enum variant can have tuple-like properties (Monday–Friday) or named properties (Saturday and Sunday). Now that the (European/Western) workdays have a different property that holds their display name, things get difficult once again! How can you get to these precious names now? The answer is by using an **impl** block.

```
impl Weekdays {

  pub fn display_name(&self) -> String {
    match self {  // the pipe ( | ) acts as an or chain of all variants
      Weekdays::Monday(name)
      | Weekdays::Tuesday(name)
      | Weekdays::Wednesday(name)
      | Weekdays::Thursday(name)
      | Weekdays::Friday(name) => name.clone(),

      Weekdays::Saturday { display_name }
      | Weekdays::Sunday { display_name } => display_name.clone()
    }
  }
}
```

In this function **display_name()**, we take a borrowed self parameter and use match (more on that later in this chapter) to extract each variant's data by assigning the value to a variable (the name for Monday– Friday, **display_name** for Saturday and Sunday). The result is a function that can be called on any variant instance of the weekdays' enum. How does one get an instance, though? Almost like a struct:

```
let monday = Weekdays::Monday("Monday".to_string());
println!("{}", monday.display_name());
let saturday = Weekdays::Saturday { display_name: "Saturday".to_string()
};
println!("{}", saturday.display_name());
```

In a typical enum, you would create a constructor (a new function without the **self** parameter) to avoid unnecessary complications when creating an enum instance. We are going to rely on enums a lot for the remainder of the book, not least because of their importance in Rust's error handling.

Handling errors with enums

The ability to add typed data to each variant allows for something very powerful: `Options` and `Results`. Both types are part of Rust's error handling strategy, and both are enums. Rust, as a safe language, cannot allow null since it would lead to pointers that lead nowhere (more on safety in the upcoming chapter), and it makes programming especially complicated and inconsistent. As an example, think of a search function that looks for a substring in a string: If the substring is found, the index is returned; if not, the typical result is **-1**. However, what is returned when one of the parameters (or both) is null? Usually—it is null. Consequently, a lot of is-not-null checks are necessary, so the program does not crash since null is not a valid memory address.

Functional languages already provide a type that encapsulates valid and invalid outcomes—and so does Rust. Any expression can return a `Result`, which is an enum with two generic types attached—so `Result<T, E>` is technically correct. The generic types (more on that in *Chapter 15, Working with Generics* are T, which is the positive result, and E for the error type that comes back. Similarly, `Options` are actually defined as `Option<T>` where T is the positive case, and `None` represents the negative case.

Let us see their actual definitions from the standard library:

```
enum Result<T, E> {
    Ok(T),
    Err(E),
}

enum Option<T> {
    None,
    Some(T),
}
```

Both of these enums come with a range of functions to convert, chain, and change the various outcomes. Keep an eye out for when we use these throughout the book to write concise code while maintaining type safety. The available functions are ever-expanding, too, so check out the respective docs on `Option` (doc.rust-lang.org/std/option/enum.Option.html) and `Result` (doc.rust-lang.org/std/result/enum.Result.html).

We will go over using `Option` and `Result` next because both types wrap the actual value in one of their variants. For when crashing the program is ok, getting the value out from both type's positive (**Ok**/**Some**) variants can be done using the **unwrap()** function:

```
Some(100).unwrap(); // 100
Ok(100).unwrap(); // also 100
Err(100).unwrap(); // panic/crash
```

As you have noticed, the **Result** type requires an E (generic) type to communicate an error. Rust actually features an `Error` (doc.rust-lang.org/std/error/trait.Error.html) trait that can be used—but you had been losing additional information if you do since the trait only has the least common denominator of information available (that is, a message and maybe stack trace). There are also third-party libraries (called crates) ready to assist in transporting errors properly. However, enums can provide an easy alternative for when those crates are not available:

```
enum ApplicationError {
  Code { full:  usize, short: u16 },
  General(String),
  IOError(std::io::Error),
  Unknown
}
```

This enum can wrap up important errors for your application, and you can then easily generalize how those errors are communicated to the user. In order to extract the value of the **Some** and **Ok** variants, Rust has a special operator: the question mark (?). This operator allows you to skip the tedious steps of matching for the positive case and extracting the value while returning the error right away—something that you will do a lot as a Rust developer. Working with this operator cleans up the code significantly, as you can see here:

```
fn something_fallible(fail: bool) -> Result<u8, u8> {
  if !fail {
    Ok(1)
  }
  else {
    Err(0)
  }
}
assert!(something_fallible(false)? == 0)
```

Note that if the parameter is true, the error is returned from the caller. The Rust book provides a deep dive into this matter at doc.rust-lang.org/book/ch09-02-recoverable-errors-with-result.html.

If you use a custom enum, you will have to extract the data differently.

Matching patterns to extract data

When a struct can be one of the multiple variants, there needs to be a way to retrieve these variants again—match them, if you will. This requires some additional syntax which Rust provides. Prepare for additional versions of if and while, as well as match.

First, let us look at if let and while let. Both expressions are tests and assignments at the same time—if the test matches. So what is the test? The answer is a type match! Going back to the earlier enum Option. Remember the variants:

```
enum Option<T> {
  None,
  Some(T),
}
```

Both if **let** and **while let** let you get the T inside the *Some* variant as a variable to use within their scope.

For that, you use the following syntax:

```
let a_wrapped_value = Some(100_usize);

if let Some(the_value) = a_wrapped_value {
  println!("{} was the wrapped value", the_value);
} else {
  println!("No value was wrapped");
}
```

Similarly, **while let** continues the looping as long as the expression that feeds the **let** clause returns the desired variant—this is something that we will encounter again in *Chapter 6, Working with Collections*. This destructuring can be done with a range of types in Rust, including structs and the match is the most powerful form:

```
let a_wrapped_value = Some(100_usize);

match a_wrapped_value {
  Some(the_value) => println!("{} was the wrapped value", the_value),
  None => println!("No value was wrapped")
}
```

The match expression is typically used for responding to all variants (the compiler forces you to add all variants) of a provided enum, just like with the display names example from earlier in this chapter:

```
impl Weekdays {

  pub fn display_name(&self) -> String {
    match self {  // the pipe ( | ) acts as an or chain of all variants
      Weekdays::Monday(name)
      | Weekdays::Tuesday(name)
      | Weekdays::Wednesday(name)
      | Weekdays::Thursday(name)
      | Weekdays::Friday(name) => name.clone(),

      Weekdays::Saturday { display_name }
      | Weekdays::Sunday { display_name } => display_name.clone()
    }
  }
}
```

This one is a bit more tricky: first, the match itself is applied to the **self** parameter, which is a reference to the current instance. match automatically translates that to the "owned type", which are the variants listed inside of the match block (that is, the weekdays). Each arm is an expression that is introduced by a =>, and the part leading up to it is what is matched. In this example, the Weekdays variants are specified individually and connected with the pipe/OR operator (|), and the display name (it is a tuple with one element) is assigned to the name, a variable that is only valid inside the match arm. Consequently, the days Monday–Friday can be matched in the same arm, as they use the same tuple-based variable.

Saturday and Sunday, however, use a struct-like property assignment with names (**dispaly_name** is the name of the property as well as the newly assigned variable), and these can be individually assigned to new variables. Either way—thanks to the uniformity, we can just take one variable name for each of the arms to assign it to the same thing and return a clone.

However, match can do more. Much more:

```
fn number_match(number: usize) -> String {
  match number {
    0 | 1 => "zero or one".to_string(),
    2 ... 9 => "two to nine".to_string(),
    10 => "ten".to_string(),
    _ => "anything else".to_string()
  }
}

fn str_match(text: &str) -> String {
  match text {
```

```
        " 🐎 " => "UNI".to_string(),
        " 🦀 " => "Rustacean".to_string(),
        " 💀 " => "BJJ".to_string(),
        _ => "Nothing specific".to_string()
    }
}

fn tuple_match(tuple: (u32, u32, u32, u32)) -> String {
    match tuple {
        (first, _, third, _) => format!("[{}, ..., {}, ...]", first, third)
    }
}

pub fn main() {
    println!("number match for 0: {}", number_match(0));
    println!("number match for 10: {}", number_match(10));
    println!("number match for 100: {}", number_match(100));

    println!("Tuple match: {}", tuple_match((10, 0, 10, 123)));

    println!("Str match for 💀 : {}", str_match(" 💀 "));
    println!("Str match for 🐎 : {}", str_match(" 🐎 "));
    println!("Str match for 🐂 : {}", str_match(" 🐂 "));
    println!("Str match for 🅱 : {}", str_match(" 🅱 "));
}
```

This is not even all, match also has guards, which allows running if conditions on variables of the match arm, it can skip properties and parts of tuples with a .. (two dots), and - most importantly—the arms are matched top to bottom. This means that the **catch-all** _ always has to place last to get all remaining variants. Check the official Rust book for all of these operators and how to use them: doc.rust-lang.org/book/ch18-03-pattern-syntax.html.

So, which ones have you seen in the previous snippet:

- | represents an OR, so either of the variants will match.
- .. (and ..=) will match a range of numbers.
- str literal are matching the exact words.
- _ the catch-all for whatever would take its place (match arm or values).

These helpers allow for the creation of sophisticated matching strategies; however, keep in mind that match is an expression, so all arms have to return the same type in order for the compiler to accept it. This may require some practice…

Finally, there is still some destructuring we did not look into. While each match arm that assigns variables from members is already doing that, a regular let can do similar things. Let us go back to the struct we had earlier:

```
struct SimpleConfiguration {
  no_threads: usize,
  verbosity: u8,
}
```

Retrieving the individual values (**no_threads** and verbosity) can be a bit verbose if the structs get larger and more nested. However, we already know the type, and without any metadata, the properties are right there, so why not extract the data into individual variables? Like so:

```
fn main() {
  let SimpleConfiguration {
    no_threads, verbosity
  } = Default::default();
  println!("no_threads: {}, verbosity: {}", no_threads, verbosity);
}
```

Which prints:

```
no_threads: 2, verbosity: 1
```

The preceding snippet also has some bonus content: calling the **Default::default()** function, which automatically finds the type's implementation if available. Since we created one earlier in this chapter, using that implementation leads to the outcome shown in the snippet. Alternatively, **SimpleConfiguration::default()** would have resulted in the same outcome. Destructuring is definitely a helpful tool for working with types, and it will not be the last time you will see the match, if let, and destructuring in this book or your Rust career. For now, let us recap what we touched on in this chapter.

Conclusion

Traits are interfaces—sometimes likened to contracts—between two code components that can both rely on these definitions and provide their own implementations. This enables a large piece of software to cleanly separate the what from the how—in addition to grouping functions semantically (separating by concerns). Traits in Rust can provide a default implementation as well as an associated type for leaving the necessary flexibility to the developer that implements the actual component.

To recall, here is the previously mentioned example. Use these traits in your component design to formalize things better:

```
trait MyTrait{
  type Associate;

  fn function_a();

  fn function_b();
}
```

Implementing the trait's functions (and specifying the associated type) is done in an **impl** block that couples the implementor with the trait:

```
impl MyTrait for MyStruct {
  type Associate = usize;

  fn function_a() {
    // do stuff here
  }

  fn function_b() {
    // do stuff here
  }
}
```

However, Rust does not only feature structs but also enums. An enum is a handy way to express (limited) variations of a certain type that the compiler can check and enforce—think categories, weekdays, and so on. In Rust, these variations can come with properties of their own to include data beyond their own variant. Here is a more advanced enum example:

```
enum Link {
  Next(Box<Data>),
  Empty
}
struct Data {
  value: u128, // we'll make this generic soon enough!
  next: Link
}
```

Linked lists are straightforward collections to store generic items in, and they come with two different node types. These can be built with enums fairly easily (with some major flaws, but more on that in *Chapter 6, Working with Collections*, and in a very readable fashion as well. Simply by examining the enum, you may be able to guess how the collection works internally and that each element is stored together with a pointer to the next element (except for the last). As a side note, this implementation of the linked list is a bad idea—check the *Further Reading* section at the end of the chapter for some resources as to why that is the case.

A more obvious choice for using enums is error handling—with Rust's `Option<T>` and `Result<T, E>` types. They provide ways to return multiple types in a structured way and communicate (semantically) whether a particular outcome was not successful or just exited normally but will not return anything. This lets you integrate errors into a regular workflow—instead of having to deal with them in different ways.

One way to achieve this integration is by using if let to unpack a positive (or negative) result and work in the else block with the other alternative, whereas `let` provides the ability to do the same but continue looping instead of a single run-through. Finally, there is the most powerful of all: match. With match, the compiler forces you to deal with every variant in the enum (or use a wildcard) and still return the same type within each arm. These arms can be further augmented to extract specific bits of information by destructuring the arm's variant.

However confusing and brief this introduction may have been, you will use these language features a lot in your Rust career. We will kickstart this in the upcoming chapter by diving into the core of the Rust programming language: borrowing and ownership.

Challenge

Let us build out the challenge from the previous chapter some more. If you recall, it was about the bubble sort sorting algorithm, and the last step was to modularize it. However, as we learned in this chapter, modules are not always enough to de-couple code sections (that is, split the what from the how), so let us add a trait sorter in this chapter together with a function to take and sort slices.

Feel free to get creative here too, and—if you dare—use associated types or enums to accomplish the task. Creating intuitive code in Rust is sometimes really tricky and may require a lot of practice to get right. Here is some starting code:

```rust
mod sorting_algorithms {

  pub trait Sorter {
    // add a function interface here
  }


  pub struct BubbleSort {} // this is an empty struct
```

```
impl Sorter for BubbleSort {
    // implement the function you declared above
  }
}

fn main() {
  let mut haystack = [4, 6, 3, 2, 8];
  println!("unsorted haystack: {:?}", haystack);
  // Import the trait and call your function to sort the haystack

  println!("  sorted haystack: {:?}", haystack);
}
```

Because you have now used traits and worked a little with types—would you have implemented the **Sorter** trait differently? For example, as a part of the collection?

Further reading

One excellent resource on learning Rust and more about the linked list data structure can be found here: cglab.ca/~abeinges/blah/too-many-lists/book/README.html.

CHAPTER 5

Borrowing Ownership with Scopes

As you have probably seen when running some of the examples, Rust is a particularly picky language. Even though the compiler tries to be helpful, some error messages can be confusing, especially because we never explored Rust's approach to managing memory, which is fundamentally different from other languages. We will remedy this in the following sections!

As mentioned in *Chapter 1, Building the Basics*, managing memory is a fundamental aspect of programming and the compiler. The approach Rust takes is different but allows you to remain in control of the program's memory allocations. This awareness and the resulting patterns and ideas have proven useful in other programming languages—in short, and you will be a better programmer overall by understanding Rust.

Structure

In this chapter, we will be covering the following topics:

- Taking ownership of memory
  - o Working with both kinds of memory
  - o Borrowing memory
  - o Working in scopes

o   Controlling mutability

- Introducing clones

Objectives

This chapter will be about scopes, lifetimes, memory ownership, and memory borrowing in Rust. By the end of this chapter, you will understand how Rust allocates, moves, and drops memory and use it in everyday programming.

Taking ownership of memory

Rust uses an approach called borrowing and ownership as its model to request memory from and give back to the operating system. Let us talk about ownership first: What does it mean to own memory?

Ownership - in the real world - means that one owns something and therefore has power over it. In the simplest form, you own a thing, and it is within your right (as of 2022, anyway) to do almost anything with it: changing it, selling it, or using it. Similarly, you (or your variables, rather) own sections of memory as they are allocated. This ownership entitles the variable to certain actions, and just like in the real world, there can only be one owner (at least formally).

Owning memory has likely been the only way that you have used variables up to now:

```
fn main() {
  let x = 10_u32; // x owns the memory where 10 is allocated inside
}
```

Owning sections memory (and the variable as a proxy); therefore, it not only means that the variable **x** owns the number **10**, but all numbers that fit into the type—a **u_32**. This ownership is—unless moved—valid while the parent scope (the function main() in the snippet) is valid. As the execution leaves the scope, all owned variables of the scope are dropped, and the memory is no longer safe to read from. Effectively, this is one way how the Rust compiler provides its famous memory safety. As far as formal rules go, this is how the Rust book (doc.rust-lang.org/book/ch04-01-what-is-ownership.html) defines those.

First, let us take a look at the ownership rules. Keep these rules in mind as we work through the examples that illustrate them:

- Each value in Rust has a variable that is called its owner.
- There can only be one owner at a time.
- When the owner goes out of scope, the value will be dropped.

So let us look at some code to understand this better:

```
fn main() {
  let owner_a = String::from("🐙");
  let owner_b = owner_a;
  {
    let owner_c = String::from("🐉");
  } // owner_c will be dropped here
  let owner_d = owner_c; // this won't work
}
```

By using **String** variables, we can better illustrate the ownership transfers—like when **owner_a** moves ownership to **owner_b** in the preceding snippet. After this assignment, the String belongs to **owner_b**, and the compiler will object to any usage of the variable **owner_a**. After that, we open a new scope { } and assign another string to **owner_c**, which we try to assign to **owner_d** after exiting the scope. According to the rules, this will not work—**owner_c**'s memory region has been dropped by then. Let us fix this and see how we can transfer ownership properly to **owner_d** in the following snippet:

> **Note: Types where duplicating bits duplicate the value (that is, they are not references) implement the copy trait, an implicit duplication of the value. This makes them much more comfortable to use and does not show the change of ownership well. Read more in the Rust docs at doc.rust-lang.org/std/marker/trait.Copy.html.**

```
fn main() {
  let owner_a = String::from("🐙");
  let owner_b = owner_a;

  let owner_d = {
    let owner_c = String::from("🐉");
    owner_c // return ownership of owner_c's memory
  };
}
```

The first part in this snippet is identical to what is happening preceding. **owner_a**'s owned memory gets moved to **owner_b**. The next statement, however, creates a string and, after assigning it to **owner_c**, returns the memory ownership from the scope to its parent and assigns it to **ownder_d**. This moving ownership to a parent scope is possible because a **String** type is very different from a regular i32 numeric. The main difference is that by default, the **String** is allocated on the heap, whereas the i32 (and similar numeric types) reside on the stack. This division of memory types is typical, and it is time we dive a little deeper.

Working with both kinds of memory

A String in Rust has a simple layout: the number of characters it holds (length), the number of characters it can hold (capacity), and a pointer to where these characters are held. The former two are simple (unsigned) numbers, whereas the latter is an address somewhere in the heap memory. Heap memory is—as the joke goes—heaps of memory. It is the part of working memory that has a very high limit and allows for reserving large parts (gigabytes) at once, which is why programs use it to store their large in-memory stuff and point to those locations (addresses) using pointers.

These pointers are essentially addresses (type **usize**) that can be stored and read from/written to—if allowed. Because any positive integer can be considered an address (which is unsafe in Rust, as we will explore in *Chapter 16, Calling Unsafe and Foreign Functions*, the operating system makes sure that those reads and writes stay within the generally assigned memory region for that program. If this is violated, the program will crash.

The second type of memory that is assigned to a program is the stack memory. What is different from heap memory is that the stack is assigned to the execution thread to store fixed-size variables and orders of magnitude smaller than the heap. As the name stack already suggests, reserving memory, there is not a free-for-all but is tightly organized in a **Last In, First Out (LIFO)** fashion. So much so that the compiler takes care of allocating the required amounts automatically, which requires the variable size to be known at compile time. Rust has error codes dedicated to this, for example, E0620 (doc.rust-lang.org/error-index.html#E0620).

Here is a brief comparison:

	Stack	**Heap**
Allocation size	Kilobytes	Gigabytes
Organization	LIFO	Unstructured
Allocation/deallocation	Automatic	Manual
Access speed	Fast	Slow

Table 5.1: A comparison of stack and heap memory attributes

Although none of these concepts are specific to Rust, the Rust compiler makes a lot of use of the inherent capabilities of the stack, and as a systems programming language, fine-grained control is a requirement. Additionally, many of the core project maintainers strive to create important libraries in a zero-copy and allocation-free fashion in order to avoid unexpected performance pitfalls or using too much memory. Especially heap memory allocations can often slow down programs in two ways:

- The allocation itself takes longer because the operating system has to find the required space.

- Access to this space is done by hopping to the pointer location, which is an additional operation.

Moreover, you have to free (**drop()** in Rust) heap memory to avoid a buildup—we will explore this topic in a later section (*Working in Scopes*) in this chapter. Stack memory, however, is returned implicitly, especially since the overall amount of memory is very limited. Typically an operating system provides a chunk of memory as the stack, which is configurable with compiler arguments, although increasing the size is rarely a solution to a stack overflow error. One reason such an error could happen is the repeated, infinite call of a function—this will create infinite copies of the variables inside and eventually require too much memory. This will not happen in regular calls because for the execution pointer to move to another function, and it has to pop the stack, which automatically frees the previous scope's memory. Let us look at the following illustration:

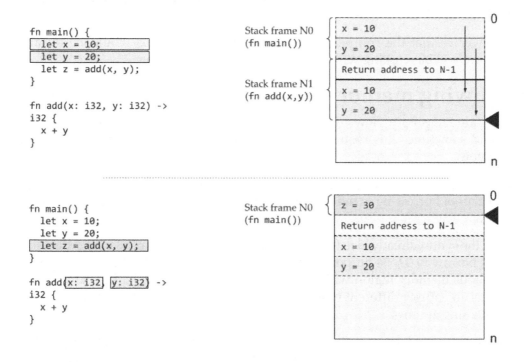

Figure 5.1: *A simplified version of Rust stack variable behavior*

The illustration contains two parts, each of which is a snapshot at the time of executing the main function, where the lower bit follows the upper one. Please note that this is a simplified version of what is actually happening. Memory management is a core part of operating systems, and this book is about Rust.

In the earlier (upper) part, the compiler automatically allocates stack memory for the variables **x** and **y** and pushes them onto the stack in order of their declaration. Once the execution pointer reaches the function (**add()**), the compiler allocates a new stack frame to move the variables into the function as parameters right after the return address (note that the stack fills up toward *n*). This means that **x** and **y**—if they were more complex types—are now unavailable for further use since they are going to be popped off (removed) the stack as soon as **add()** returns.

The thick black triangle on the right symbolizes this return where the variable z is declared with the result of the **add()** function. However, for that to be pushed into the right frame, the previous frame (N1) has to be popped off entirely—or, in other words: the function has to return.

This requirement to pop and push variables and so on to the stack in a predictable order leads to implicit guarantees like scopes but also leads to considerable problems. For example: what if we had an address to the original *x* with the plan to read from that address some other time?

The answer is: that the compiler would not let you since this would be unsafe. Instead, we will be working with something smarter: borrowing.

Borrowing memory

Borrows are temporary views of the data. They have to live shorter than the data itself, and sometimes this requires explicit lifetime annotations (the compiler will remind you).

Since memory is owned by a scope, it can provide borrows to other child scopes. The concept of borrowing is independent of memory allocation, so anything can be shared that way!

We used the syntax already: & in front of the type. Consequently, a &u8 is a particularly wasteful borrow (a 32/64 bit pointer to an 8-bit data), but a &[u8] is a reference to a continuous memory region with several u8 values. Technically a **&String** can be viewed as an entirely different type from a String, a fact that makes error messages a bit confusing at times.

Luckily, conversion back to an owned type is pretty convenient with the * operator. This dereferences the borrow and provides access to the owned type's properties, which is sometimes required (for example, to get the size of the owned type). For custom types, the operator can be implemented using the DeRef trait (doc.rust-lang. org/std/ops/trait.Deref.html)).

Let us look at an example for borrowing:

```
use std::mem;

fn how_large(s: &String) {
  println!("Size of val: {} bytes", mem::size_of_val(s));
  println!("Size of type: {} bytes", mem::size_of::<&String>())
}

fn main() {
  how_large(&String::from("Hello World"));
}
```

This snippet prints the following sizes:

```
Size of val: 24 bytes
Size of type: 8 bytes
```

According to the documentation (doc.rust-lang.org/std/mem/fn.size_of_val.html), **size_of_val()** Returns the size of the pointed-to value in bytes, which means it dereferences the reference that you pass into it. It then counts the size of the allocated memory—regardless of its location (heap or stack). Consequently, we see the size of the Hello World rather than the Strings.

The second function **size_of::<T>()** returns the static size of its type parameter **T**, and on a 64bit machine (or play.rust-lang.org), a pointer is 64 bits, or 8 bytes, in size. Thus, this is the size of **&String**.

> Note: size_of::<String>() **returns the size of its components without the actual content (type parameters cannot know what you are going to put in, they are static). If you want to know that, why not try it out?**

Now that we can own and borrow memory, let us move on to (re-)visiting scopes.

Working in scopes

We have already used the basics of Rust scopes (which covers 80% of use cases anyway) because *Chapter 1, Building the Basics,* so let us dive a little deeper here. So far, we have used lifetimes and scopes interchangeably, but that is only partly true because a scope informs the compiler about the data's lifetime.

> Note: Each reference has an implicit lifetime attached to it. In order to make the lifetime explicit (and thereby tell the compiler), you can use the syntax (a single quotation mark) plus a name for the lifetime (that is, my_lifetime). However, this is an advanced topic that fits very well with generics, so you can look forward to learning more in *Chapter 15, Working with Generics.*

The lifetime of data is responsible for when it needs to be allocated, freed, and where it is moved and borrowed from and to. In a relatively simple program flow, the question about scopes rarely comes up, but any real-life application will have one of the following:

- Closures (sometimes called lambda functions).
- Trait objects (*Chapter 12, Using Heap Memory Effectively*).
- Structs that own references.
- Multi-threading/async programming (*Chapter 13, Running Code Concurrently.*
- Generics (*Chapter 15, Working with Generics*).

Each of these constructs allow you to create more complex lifetimes (or lifetime requirements) or nest scopes that execute at different times. Let us consider the following snippet:

```rust
fn complicated_len() -> impl Fn() -> usize {
  let s = String::from("Hello World");
  || {
    s.len()
  }
}


fn main() {
  let len_fn = complicated_len();
  println!("{}", len_fn());
}
```

This snippet will not compile, and for experienced Rustaceans, it is clear why—but can you already spot the mistake (as a reminder: ||{ /* fn body */} is a closure without arguments)? Take a moment to see if you can find it. For more help, here is the compiler message:

```
Compiling playground v0.0.1 (/playground)
error[E0373]: closure may outlive the current function, but it
borrows `s`, which is owned by the current function
 --> src/main.rs:3:3
  |
3 |   || {
  |   ^^ may outlive borrowed value `s`
4 |     s.len()
```

```
   |      - `s` is borrowed here
   |
note: closure is returned here
 --> src/main.rs:1:25
   |
1 | fn complicated_len() -> impl Fn() -> usize {
   |                         ^^^^^^^^^^^^^^^^^^^
help: to force the closure to take ownership of `s` (and any other
 referenced variables), use the `move` keyword
   |
3 |    move || {
   |    ^^^^^^^
```

```
For more information about this error, try `rustc --explain E0373`.
error: could not compile `playground` due to previous error
```

Just like so many times with Rust programming, the compiler is right (the compiler working group is doing an awesome job!): The variable s will not live long enough to borrow its contents to the closure that is being returned. Consequently, the original variable s would be dropped whenever the returned closure is called, which would have led to reading undefined memory. Safe Rust will not do that.

Because the compiler messages are helpful, they also include a solution to the dilemma: using the move keyword. This keyword instructs the compiler to move the variables into the scope if they are used on the inside. Consequently, s will not be available for further use in the parent.

Here is the updated snippet:

```rust
fn complicated_len() -> impl Fn() -> usize {
  let s = String::from("Hello World");
  move || {
    s.len()
  }
}


fn main() {
  let len_fn = complicated_len();
  println!("{}", len_fn());
}
```

With the **move** keyword (which applies to the closure, not the scope), the code produces the following output ("Hello World" has 11 characters):

```
Compiling playground v0.0.1 (/playground)
Finished dev [unoptimized + debuginfo] target(s) in 1.65s
  Running `target/debug/playground`
11
```

The reason for this behavior is rooted in the fact that the compiler does not know who is taking ownership of the variable s. With the move, this is clearly defined—it is the closure itself. An alternative way would be to assign a named lifetime to the reference and thereby tell the compiler explicitly how long the variable is going to be around, which is typically a lot more complicated. We will see in *Chapter 15, Working with Generics*, how that works!

We will also touch on the remaining things on the previous list of complex lifetimes throughout the remainder of the book, as well as strategies to work around these issues. Borrowing is cheap and efficient and much preferred in a no-std scenario (for example, embedded systems, which do not have a standard—std—library available), where allocating any memory may be difficult/expensive.

However, elaborate borrowing schemes like zero-copy crates employ are great examples of how efficient Rust code can be. One example is the JSON serialization and deserialization crate Serde (github.com/rust-embedded-community/serde-json-core/).

So far, we have touched on owning and borrowing memory, but never how to actually change anything in Rust. Although the programming language favors immutable data, mutable data is easily possible but comes with certain rules and constraints. Let us explore those now.

Controlling mutability

If you tried to change any variable in the past challenges after it has been initialized, you might have faced a compiler error. The reason for this is simple—all variables are immutable by default, which makes a lot of things a lot simpler. If you recall the ownership rules from earlier, there can only be one mutable reference at a time in order to ensure that no data race condition occurs.

Not allowing these data races are what makes Rust safe and provides side-effect-free mutability. Code that violates these rules will not compile with safe Rust. Enforcing these rules gets a lot easier if the default is to prohibit mutability and require changes to be signaled explicitly via the mut keyword.

Note: Side-effects describe inadvertent changes to data in a range of circumstances, particularly in the database world. They occur when two parties want to update data based on the same original at the same time.

Consequently, you—as a developer—should be careful when you require mutable variables. As it turns out, mutability is rarely required and can be avoided by using:

- Variable shadowing.
- Copy/clone/move and just return the updated values.

Shadowing is reassigning a variable name to a different value. Here is an example:

```
fn main() {
  let x = 10;
  let x = 20; // this x shadows the first x from here on
  assert_eq!(x, 20);
}
```

Note: `assert_eq!` is a macro to assert equality. If both parameters are not equal (as defined by the `std::cmp::Eq` trait), the program crashes in a panic. So if your program runs, both parameters are equal.

This variable shadowing also allows to reuse names, so you do not have to find the 22nd letter in the (English) alphabet or open a thesaurus for synonyms. Another way to achieve the same thing as mutability is to the variable and return the result in a new variable:

```
fn main() {
  let a = String::from("Rust");
  let x = a + "acean"; // you could shadow `a` here as well
  // a has been moved here and is no longer usable
  assert_eq!(x, "Rustacean");
}
```

Finally, declaring a variable `mut` is not terrible, but it limits your options—you cannot borrow while a variable is `mut`, and the compiler will warn about unneeded `mut` declarations. However, sometimes it is necessary to update things—like a shared state or simply add something to a list:

```
fn main() {
  let mut todo = vec![];

  todo.push("Laundry");
  todo.push("Dishes");
```

```
    todo.push("Sports");

    assert_eq!(todo, vec!["Laundry", "Dishes", "Sports"])
}
```

Mutability can also be required for function parameters in order to change stuff inside the function—note that this also applies to the self parameter, where the calling struct instance has to be mutable. These mutable parameters are usually mutable references with the **&mut** syntax. Having ownership of most types also allows you to create a mutable instance yourself inside the function. Let us look at an example for a few mutable variables:

```
fn join_into(target: &mut String, separator: char, list: &[&str]) {
  let mut is_first = true;
  for elem in list {
    if !is_first {
      target.push(separator);
    }
    else {
      is_first = false;
    }
    target.push_str(elem);
  }
}

fn main() {
  let todo = vec!["Laundry", "Dishes", "Sports"]

  let mut target = String::new();
  join_into(&mut target, '-', &todo);

  assert_eq!(target, "Laundry-Dishes-Sports")
}
```

In this snippet, we created a function to join list elements together with a separator—but instead of returning a new String instance, we expand one that is provided by the caller. Therefore, **join_into** function requires a mutable String reference to write to, the separator between the items, and a list of string references to join. If you are wondering about String versus &str, the latter is a borrowed string somewhere in memory, whereas a String type is always the standard library's String type. You will come across those two a lot as a Rust developer, and the conversion between them is straightforward: **&String** can be used as **&str** and **String::from("string literals are always &str")** results in a String (or you use **to_string()**). As a side note about lifetimes: Literals use the reserved 'static lifetime. This means a **const** string literal is actually **const MY_LITERAL: &'static str = "I am a literal";**.

The snippet uses the **&str** type collection as an input parameter, iterates over it using a **for** loop, and only starts appending the separator (a char parameter) after the second iteration via a bool switch. Most of those things we have discussed before, and you will recognize them. However, the target parameter is a mutable reference to a String, so we can append the **&str** values—in fact, a clone of these values. However, the important part is that we are changing the input string thanks to its mutability—it is a heap-allocated data structure, and the function uses a reference to write directly to it.

> **Note: Thanks to Rust's strict mutability rules, a new pattern was necessary to achieve what a modern programming language's needs: an accessible shared state. The (programming) pattern that Rust uses is called the interior mutability pattern and uses a reference counter (std::rc::Rc) that wraps a cell (std::cell::Cell or std::cell::RefCell) to have something like a borrow check at runtime. Failing to pass this check will crash the program with a panic; however, it lets you own immutable references that can be turned mutable at any time. Check out the Rust book's chapter on that (doc.rust-lang.org/book/ch15-05-interior-mutability.html) or wait until *Chapter 12, Using Heap Memory Effectively*.**

Ultimately, mutability is not a difficult thing to do—it is just very constrained in its use. However, the reality of most programs is that many values are declared once and read many times, which is a perfect fit for default immutability. With the Rust compiler checking your use of mutable references, you can be sure that if the program compiles and the keyword unsafe is absent from your code, your code is free of data race conditions and side effects.

Introducing clones

This chapter also introduces a dilemma: what if a function wants ownership of a variable, but the calling scope requires ownership as well? Especially in other programming languages, this is handled implicitly, and passing data into a function typically does not result in it being gone from the scope, which is similar to borrowing.

This is where Rust requires being explicit about certain actions. In particular, if ownership of a variable is required twice—the memory area should be allocated twice. Instead of creating this copy implicitly, a call to the **clone()** function is necessary to get the program to compile.

A **clone()** implementation does not come for free either; custom types have to either derive the trait implementation:

```rust
#[derive(Clone)]
struct Fraction {
  pub numerator: usize,
  pub denominator: usize
}
```

… or implement the clone trait:

```rust
struct Fraction {
  pub numerator: usize,
  pub denominator: usize
}


impl Clone for Fraction {
  fn clone(&self) -> Self {
    Fraction {
      numerator: self.numerator.clone(),
      denominator: self.denominator.clone(),
    }
  }
}
```

Cloning typically creates a deep copy of the type's data, so if you clone a byte array with 2 GiB in size, you will need 4 GiB to fit both copies in memory. The main implication is that this will impact performance, fill up space, and is probably not very elegant either. If using references is not handy, the Rust standard library offers types like the reference counter (**std::rc::Rc** - doc.rust-lang.org/std/rc/struct.Rc.html), copy-on-write (std::borrow::Cow—doc.rust-lang.org/std/borrow/enum.Cow.html), as well as Cells and RefCells (both in std::cell—doc.rust-lang.org/stable/std/cell/).

We will look at using these types and the interior mutability pattern in a later chapter (*Chapter 12, Using Heap Memory Effectively*. For now, know that if ownership is absolutely required by a function, crate, or some type, using **clone()** is an option if the data is reasonably small. If that is not the case, wrappers such as Rcs or Cows can provide a solution. If none of that helps, rewrite the function or replace the crate.

Conclusion

Let us quickly recap what borrowing and ownership in Rust are: Rust's memory management concept is much more strict than that of other languages, and it already kicks in during compilation. Scopes create implicit lifetimes during which a variable can own a memory region. Although these lifetimes are active, the owner can borrow a reference.

As far as syntax goes, borrowing uses a & to denote (and create) a reference (borrow) and a * to get back to the owned data when needed. If you declare lifetimes explicitly, we will explore this topic in *Chapter 15, Working with Generics*; you can tell the compiler when a variable's ownership expires by binding it to a scope.

Alternatively, the move keyword moves ownership into a sub-scope that may outlive its parent. In order to mutate memory, ownership is not required—a mutable borrow is just as good. However, the borrow checker component of the compiler will enforce the rules (from doc.rust-lang.org/book/ch04-01-what-is-ownership.html):

- Each value in Rust has a variable that is called its owner.

- There can only be one owner at a time.

- When the owner goes out of scope, the value will be dropped.

Eventually, you will find that practice lets you see lifetimes and borrow check yourself in your head while writing code. Since this is part of Rust's steep learning curve, do not worry if some things do not make intuitive sense yet. Keep practicing, for example, with the challenge for this chapter. The challenge also provides a small preview as to what the next chapter contains, which are collections like the **Vec<T>**, maps, and sets.

Challenge

For this chapter's challenge, we stay in the realm of classic algorithms and data structures. After the sorting algorithm in the last few chapters, we are looking at the data structures part—something which will be helpful for the upcoming chapter as well. In this challenge, you have to finish and use a data structure that you already saw in *Chapter 4, Interfacing with Code and Errors*: The linked list!

The linked list is a data structure that contains the current value of what it stores together with a pointer to the next value. The challenge here is to implement a few basic operations to manipulate the list and use what you learned in this and previous chapters to complete it. Be sure to use play.rust-lang.org or a local Rust installation (if available) in order to see if the provided asserts work. However, most importantly: Have fun!

```rust
enum Link {
  Next(Box<Data>),
  Empty
}

struct Data {
  value: u128,
  next: Link
}

impl LinkedList {
  pub fn new() -> Self {
    LinkedList { head: None }
  }

  pub fn append(&mut self, value: u128) {
    // Add an element to the end of the list
    // use Box::new() to allocate data
  }

  pub fn count(&self) -> usize {
    // Count the elements and return how many you found
    0
  }

  pub fn pop(&mut self) -> Option<u128> {
    // Remove the last element and return the value, or None if empty
    Some(0)
  }
}

struct LinkedList {
  head: Option<Link>
}

// By default, a data structure is dropped recursively
// Which leads to a stack overflow.
```

```rust
impl Drop for LinkedList {
  fn drop(&mut self) {
    let n = self.count();
    if n > 0 {
      for _ in 0..n {
        let _ = self.pop();
      }
    }
  }
}

fn main() {
  let mut list = LinkedList::new();
  list.append(1);
  list.append(2);
  list.append(3);

  assert_eq!(list.count(), 3);
  assert_eq!(list.pop(), Some(3));
  assert_eq!(list.pop(), Some(2));
  assert_eq!(list.pop(), Some(1));
  assert_eq!(list.pop(), None);
}
```

In this list, each element (**Data** instance) holds a pointer to the heap allocation (a **Box** allocates stuff on the heap) of the next element. This avoids a potential infinite size because otherwise, an element contains an element, contains an element, contains an element…). A similar problem plagues the automatically implemented **Drop**, which uses recursion (www.geeksforgeeks.org/recursion/) to free each element, and that can overflow the stack really quickly. If all of that sounds confusing to you, experiment! We will get to testing soon enough, but using extreme values is already a great start to find out what breaks when.

This example was inspired by *A Bad Stack from Learning Rust with Entirely Too Many Linked Lists* (rust-unofficial.github.io/too-many-lists/first-final.html). Feel free to use it to solve the preceding challenge. Rightfully, this is not a great implementation of a linked list. Let us explore better implementations in the upcoming chapter.

CHAPTER 6

Working with Collections

In previous chapters, we used collections of different types only sometimes, which is something that we want to remedy now. The Rust standard library contains a wealth of collections, and each one of them has different strengths and weaknesses. It is time to get some clarity around the different variations, when and how to use them, and even some implementation details.

Data structures (such as collections of all sorts) are important parts of solving problems with software, especially if they come as part of a standard library. There, you can assume that many people spent time optimizing the related algorithms, so a tree structure is as efficient as it reasonably gets. Instead of building your own lists, maps, trees, and so on, it is much better to learn what is already available.

As the saying attributed to Isaac Newton goes: *If I have seen further, it is by standing on the shoulders of Giants* (spelling modernized). Let us start climbing.

Structure

In this chapter, we will be covering the following topics:

- Using sequential collections: slices and Vec<T>
    - o Operating The Vec<T>
        - ▪ Initialization

- Adding, removing, and accessing elements
   o Borrowing The Vec<T>: Slices
- Deriving keys from values with sets and maps
   o Sorting keys: trees and hashes
   o Using sets and maps
- Iterating over any collection
   o Chaining iterators together
   o Collecting the results

Objectives

By the end of this chapter, you will have explored the various collections that Rust offers, such as BTreeSets and BTreeMaps, HashMaps, HashSets, Vec<T>, and the all-important slice.

Using sequential collections: slices and Vec<T>

In *Chapter 1, Building the Basics*, we saw the first type of sequential collection in Rust: the array. Arrays are common data types across all programming languages and technologies because they are a repetition of one type and can exist on the heap as well as on the stack memory. However, because they are allocated in one big chunk, resizing is tricky (and impossible on the stack), which is an obvious drawback!

To recap, here is an array declaration (and definition):

```
let my_array: [u8; 3] = [1, 2, 3];
```

The **Vec<T>** is always allocated on the heap and can be grown as required and if space is available. Internally, the **Vec<T>** is organized just like an array and almost as fast.

With two sequential collection types that are somewhat different in structure but not in use, Rust faces an issue: can there be a universal type that developers can use for borrowing? The answer is yes; it is called a slice. A slice is like a view into whichever memory (it is a reference type without an explicit owned type) and typically denoted **&[T]** (**T** being the generic type). Both types can hold a maximum of **usize** number of items.

The declaration is similar to an array's but without a defined length. Slices can also be mutable and change values in place if required; however, not all collection types can be borrowed that way. What is required is a continuous chunk of memory, which is not always available (for example, in HashSets or BTreeSets).

Slices are great for function declarations (for example, instead of a borrowed &Vec<T>) but are somewhat complicated to handle as struct members because they are borrowed types, after all…

Operating the Vec<T>

Let us start with the **Vec<T>**. It is a versatile list for all data types, and you will be using it a lot. Generally, the **Vec<T>** uses a continuous chunk of memory to store data that it pre-allocates on insert. Consequently, an empty **Vec<T>** requires practically no space until the first insert.

Just like the String, a **Vec<T>** has a length and capacity, the latter of which signals the potential number of elements it can store. Whenever length equals capacity on insert, the **Vec<T>** allocates more than the previous capacity to accommodate the projected increase in length. Next, the data are copied into the new memory region, and the—now old—region is freed. Because this has an obvious performance impact, you should try to initialize the **Vec<T>** with an appropriate capacity.

A particular growth strategy is not guaranteed, but the **push()** function retains its runtime complexity on reallocation. Read more at doc.rust-lang.org/std/vec/struct. Vec.html#guarantees.

Initialization

Other than the conventional **Vec::new()** (or with a specified capacity **n** using **Vec::with_capacity(n)** you can use a macro **vec![]**. Internally, the macro creates a mutable **Vec<T>,** and if you specify items inside the **[]**, these items get added. Alternatively, you can initialize a **vec![0; 5]** to get a **Vec<T>** with length 5 and all 0 values. Here is a summary in the following snippet:

```
fn main() {
    assert_eq!(vec![], Vec::new());
    assert_eq!(vec![], Vec::with_capacity(5));
    assert_eq!(vec![0; 5], vec![0, 0, 0, 0, 0]);
}
```

Once initialized, the **Vec<T>** allocates a struct with three **usize** variables (that is, three times 8 bytes on a 64-bit system). This is what the Rust standard library's source code defines the struct(s) as (edited for brevity—find a link to the source code in the *Further Reading* section):

```
// A pointer to the data and the capacity
pub struct RawVec<T, A: Allocator = Global> {
```

```
    ptr: Unique<T>,
    cap: usize,
    alloc: A,
}
// The actual Vec, with the length
pub struct Vec<T, A: Allocator = Global> {
    buf: RawVec<T, A>,
    len: usize,
}
```

Disregarding the allocator bits (which are required to allocate memory in special environments), the **Vec<T>** is very lean and—if nothing is inserted—requires 24 bytes in size. Heap memory is only reserved once you are adding elements.

Adding, removing, and accessing elements

You can mutate a **Vec<T>** using many different operations, but in this section, we explore some basic ones: **push()**, **insert()**, and **remove()**. All of these require the variable to be declared **mut**, and all of them require some time to do. This time requirement is typically described as the Big-O-Notation and denotes the performance for when the collection size increases/decreases. We will use *e* as the input parameter for the element and *i* for the index.

> **Note: The Big-O-Notation is a way of describing the growth curve of an operation, where the exact measurement is either size or time required—depending on the context. There are major classes of how this measurement develops if you repeat the operation many times, and the most important classes—fastest first—are constant (O(1)), linear (O(n)), quadradic (O(n^2)), or exponential (O(2^n)). Read more over at www.geeksforgeeks.org/analysis-algorithms-big-o-analysis/.**

Adding data to the end of the **Vec<T>** is done via the push(e) function. This function takes an element and has a complexity of O(1), which means that this operation will take the same amount of time, regardless of the collection size.

Alternatively, you can use **insert(i, e)** to add an element at the specified position. Because this requires the remainder of the collection to move, the worst-case complexity is O(n) (inserting at the front), and the best case complexity is O(1) (inserting at the back).

Removing items works just like the reverse of the insert function: **remove(i)**. Calling the function with a valid index will return the element that has been removed while also shifting the elements into their new place (that is, left). Thus, the runtime complexity mirrors that of **insert()**: O(n) in the worst case and O(1) in the best.

One other important task is to retrieve the element at a specified index. The Rust **Vec<T>** implements the trait for using the **[ ]** operator (for example, **vec[i]** gets the element at position **i** from the **Vec<T> vec**). However, using the **[ ]** leads to a panic in case the index does not exist—which is not ideal for robustness. Instead, you can use the **.get(i)** function that returns an Option type. However, the indexing operator allows direct access to a member, which includes assignments.

Let us put all those functions together into one snippet. You should experiment and get familiar with the different functions:

```
fn main() {
    let mut animals = vec!["🐙", "🦄", "🐛"];
    // Direct assignments using the indexing operator
    animals[2] = "🐌";
    // Insert a pufferfish at the end
    animals.push("🐡");
    // Remove the unicorn (spot nr 1)
    let unicorn = animals.remove(1);
    // Insert the unicorn at spot nr 2
    animals.insert(2, unicorn);
    // Fetch the crab
    let crustacean = animals[0];
    assert_eq!(crustacean, "🐙");
    assert_eq!(animals, vec!["🐙", "🐌", "🦄", "🐡"]);
    assert_eq!(animals.get(10), None);
}
```

These are just the basics of what you can do with the Rust **Vec<T>**; there are many more operations that you can read up on. The best place to start is by looking at the docs (doc.rust-lang.org/std/vec/struct.Vec.html) or moving on to slices in the next section.

Borrowing the Vec<T>: slices

Although ownership of a collection is great, it is sometimes expensive to move around. Think about a 100,000 element collection that requires gigabytes in memory—a clone is going to take some time. Additionally, if you only need 16 elements from somewhere in the middle of these 100,000 elements, creating a new **Vec<T>** instance is also kind of wasteful—and this is where the slice comes in. As we already discussed, slices are borrowed, and they allow a view into a collection's memory. This view can provide part of a collection or the whole thing—no reallocation required.

Here is an illustration of a slice's view into a **Vec<T>**. In this case, the slice is constructed with **&vec[1..4]**:

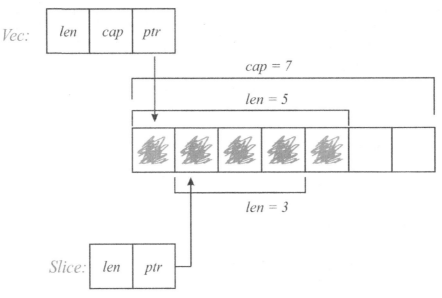

Figure 6.1: *A slice is a view into a sequential collection such as a Vec<T>*

Good API design prefers slices over actual types whenever possible. Consequently, slices are what you will be working with a lot—just bear in mind that their manipulation options are limited to individual elements at certain indices. Here is an example:

```rust
fn replace_index_with_5(data: &mut [u8], idx: usize) {
  data[idx] = 5;
}

fn sort_in_place(data: &mut [u8]) {
  data.sort()
}

fn main() {
  let mut v = vec![1, 2, 3, 4, 5];
  replace_index_with_5(&mut v, 1);
  assert_eq!(v[1], 5);
  assert_eq!(v, vec![1, 5, 3, 4, 5]);
  sort_in_place(&mut v);
  assert_eq!(v, vec![1, 3, 4, 5, 5]);
}
```

This is due to slices only having a view on memory—it is possible to move elements around and replace them, but the overall area cannot be grown or shrunk. However, because the conversion from a **Vec<T>** is quick and efficient, you should just do it there. For all other operations (chunking, splitting into multiple slices, and so on) check the documentation at doc.rust-lang.org/stable/std/primitive.slice.html. For now, let us take a closer look at sets and maps.

Deriving keys from values with sets and maps

Storing a list of something is a quintessential solution for many things in computer science (and real-life). Who does not have a to-do list, an address book, or a shopping list? The issues usually do not start with making a list but with actually finding anything in it. Did you use a nickname or the full name of an estranged aunt? Is broccoli already on your shopping list? These problems are just as present in sequential collections in computer science—and therefore Rust—as in real life. Scanning through a collection of names to see which one is the one you are looking for starts to become a hassle after some 20 names or so, likewise with a long shopping list.

One solution to this issue is to derive a key to identify a particular item. In an address book, this could be the nickname (for all entries) or, in a shopping list, the entire shopping item. Disregarding the details of these examples, the principle of using a key to enforce uniqueness and optimizing for retrieval is what we are looking for. Each key represents one item and follows a well-known format and size (for example, a single field from the address book entry) to achieve quick retrieval by sorting or hashing. Now, what are sets and maps?

A set is a collection of items without duplications. Consequently, an insert has to check for the presence of an item before actually inserting, a perfect scenario for a fast lookup of a derived key. These sets are typically used for checking memberships, creating intersections and unions, or simply making sure that you have a unique collection of elements.

A map, on the other hand, maps a key to a value—and they are everywhere in real life. Think of an employee or student ID, which are the keys to your company or university profile (the value). Sometimes these keys can be derived from the value directly (for example, birth year or year of inscription), but—depending on your use case—it is not absolutely necessary. The goal usually is to find identical values just by their keys, or sometimes it is about having a very fast lookup ability.

In this view, the index of an element in a **Vec<T>** is the key to the stored element (the value), but with a major difference: They change on insert (remember the shift to the right/left?). So clearly, sets and maps need additional data structures to work as designed and achieve the promised speed. In the Rust standard library (in `std::collections`), there are two implementations: `BTreeSets` and `BTreeMaps`, as well as `HashMaps` and `HashSets`. How do they work?

Sorting keys: trees and hashes

As we have established, walking through a collection and comparing each element to what you are looking for takes time—which might be negligible for small data but will not work well for large collections (linear search is O(n)). One way out of this is sorting the collection and then using this new order to derive the most likely position of the element you are looking for. This concept can be elevated to a higher level of abstraction to create new data structures: trees. A balanced binary tree, for example, is a collection where the median element represents the root and has two children—one with a smaller (than) and one with a larger value than their parent. Each of these children has children that follow these rules on their own, leading to a structure that looks like a tree with the root up high:

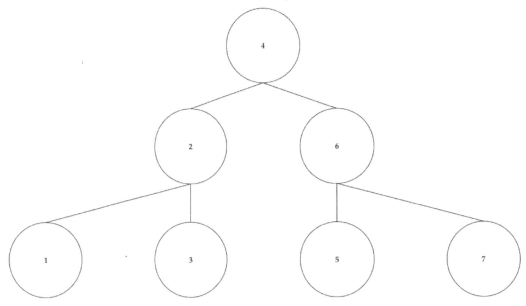

Figure 6.2: *A balanced binary tree data structure*

This data structure allows going through all items without even looking at most of the elements. Consequently, search (that is, retrieving a single element) can be much faster (O(log(n))), which is ideal if you want to retrieve elements by some kind of identifier. As long as there is a definitive order that the data structure can create using the identifier, a tree structure is highly efficient—although it is most likely not a binary tree. In Rust's case, it is a B-Tree data structure (read more at www.geeksforgeeks.org/introduction-of-b-tree-2/) that is used for `BTreeSet` and `BTreeMap`, and they work in a similar fashion.

What if the keys are not sortable? Maybe it is impossible to only use a single value, or comparing two elements is inefficient. In this case, we have to actually derive a key from the provided value, and one such method is hashing. In essence, hashing is when you use a hash function to create a typed key from some inputs. Creating hashing algorithms is the content of academic research, and each algorithm has many properties, like how well it spreads or groups keys of similar values. Typically, the notation `H(v) = k` illustrates that the value `v` has to go into a hash function `H` to get key `k`.

In many situations, making the right choice for a hashing algorithm can have a huge impact so let us look at an example where the hash of a String is simply its length (with terrible results):

```
fn main() {
  let max_buckets = 3;
  let mut naive_hashmap = vec![Vec::<String>::new(); max_buckets];
  let data = "blog.x5ff.xyz".to_string();
  let hash = data.len();
  let hashmap_position = hash % max_buckets; // modulo operation
  naive_hashmap[hashmap_position].push(data.clone());
  assert_eq!(naive_hashmap, vec![vec![], vec![data], vec![]])
}
```

In this code snippet, we utilize a **Vec<T>** to store another **Vec<T>** at each index. This allows storing multiple data entries at each index, which will be necessary with the large overlaps this "hash" function produces. By using the modulo operator (it simply retrieves the remainder of a division of both operands), we find the position for the entry in the collection without overflowing. By doing this procedure (getting the length and calculating the modulo), each retrieval operation will end up in the same bucket, after which retrieving the actual value requires a linear search. Depending on how full the bucket already is, this adds time to the retrieval, and cutting this time down has been a topic of extensive research.

Yet, in real-world scenarios, the length of a string will not be a great choice for a hashing algorithm since it produces the same hash for many strings. Instead, the Rust HashMap uses SipHash (find the inventor's C implementation here: github. com/veorq/SipHash/) by default, but it is also easy to use another algorithm when required.

> **Note: While technically possible, a complex hashing algorithm like SHA256 (to dive deep, read more at datatracker.ietf.org/doc/html/rfc4634) is not great for maps. Each algorithm was designed with a purpose in mind, SHA256's is message authentication.**

In Rust's standard library, the `HashMap` and `HashSet` share most of their implementation, and the hashing algorithm can be swapped if necessary. Because working out the details of either set or map would certainly exceed this chapter (and book, really), please check out the excellent documentation (doc.rust-lang.org/std/collections/hash_map/struct.HashMap.html and doc.rust-lang.org/std/collections/struct.BTreeMap.html). The `std::collections` module where we will import the types from features a decision guide as well: doc.rust-lang.org/std/collections/index.html.

Let us look into how these specialized collections can be used.

Using sets and maps

Maps have countless use cases that mostly revolve around providing either quick access to data via an ID or using them to group similar/the same elements together (for example, for counting them).

Sets (`HashSet`, `BTreeSet`) provide an **insert(e)**, **contains(&e)**, and **remove(e)** function but their main functions are common (mathematical) set functions:

- **intersection(&other)** returns all elements that are in both.
- **difference(&other)** returns elements contained in one but not the **&other**.
- **union(&other)** returns all elements of both.
- **symmetric_difference(&other)** returns elements that are in either but not both.

The internal structure of these set-type collections allows for much better performance than recreating them using regular sequential collections. Here is an example of how to use the set:

```
use std::collections::BTreeSet;

fn main() {
    let mut a: BTreeSet<usize> = vec![1, 2, 3].into_iter().collect();
    let mut b: BTreeSet<usize> = vec![2, 3, 4].into_iter().collect();

    assert_eq!(a.insert(4), true);
    assert_eq!(a.insert(4), false); // no insert because it's already
there
```

```
    assert_eq!(a.contains(&4), true);

    // Set operations return an iterator that has to be collected before
use
    assert_eq!(a.intersection(&b).collect::<Vec<_>>(), vec![&2, &3, &4]);
    assert_eq!(a.difference(&b).collect::<Vec<_>>(), vec![&1]);
    assert_eq!(a.union(&b).collect::<Vec<_>>(), vec![&1, &2, &3, &4]);
    assert_eq!(a.symmetric_difference(&b).collect::<Vec<_>>(), vec![&1]);
}
```

In this snippet, we used the previously mentioned functions together with **assert_
eq!()** to show the outcomes. Sets are a great choice when a unique collection
of elements is required and when they have to be compared. Also, note that the
operations yield an iterator with borrows of the set's values, which means that a deep
copy (**clone()**) is often necessary to get ownership over the result. Furthermore,
these operations are exactly the same on a HashSet, but the output would not be
ordered.

The map works in similar ways, with the available functions being **insert(k, v)**,
remove(k), and **get(&k)**. However, there are no specialized applications other than
those. Instead, Rust makes a lot of use of the Iterator trait, which we will discuss
in the following section. But first, let us look at using basic data manipulation
operations on a map:

```
fn main() {
    let mut animal_counter = BTreeMap::new();
    animal_counter.insert("🐙", 1_usize);
    animal_counter.insert("🐢", 1_usize);
    animal_counter.insert("🐛", 1_usize);

    // Direct assignments using the indexing operator
    assert_eq!(animal_counter.get("🐑"), None);
    assert_eq!(animal_counter.keys().collect::<Vec<_>>(), vec![&"🐛", &"
🐙", &"🐢"]);
    animal_counter.insert("🐙", 2_usize);
    animal_counter.insert("🐛", 1_usize);
    for (k, v) in &animal_counter {
        println!("{} has been seen {} time(s)", k, v);
    }
    assert_eq!(animal_counter.remove("🐢"), Some(1));
    assert_eq!(animal_counter.into_iter().collect::<Vec<_>>(), vec![("🐛
", 1), ("🐙", 2)]);
}
```

This snippet shows a few ways of working with a map's key-value pairs. Most operations in a map require only the key in order to get the value—kind of like a search index.

> **Note: The** `BTreeMap` **is different from a HashMap in that it allows range queries for keys/set members.** `HashMaps` **are inherently unordered and therefore lack the concept of a range. Trees, however, are very orderly and thus have a** `range()` **function: doc.rust-lang.org/std/collections/struct.BTreeMap.html#method.range**

However, searching for stuff is much easier if you have a chance to enumerate all (or most) of the elements (that is, an exhaustive search). Iterators are a mechanism for doing that, and, as promised in *Chapter 4*, *Interfacing with Code*, we are exploring the Iterator trait now.

Iterating over any collection

Enumerating all elements in a collection is a traditional domain of a for a loop. In early programming languages (for example, C), it was common to use simple pointer math together with the properties of zero-overhead collections to get to every element in a collection. The math is not very complex: **start_address + type_size * index = target_address** and can still be done in unsafe Rust.

In modern programming languages, the concept of enumerating all possible values of a collection is abstracted over all possible data structures. These include maps and sets even though they do not have a fixed order and typically are not stored sequentially. Especially trees have multiple ways to iterate over all elements: bottom-to-top, top-to-bottom, left-first, right-first, and so on. As a consequence, the iterator is a generic way of implementing such an enumeration for every collection.

In Rust, the Iterator trait provides an opportunity to do that, and it comes with a large amount of operations that build on the single function you have to implement: `next()`. Iterators are a behavioral design pattern captured by the "Gang of Four" (Erich Gamma, Richard Helm, Ralph Johnson, John Vlissides) in their '94 classic: Design Patterns.

The trait has around 70 functions, but only **next()** is mandatory to implement:

```rust
impl Iterator for MyCollection {
  type Item = ...; // The Result type goes here

  fn next(&mut self) -> Option<Self::Item> {
    // Return Some(item) or None when done
  }
}
```

Because an iterator can be finite or infinite, the return type is an Option that contains the associated type. The associated type is typically the collection's element type—or a reference to it. For example the **Vec<T>** features an **iter()** function (for references) as well as an **into_iter()** function. The latter consumes the collection and returns owned elements, and it is what the for loop uses. The function is defined in the **IntoIter** trait (refer to *Chapter 4, Interfacing with Code*.

A slice cannot provide ownership for elements to iterate over, which is why its **into_iter()** implementation will always yield borrows. If a mutation is necessary, **iter_mut()** is a typical function that provides mutable access to each element.

Chaining iterators together

Since advancing an iterator is just a function call to **next()** - what would happen if this **next()** calls another **next()** internally? Here is where we encounter another pattern—the decorator pattern (from the same book, *Design Patterns by the Gang Of Four*). This pattern describes ways to chain iterators together by essentially wrapping them into each other. This has two consequences:

- Any iterator function becomes compatible with another.

- The iteration has to be lazy (evaluated only when called).

The first aspect is very useful, and we will see in the next snippet how it simplifies code significantly. The second aspect, however, requires some rethinking of certain aspects of working with collections, and we will look at them in the next section.

Before writing any code, let us define the (subjectively) most important functions:

- **enumerate()**: A practical function to add an index to the current iterator.

- **map()**: Takes a closure to transform each element into another.

- **fold()**: Also known as **reduce()**, takes a closure with the previous and current element and folds everything into a single result.

- **filter()**: Include or exclude elements based on a predicate.

The **Iterator** trait has about 70 functions and is constantly expanding, so for specific problems, it is recommended to check the documentation for useful functions and examples (doc.rust-lang.org/stable/std/iter/trait.Iterator.html). For now, let us look at an example of how to create those chained iterators:

```
fn main() {
    let v = vec!["zero", "one", "two", "three", "four", "five"];
    let odd_squared_sum = v.iter()
        .enumerate()
```

```
    .filter(|(i, _)| *i % 2 == 1) // i has type &usize
    .map(|(i, _)| i * i)
    .fold(0, |prev, cur| prev + cur);
  assert_eq!(odd_squared_sum, 1 * 1 + 3 * 3 + 5 * 5); // = 35
}
```

The snippet shows a few things: First, we define a **&str** (literal) list with the numbers spelled out. After that, an iterator over the borrowed content (calling **.iter()**), chained together with an **enumerate(),** yields a tuple from thereon. This tuple contains the index (preceding variable **i**) added by the **enumerate()** alongside the element. With a **filter()**, the predicate closure filters out all even numbers. Note here that an assignment to _ as a name tells the compiler to ignore it.

In the call to **map()**, the closure unpacks the tuple (again) and returns the index, squared. Finally, **fold()** uses the closure to unpack the arguments (the previous value and the current value, **prev** and **cur**, respectively) and sums them up. The first argument and later the result of the closure is being passed as **prev** for the next call.

The snippet ends by showing the sum that is effectively calculated in this (toy) example. However, **filter()** and **map()** are often very useful for data processing in exactly this fashion. In many of those scenarios, you will want to collect the results in a list, map, or scalar number—we will cover that in the following section.

Collecting the results

In order to fully enumerate an iterator and assign the results to a collection or other variable type, you will have to implement the **FromIterator** trait. That trait allows using the **collect()** function to create your type.

All of the types discussed here implement this trait, but they may require a specific format to collect from. Specifically, a map is typically constructed from tuples (for example, **("mykey", "my_value"))**, whereas a **Vec<T>** can be collected from anything list-like. In addition to that, you can collect Option and Result types from different constellations (refer to doc.rust-lang.org/std/option/enum.Option. html#impl-FromIterator%3COption%3CA%3E%3E for an example).

Let us look at an example for collecting into other collections:

```
use std::collections::{BTreeMap, HashSet};

fn main() {
  let a_set: HashSet<_> = vec![1, 2, 3, 4].into_iter().collect();

  let a_map: BTreeMap<_, _> = vec![("one", 1), ("two", 2), ("three", 3),
("four", 4)]
```

```
    .into_iter()
    .collect();

  let only_one: Option<usize> = vec![1, 2, 3, 4].into_iter().next();
}
```

The **a_set** is a **HashSet<i32>** (the _ signals the compiler to infer the type automatically) created from a **Vec<T>** using the ownership iterator, deduplicating entries automatically. **a_map** contains a mapping from **&str to i32** from a tuple collection, and finally, an **Option** is constructed from a single element of a **Vec<T>** with the **next()** function.

Given how handy converting between these collections is, you will encounter these functions a lot—especially in this book. Therefore, let us move on and discover the rest of it.

Conclusion

Data structures are an essential part of solving sophisticated problems in computer science. Rust's **Vec<T>** provides a solid base for storing sequential data in an efficient manner. Borrowing a **Vec<T>** to a function makes use of the slice type that can be used universally to provide a—also mutable—view into the sequential memory region by passing a reference, which is much cheaper than cloning the real thing.

Manipulating **Vec<T>** can be done using functions such as **push()**, **insert()**, or **remove()**, and the **Vec<T>**'s allocated memory area grows correspondingly. For slices and **Vec<T>**s, fetching and changing values via direct indexing (for example, **my_vec[i]**) and in-place functions are options too (for example, **sort()**).

In Rust's standard library, you can also find maps and sets for more complex use cases. Sets are generally used for unique collections that have to test for membership quickly and efficiently, whereas maps provide a mapping of a set of keys to a collection of values. This enables a fast search for a particular item that has a known key without even looking at all keys! The variations for maps and sets in the Rust standard library are **HashMap** and **HashSet**, as well as **BTreeMap** and **BTreeSet**, all of which have their own up- and down-sides depending on the use cases; follow the decision guide in the documentation: doc.rust-lang.org/std/collections/index.html.

Finally, we explored the Rust **Iterator** (trait) that provides a powerful and composable mechanism to iterate over a collection. This iteration includes:

- **map()** function to map one collection onto another.
- **fold()** which folds all elements into a single type.
- **enumerate()** to simply add an index to the iteration.
- **filter()**, a way to exclude/include elements based on a predicate.

More examples include flattening a collection or creating a sliding window, or simply taking a defined number of elements from the iterator. However, their use requires a different style of programming—a more functional one. The main trade-off is the fact that those one-liners can turn out hard to read and reason about, especially if they require workarounds that would "just work" in a regular for loop. Play with them to find out their strengths and weaknesses; the challenge that follows might be a great place to do that.

After solving the challenge, the upcoming chapter awaits with managing input and output with Rust.

Challenge

For this chapter's challenge, we will improve the LinkedList type further by implementing the Iterator and **IntoIterator** traits. As before, use the provided main function to check your implementation and use the material in this chapter (or anywhere else) to complete the following code. Once again, use play.rust-lang. org or a local Rust installation (if available, not covered—yet) to run the code. Most importantly, however, have fun!

Here is the code:

```rust
enum Link {
  Next(Box<Data>),
  Empty
}

struct Data {
  value: u128,
  next: Link
}

impl LinkedList {
  pub fn new() -> Self {
    LinkedList { head: None }
  }

  pub fn append(&mut self, value: u128) {
    // your previous implementation
  }

  pub fn count(&self) -> usize {
    // your previous implementation
    0
  }
}
```

```rust
  pub fn pop(&mut self) -> Option<u128> {
    // your previous implementation
    Some(0)
  }
}

struct LinkedList {
  head: Option<Link>
}

struct LinkedListIterator {
  // properties go here
}

impl Iterator for LinkedListIterator {
  Item = u128;

  fn next(&mut self) -> Option<Self::Item> {
    // Return None when finished, otherwise Some(current item)
    // Also, start at the front
  }
}

impl IntoIterator for LinkedList {
    type Item = u128;
    type IntoIter = LinkedListIterator;

    fn into_iter(self) -> Self::IntoIter {
      // Return your iterator type
    }
}

// By default, a data structure is dropped recursively
// Which leads to a stack overflow.
impl Drop for LinkedList {
  fn drop(&mut self) {
    let n = self.count();
    if n > 0 {
      for _ in 0..n {
        let _ = self.pop();
      }
    }
  }
}

fn main() {
  // Using the LinkedList in a for loop
```

```rust
let mut list = LinkedList::new();
list.append(1);
list.append(2);
list.append(3);

assert_eq!(list.count(), 3);
// into_iter() takes ownership of the list
for elem in list {
  println!("> {}", elem);
}

// Using Iterators to manipulate
let mut list = LinkedList::new();
list.append(4)
list.append(5);
list.append(7);

let odd_squared_sum = list.into_iter()
  .filter(|(i, _)| *i % 2 == 1) // i has type &usize
  .map(|(i, _)| i * i)
  .fold(0, |prev, cur| prev + cur);

assert_eq!(odd_squared_sum, 5 * 5 + 7 * 7); // = 74

// Collect to HashSet
let mut list = LinkedList::new();
list.append(4);
list.append(4);
list.append(5);
list.append(7);

// Convert to a HashSet using Iterators
let a_set: std::collections::HashSet<_> = list.into_iter().collect();
let mut set_elems = a_set.into_iter().collect::<Vec<_>>();
set_elems.sort(); // HashSets are unsorted, so it's hard to compare
assert_eq!(set_elems, vec![4, 5, 6])

// Additional exercise: FromIterator
//let list: LinkedList = set_elems.into_iter().collect();

// Tests from the previous chapter
let mut list = LinkedList::new();
list.append(1);
list.append(2);
list.append(3);

assert_eq!(list.pop(), Some(3));
```

```
assert_eq!(list.pop(), Some(2));
assert_eq!(list.pop(), Some(1));
assert_eq!(list.pop(), None);
}
```

Iterator implementations are often their own struct since they need to store the state of the iteration somewhere. To give you some ideas, here, the iterator could use a shrinking list as its state since **into_iter()** will consume the list anyway (the self parameter is not a borrow), or alternatively store a pointer to the next node, returning the current value. In either case, the returned item has to be the payload to keep anyone who is building on your LinkedList from relying on internal structures, as these might change in later chapters.

For more ideas on implementing the traits, read up on the traits in the Rust documentation:

- doc.rust-lang.org/std/iter/index.html#implementing-iterator

- doc.rust-lang.org/std/iter/trait.IntoIterator.html#examples

- doc.rust-lang.org/std/iter/trait.FromIterator.html#examples

The last point is for the curious: You can implement **FromIterator** as an additional challenge to complete the cycle of LinkedList -> HashSet (or anything else) -> LinkedList! Alternatively, you can move on to the upcoming chapter.

Further reading

Here are the links to go deep on the **Vec<T>**'s inner workings:

- **Vec<T> source:** doc.rust-lang.org/src/alloc/vec/mod.rs.html#396-399

- **RawVec<T> source:** doc.rust-lang.org/src/alloc/raw_vec.rs.html#52-55

CHAPTER 7
Reading Input and Writing Output

Since the start of this book, we have come a long way. In the previous six chapters, we went from simple variables to creating a custom LinkedList data structure. However, so far, we have used only a few interactions with the user.

Aside from the occasional **println!()**, there were hardly any outputs on-screen, and we have not dealt with user input at all so far. In this chapter, we are going to remedy all of this and focus on making interactive programs as well as using the classic "print debugging" strategy (only as a last resort, of course!).

Structure

In this chapter, we will be covering the following topics:

- Reading from and writing to I/O streams
  - Console, networking, and file systems
  - Using formatted print
    - Printing custom types
- Configuration options for programs
  - Using command-line arguments
  - Using environment variables

Objectives

In this chapter, we will explore passing command line arguments, reading from and writing to streams such as the console, and we will learn about handling environment variables.

Reading from and writing to I/O streams

In Rust, I/O is centered around two traits: **std::io::Read** and **std::io::Write**. As their names suggest, they are concerned with input and output (respectively). Similar to the Iterator trait, they only require a single function to be implemented in order to use the full suite of structs that build on those.

The **std::io::Read** trait needs a function **read()** to be implemented to gain access to (read more at doc.rust-lang.org/std/io/trait.Read.html):

- **read_to_string()** that reads and interprets the byte input into a String.

- **read_to_end()** keeps reading until an EOF byte is detected.

- **read_exact()** reads the exact number of bytes provided.

Looking at the function's signature, the body of the **read()** function is expected to fill an input buffer and return the number of bytes that it was filled with. Consequently, your type has to have some kind of source that it can fill the buffer from—with a blocking or non-blocking operation:

```
impl std::io::Read for MyType {

  fn read(&mut self, buf: &mut [u8]) -> Result<usize> {
    // implement here
  }
}
```

This is what the docs (doc.rust-lang.org/std/io/trait.Read.html#tymethod.read) say about whether to block or not:

> **Note: This function does not provide any guarantees about whether it blocks waiting for data, but if an object needs to block for a read and cannot, it will typically signal this via an Err return value.**

Especially when working with networking streams, this is a very important aspect given the unpredictability of networking delays or even outages. Bear that in mind when implementing and using **read()**.

On the other side is **std::io::Write**. This trait works in a similar fashion as read but in reverse. Writing to an object involves two steps: writing and flushing. The first part may write into a buffer, whereas the latter refers to force-writing the buffer to the underlying medium (remember the safely remove hardware concept in Windows?). Both of these methods may block until everything is written, but that depends on the trait's implementor.

As a consequence, the **std::io::Write** trait requires you to implement both of these functions:

```
impl std::io::Write for MyType {

  fn write(&mut self, buf: &[u8]) -> Result<usize> {
    // write the buffer to an internal storage
  }

  fn flush(&mut self) -> Result<()> {
    // flush it to the medium
  }
}
```

Similarly to **read()**, the **write()** function is expected to write data from the provided buffer into the underlying medium or an intermediary data structure and return how many bytes it managed to write.

These two traits provide the foundation for Rust's streams, and they can be wrapped into structs such as **BufReader** or **BufWriter** (doc.rust-lang.org/std/io/index.html) for additional functionality or used in convenience functions such as std::io::copy (doc.rust-lang.org/std/io/fn.copy.html). As a side note: the **Vec<T>** also implements Read and Write, which works great as an actual stream replacement for testing. However, let us move from the hypothetical to the practical: what about networking and file system access?

Console, networking, and file systems

Having these **Read** and **Write** traits available makes many streams equal in terms of treatment. This means that, for example, files, network sockets, and consoles (standard input/output) can all be treated exactly the same. In fact, a popular mechanism on Linux is to stream data to a program using standard input (for example, something like **cat myfile | grep -i "hello"**), so the distinction is quite blurry.

Let us start off with networking. The Rust standard library provides a listener (doc.rust-lang.org/stable/std/net/struct.TcpListener.html) and a stream for TCP connections, the latter of which implements the Read and Write traits. The listener provides the classic accept() function to return a TCP stream on the server-side as well. Let us look at a simple echo server implementation using Rust's standard library (this will not work on play.rust-lang.org for security reasons):

```rust
use std::io::{Read, Write};
use std::net::{Shutdown, TcpListener};

fn main() -> std::io::Result<()> {
    let listener = TcpListener::bind("127.0.0.1:43280")?;
    println!("Listening to {:?}", listener.local_addr()?);
    loop {
        // a simple, sequential TCP server that returns what it receives
        match listener.accept() {
            Ok((mut stream, addr)) => {
                println!("{:?} connected", addr);
                let mut buf = vec![0; 100];
                let bytes_read = stream.read(&mut buf)?;
                let bytes_written = stream.write(&buf[0..bytes_read])?;
                println!(
                    "Received {} bytes, sent {} bytes.",
                    bytes_read, bytes_written
                );
                stream.shutdown(Shutdown::Both)?;
            }
            Err(e) => eprintln!("Error accepting client connection: {:?}", e),
        }
    }
}
```

This iterative server accepts connections sequentially on port **43280** and reads into a buffer (a mutable 1,000 bytes Vec<T>), sends back what it received, and then closes the connection. Any client simply has to connect, send something, and wait for a response. Obviously, because it is an iterative server, it can only handle a limited number of connections. Let us take a look at the following client code:

```rust
use std::io::{Read, Write};
use std::net::{Shutdown, TcpStream};

fn main() -> std::io::Result<()> {
    match TcpStream::connect("127.0.0.1:43280") {
        Ok(mut stream) => {
            let payload = b"Hello Rust";
            println!(
```

```
            "Connected to the server! Sending '{}'",
            String::from_utf8_lossy(payload)
        );
        let bytes_written = stream.write(payload)?;
        let mut received = String::new();
        stream.read_to_string(&mut received)?;
        println!("Received: {}", received);
        stream.shutdown(Shutdown::Both);
        Ok(())
    }
    Err(e) => {
        eprintln!("Couldn't connect to server...");
        Err(e)
    }
  }
}
```

This code uses a byte literal **(b"Hello Rust")** to send (and for printing, we interpret it as a UTF-8 string) via the regular **write()** function. The (blocking) **read()** function then waits for the server's response, and the reverse is happening on the server (see the previous snippet). However, on the client, we are using the convenience function **read_to_string()** to read to a String directly before closing the connection.

When running the server and client simultaneously, you will see the following client output:

```
    Finished dev [unoptimized + debuginfo] target(s) in 0.48s
      Running `target/debug/playground-client`
Connected to the server! Sending 'Hello Rust'
Received: Hello Rust
```

Figure 7.1: The client's output

Whereas the server's output looks like that (showing three requests):

```
    Compiling playground v0.1.0 (/private/tmp/playground)
    Finished dev [unoptimized + debuginfo] target(s) in 0.75s
      Running `target/debug/playground`
Listening to 127.0.0.1:43280
127.0.0.1:63897 connected
Received 10 bytes, sent 10 bytes.
127.0.0.1:63954 connected
Received 10 bytes, sent 10 bytes.
127.0.0.1:63961 connected
Received 10 bytes, sent 10 bytes.
^C
```

Figure 7.2: The server's output

This indicates that all the **println!** calls succeeded, and the server did what we built it to do: Echo the incoming message. Because this usage of the Read and Write traits was not surprising, let us move on to input and output from and to files and the console.

Writing to files and reading from their works are great without using any additional abstraction. However, in order to get the best speeds, using buffered writes and reads has shown good results. So for the next snippet of writing and then reading a file, let us use a **BufReader**/**BufWriter** (see doc.rust-lang.org/std/io/struct.BufReader. html and doc.rust-lang.org/std/io/struct.BufWriter.html).

First, the **File** struct is part of the **std::fs** module (doc.rust-lang.org/std/fs/struct. File.html), and occasionally, there can be differences between Windows and POSIX (UNIX/Linux) systems due to the different file systems they use. This should not be the case here, but keep this in the back of your head for the occasional error.

```rust
use std::io::{Read, Write, BufReader, BufWriter};
use std::fs::File;

fn write(content: &str, file: impl Write) -> std::io::Result<()> {
  let mut buf_writer = BufWriter::new(file);
  buf_writer.write(content.as_bytes())?;
  Ok(())
}

fn read(file: impl Read) -> std::io::Result<String> {
  let mut buf_reader = BufReader::new(file);
  let mut contents = String::new();
  buf_reader.read_to_string(&mut contents)?;
  Ok(contents)
}

fn main() -> std::io::Result<()> {
  let content = "Hello ⬛";
  {
    let file = File::create("testfile.txt")?;
    write(content, file)?;
  } // Running out of the scope will close the file
  {
    let file = File::open("testfile.txt")?;
    let outcome = read(file)?;
    assert_eq!(content, outcome);
  } // Running out of the scope will close the file
  Ok(())
}
```

This snippet uses both **read()** and **write()** functions with the corresponding traits as input parameters to write to and read from a file. The String itself is not important because it is converted to bytes in the **write()** function right before sending them to the file. Within the main function, each file opening (or creating) is encapsulated in its own scope in order to avoid dangling file pointers. The assert, in the end, ensures that the file's content is what we wrote. Now, these functions work just as well with a network stream or **std::io::stdin()**:

```rust
use std::io::{Read, Write, BufReader, BufWriter};
use std::fs::File;

fn write(content: &str, file: impl Write) -> std::io::Result<()> {
  let mut buf_writer = BufWriter::new(file);
  buf_writer.write(content.as_bytes())?;
  Ok(())
}

fn read(file: impl Read) -> std::io::Result<String> {
  let mut buf_reader = BufReader::new(file);
  let mut contents = String::new();
  buf_reader.read_to_string(&mut contents)?;
  Ok(contents)
}

fn main() -> std::io::Result<()> {
  let content = "Hello 🐙";
  {
    let mut file = std::io::stdout();
    write(content, &file)?;
    file.flush();
  }
  {
    println!("\ninput text above, evaluate with CTRL-D ...");
    let file = std::io::stdin();
    let outcome = read(file)?;
    assert_eq!(content, outcome);
  }
  Ok(())
}
```

In this snippet, we had to add two modifications: first, a **flush()** was necessary after writing to **stdout** to print the text. The console output file handle is never really closed, so flushing makes things appear right away. The second is the addition of a **println!** call to instruct the user what to do since a **read_to_string()** (or any read) will block the caller without any warning and expect input on the **Read** type. Because this type is console input, this input has to come from the user (in this case), and it is terminated by sending the EOF character, which is typically *Ctrl + D*. Here is what it can look like:

```
    Finished dev [unoptimized + debuginfo] target(s) in 1.09s
     Running `target/debug/playground`
Hello 🦀
input text above, evaluate with CTRL-D ...
Hello 🦀^D
thread 'main' panicked at 'assertion failed: `(left == right)`
  left: `"Hello 🦀"`,
 right: `"Hello 🦀\n"`', src/main.rs:28:5
note: run with `RUST_BACKTRACE=1` environment variable to display a backtrace
```

Figure 7.3: Output when running the command line I/O sample

> **Note: The failed assertion in this output is easily mitigated by calling** `trim()` **on the outcome variable.**

With users of a program, it is pivotal to provide instructions and print information in a usable fashion. One of the methods for doing that is using formatted print in order to take control over a data type's representation on screen.

Using formatted print

When writing strings, formatting is an important concern. Whatever the use case, be it debugging, user interaction, or generating HTML pages, integrating variables into an output string is very important. For this, Rust uses macros (which we will cover in *Chapter 11, Generating Code with Macros*), and we have already used some of them.

Here is an overview of the macros that support formatting:

- **`println!`/`print!`** write to the console (standard out), appending a newline or not (respectively).

- **`eprintln!`/`eprint!`** write to the console (standard error), appending a newline or not (respectively).

- **`writeln!`/`write!`** write to the provided stream appending a newline or not (respectively).

- **`format!`** allocates a new String from the formatted values.

- **`panic!`** halts the current thread, displaying a formatted message.

So what is formatting? Essentially it is a template that has a value rendered into it wherever a placeholder is provided. Because the displaying of a variable can be vastly different from the information it actually holds, formatting is a great way of controlling what is being written.

Rust's standard library provides a number of formatting options for different applications. The full list can be found at (doc.rust-lang.org/stable/std/fmt/index. html), but let us cover a useful subset here:

- {} / {name} writes the **std::fmt::Display** output of the *n*th parameter or the named parameter.

- {:?} displays an instance's **std::fmt::Debug** implementation.

- {:x} renders lower-cased Hex if supported. Alternatives are O for octal, b for binary, or e for exponent display (4.2e1), as well as their upper-case variants for upper-casing letters ({:X} for upper-case Hex, and so on).

- {:5.2} defines left spacing (5) and decimal places (2).

These signs are all used in the first part of a formatting macro, and they are typically literals (although they can be parameters, too!). Here is a complete example:

```
fn main() {
    println!("My name is {name}", name="Arthur Dent");
    println!("Pi = {pi:30.10}", pi=std::f64::consts::PI);
    println!("blog.x{:x}.xyz", 1535);
    println!("{:b}", 1535);
    println!("{:?}", vec!["hello", "world"]);
}
```

The preceding snippet produces the following output:

```
My name is Arthur Dent
Pi =                     3.1415926536
blog.x5ff.xyz
10111111111
["hello", "world"]
```

The first line simply substitutes the {name} placeholder with the provided **&str**, whereas the second **println!** prints the named parameter pi with a total length of 30 (aligned to the right) and 10 decimal places. The remaining lines transform the number 1535 into a hex ({:x}) and binary ({:b}) representation and the snippet ends with a debug print of a Vec<T>.

These format strings can be used in exactly the same way for the other macros mentioned preceding; however, formatting custom types requires implementing specific traits, the most important of which we already mentioned: **std::fmt::Display** and **std::fmt::Debug**.

Printing custom types

If you create your own type, there is no default formatting implemented, and any attempt to print it will fail with a compiler error. Even if all members of your type are standard types (for example, **usize** or **String**), there will not be any default way of printing the type.

That is unless you derive the **Debug** trait implementation. We will discuss the derive macros in *Chapter 11, Generating Code with Macros*; for now, just know that a **#[derive(Debug)]** statement automatically implements the **Debug** trait by recursively printing each member (this also works for other traits). Here is an example:

```rust
#[derive(Debug)]
struct Account {
  name: String,
  password: [u8; 5] // use 32 for a 256 bit hash (SHA-256)
}


fn main() {
  let me = Account { name: "Arthur".to_string(), password: [0; 5]};
  let output = format!("{:?}", me);
  assert_eq!(output, "Account { name: \"Arthur\", password: [0, 0, 0, 0, 0] }");
}
```

However, printing passwords into logs is a huge security flaw, so we cannot just use the derived **Debug** implementation but implement **Display** by hand. Let us see the updated version of the code:

```rust
#![allow(dead_code)]

use std::fmt;

struct Account {
  name: String,
  password: [u8; 5] // use 32 for a 256 bit hash (SHA-256)
}

impl fmt::Display for Account {
  fn fmt(&self, f: &mut fmt::Formatter<'_>) -> fmt::Result {
    write!(f, "Account ({name})", name = self.name)
  }
}
```

```
fn main() {
  let me = Account { name: "Arthur".to_string(), password: [0; 5]};
  let output = format!("{}", me);
  assert_eq!(output, "Account (Arthur)")
}
```

By implementing the **fmt()** function of the Display trait, we make the function available to format the most basic placeholder {} in the formatting macros. For the individual modifiers (Hex, binary, octal, and so on), there are additional traits that function exactly the same as **Display**, and you can implement them if they seem handy for your custom type. Learn more on the **std::fmt** docs page (doc. rust-lang.org/stable/std/fmt/index.html#formatting-traits), and we will move on to configuration options in the meantime.

Configuration options for programs

Passing different configuration options into programs is a great way to save yourself from Rust's infamous long compilation time. In a world of containers, environment variables have become a staple in passing these configuration options into programs, just as much as regular command-line arguments are. For this reason, we will look at both concepts in their simplest form by using the standard library.

In real-world projects, you will be working with various third-party crates to achieve type safety even for sophisticated types and have multiple variations available (for example, JSON files, TOML files, and environment variables). However, knowing the basics will make using these crates much easier and gives you a basis to understand what is going on. Let us start with command line arguments.

Using command-line arguments

Command-line arguments are those parameters that you can add after calling a binary via the command line (Windows and Linux/Unix). Typical examples include cargo run (run being the argument here) or curl—help where—is used to signal a configuration parameter. This is a convention, though; PowerShell uses single—to denote those. Regardless, the API in the standard library returns a list of strings without any additional parsing or filtering.

> **Note: We recommend using PowerShell on Windows if you want to run the following examples because declaring and using environment variables is much more like on Linux/Unix systems (where PowerShell is available as well). Read more at docs.microsoft.com/en-us/powershell/module/microsoft.powershell. core/about/about_environment_variables.**

In Rust, working with a collection of command-line arguments is as simple as working with any iterator. In our case, we want to collect the variables into a **Vec<String>**, so using the **collect()** function will do just that. Here is the example (unfortunately, this will not work on play.rust-lang.org):

```rust
use std::env;

fn main() {
  let args: Vec<String> = env::args().collect();
  println!("{:?}", args);
}
```

As the preceding snippet shows, after collecting the values as Strings, you can parse them appropriately to get the types you need. Because this can be quite cumbersome, Rust's clap crate provides types and abstractions for various use cases in and around command-line argument parsing (see github.com/clap-rs/clap). Additional information about the Rust command-line arguments can be found at doc.rust-lang.org/book/ch12-01-accepting-command-line-arguments.html.

An alternative way of configuring your application is to use environment variables, which have been the default for containerized applications for a while now. Let us look at how to read from the environment.

Using environment variables

Environment variables are variables that are provided and injected by the operating system. They are typically strings and exist in the current context of the program, but any program or script can read or write to this storage, and because the read operation calls the operating system directly, the returned value can change at runtime.

```rust
use std::env;

fn main() {
  let path = env::var("PATH").expect("PATH variable not found");
  let paths = path.split(":").collect::<Vec<_>>();
  assert_eq!(paths, vec![
    "/playground/.cargo/bin",
    "/playground/.cargo/bin",
    "/usr/local/sbin",
    "/usr/local/bin",
    "/usr/sbin",
    "/usr/bin",
    "/sbin",
```

```
    "/bin",
  ]);
}
```

The **std::env::var()** function provides easy access to environment variables by returning an **Option<String>** type, which can be used to parse other types (**usize** or even JSON), just like command line parameters. Just like for command-line arguments, there are crates that allow a different syntax (for example, using declarative macros); however, there is no one crate that everybody uses. Check crates.io for what is available and pick whatever fits your use case.

Conclusion

In this chapter, we worked with user input and output for and from different places. The techniques can be used in any context, but they have made the book for their practicality: Modern, containerized applications use environment variables for configuration, whereas great tools with direct user interaction require command-line arguments. Meanwhile, Rust's meager support for debugging makes the use of **println!** statements across the code a common sight, and with that, the implementation of **std::fmt::Display** or **std::fmt::Debug** is a staple of many programmers.

However, the use of the **std::io::Read** and **std::io::Write** is still the most important part. In order to write maintainable code and make unit-testing a habit, using multiple types as a parameter has to be simple. Therefore, instead of requiring a **File** type, why not work on the stream alone and use **impl Write**? Read should occupy a similar position in your repertoire.

If the standard library does not satisfy your I/O needs, a third-party crate just might. We will explore how to add those in the upcoming chapter.

Practice makes perfect, though, which is why we are going to move on to the challenge.

Challenge

Over the previous chapters, we have built a LinkedList type that can hold data; it should be traversable and, by using the power of iterators, even searchable. One thing is missing, though: storing data.

For this chapter's challenge, we had like to encourage a program that uses your list to store and print a file. There are a few changes you have to make to your list in order to store a String instead of a u128, and then you can read a file line-by-line and store each line as a node. You should then print what you read using the **println!**

macro—ideally by implementing the **Display** trait or some other method. Here is some code to get you started:

```rust
use std::io::{Read, BufReader, BufRead};
use std::fs::File;

enum Link {
  Next(Box<Data>),
  Empty
}

struct Data {
  value: String,
  next: Link
}

impl LinkedList {
  // ... your previous implementation goes here
}

struct LinkedList {
  head: Option<Link>
}

struct LinkedListIterator {
  // ... your previous implementation goes here
}


fn main() -> std::io::Result<()> {
  let mut list = LinkedList::new();
  let file = File::open("testfile.txt")?;

  let mut buf_reader = BufReader::new(file);
  let mut line = String::new();
  while let Ok(_bytes_read) = buf_reader.read_line(&mut line) {
    list.append(line.clone());
  }
  println!("Your file contains: {:?}", list);
  Ok(())
}
```

CHAPTER 8
Using Crates with Cargo

So far, the examples in this book have mostly been doable without even touching Rust's main tool: `cargo`. `cargo` is a command-line application that manages third-party dependencies, orchestrates their build, and can even publish crates to crates.io, the main package repository.

Although there are many tasks that a build system can take over, this chapter will look at covering a wide base, so working on specific platforms or CPU architectures are covered, as well as using an entirely custom build process. In theory, you could use `cargo` to build your C project as well.

Structure

In this chapter, we will be covering the following topics:

- Creating crates with `cargo`
  - o Writing the build manifest
  - o Adding third-party crates
- Going deeper into `cargo`
  - o Customizing the build
  - o Using workspaces for large projects

Objectives

By the end of this chapter, we will have created our first `cargo`-based Rust project (first in this book, anyway) and learned about the manifest, the build process, managing dependencies, and extending cargo using additional tools.

Creating crates with cargo

Install `cargo`, `rustc`, and everything essential for building and running Rust projects by following the instructions at rustup.rs.

`cargo` is Rust's main build tool and it orchestrates the processes with `rustc` (the Rust compiler) and native linkers and downloading and updating third-party dependencies. You can change most of these steps in the manifest file (**Cargo.toml**) and look at the dependency tree in `Cargo.lock`. However, before we get into these, let us look at the basic build process.

As mentioned in *Chapter 1, Building the Basics*, Rust is a compiled language where a compiler outputs native bytecode for the operating system to interpret. This is pretty simple when there is only a single file involved: Read all text, parse into tokens, build the syntax tree, translate into binary instructions, and output as a file. Because Rust also has modules, things get a little more difficult now there are imports that need to be verified, dependency graphs need to be created, and so on—all of which make it difficult to manage individual `rustc` calls. Additionally, third-party dependencies are typically downloaded in a raw state, so they need to be compiled as well, which begs the question of ordering these so the imports will not fail.

`cargo` is maintained by the Rust team, and it comes with its own book at doc.rust-lang.org/cargo/. For detailed questions, that is definitely the right place. Until then, let us cover the necessities for most projects, starting with a binary application:

```
$ cargo new myproject
    Created binary (application) `myproject` package
$ tree myproject/
myproject/
├── Cargo.toml
└── src
    └── main.rs

1 directory, 2 files
```

This sets up everything for a simple command-line program, including a `Hello, World` sample in **myproject/src/main.rs**. This also corresponds to the preferred setup for a folder structure and entry point. Although both can be customized, this src/main.rs structure is very common. The **Cargo.toml** file is uneventful, too (comments removed):

```
[package]
name = "myproject"
version = "0.1.0"
edition = "2021"

[dependencies]
```

The other project type for Rust projects is a library. As the name suggests, a library is made for integrating with executable binaries (or other libraries) to encapsulate specific tasks or other code. If a module is a collection of structs, a library is a collection of modules. The `cargo` new command creates a binary by default, so for a library, we have to add a --**lib** flag:

```
$ cargo new mylib --lib
    Created library `mylib` package
$ tree mylib/
mylib/
├── Cargo.toml
└── src
    └── lib.rs
1 directory, 2 files
```

`cargo`'s default settings for libraries is to find a file called **lib.rs**, which is why the manifest looks like that of a binary project (with comments removed):

```
[package]
name = "mylib"
version = "0.1.0"
edition = "2021"

[dependencies]
```

An obvious difference between the two is that certain commands work in either one or the other project. Here are a few examples for the library project:

```
$ cargo run
error: a bin target must be available for `cargo run`
$ cargo test
   Compiling mylib v0.1.0 (/private/tmp/learn-rust-programming/mylib)
    Finished test [unoptimized + debuginfo] target(s) in 0.80s
     Running unittests (target/debug/deps/mylib-ba97c7fc1b10e4b3)

running 1 test
test tests::it_works ... ok
```

```
test result: ok. 1 passed; 0 failed; 0 ignored; 0 measured; 0 filtered
out; finished in 0.00s

   Doc-tests mylib

running 0 tests

test result: ok. 0 passed; 0 failed; 0 ignored; 0 measured; 0 filtered
out; finished in 0.00s
$ cargo build
    Finished dev [unoptimized + debuginfo] target(s) in 0.00s
```

Contrast that with running the same commands in the binary project:

```
$ cargo run
   Compiling myproject v0.1.0 (/private/tmp/learn-rust-programming/
myproject)
    Finished dev [unoptimized + debuginfo] target(s) in 0.23s
     Running `target/debug/myproject`
Hello, world!
$ cargo test
   Compiling myproject v0.1.0 (/private/tmp/learn-rust-programming/
myproject)
    Finished test [unoptimized + debuginfo] target(s) in 1.13s
     Running unittests (target/debug/deps/myproject-485563a462792de9)

running 0 tests

test result: ok. 0 passed; 0 failed; 0 ignored; 0 measured; 0 filtered
out; finished in 0.00s
$ cargo build
    Finished dev [unoptimized + debuginfo] target(s) in 0.03s
```

As the preceding snippets show, a library project cannot be run, whereas the binary project is running just fine. Both types can use unit tests and the `cargo build` command to compile and test the code (`cargo run` also does a `cargo build`). Although there are many more tasks that cargo offers (and it is extensible), here is a summary of some of the most frequent ones you are going to use to create, build, and run or test a Rust project:

- **run** runs the current project.

- **new** creates a new project in a subfolder of the current directory.

- **init** initializes a new project in the current directory.

- **build** builds the current project.

- **test** runs unit- and integration tests (see *Chapter 9, Testing What You Build*).

- **clean** cleans the build directory (**target/**).

- **doc** generates the current project's documentation (see *Chapter 10, Documenting What You Build*) as HTML.

cargo uses a lot of sane defaults, which can be changed by adding or editing the respective options in the build manifest: **Cargo.toml**. Let us take a closer look at what it offers.

Writing the build manifest

Cargo and a given project can be configured separately with a global configuration and a local manifest. Each has its own options (some may overlap), but both follow the TOML markup (which is similar to **.ini** files). We already saw the default **Cargo.toml** in the previous section:

```
[package]
name = "mylib"
version = "0.1.0"
edition = "2021"

[dependencies]
```

These keys are almost the bare minimum (name and version, edition defaults to 2015) of what needs to be present before cargo refuses to work. However, there are many more aspects that can be configured in this file, such as dependencies, links to other resources, build profiles, and even a lengthy description. Let us look at a few important ones:

The package provides metadata for the package, such as name, version, and authors, a link to the documentation (defaults to docs.rs when published), and keywords. The website crates.io uses this information to create a package index, including a small description site and links to more information. Important fields are as follows:

- **edition** states the target edition for the package. Available values are 2015 (the default), 2018, ad 2021, and they represent breaking changes to the language. Read more here: doc.rust-lang.org/edition-guide/

- **version** provides the package version in the form of a triple separated by a dot (.): **<major>.<minor>.<patch>**. Rust strongly encourages semantic versioning.

- **name** is the package's name.

- **license** informs registries about the software license of the package.

- **metadata** provides metadata for external tools such as Linux distribution packages, Android apps, and so on.

There are many more fields to configure the presentation on crates.io, compiler versions, or external build scripts. Read more about those fields at doc.rust-lang. org/cargo/reference/manifest.html#the-package-section.

Another interesting section is the metadata table in **package.metadata**, because it is ignored by cargo. This means that projects can store their own data in the manifest for the project—or publishing-related properties—for example, for publishing on Android's Google Play Store or information to generate Linux packages.

Profiles govern the way rustc compiles the package. A typical profile is the release profile, which you can turn on with a --release switch (for example, cargo build --release), with the default profile being dev (invoked by cargo build or cargo run). We will get to writing and running tests in the next *Chapter 9, Testing What You Build*, which use the test (and bench) profiles. All these profiles come with reasonable defaults, yet you might want to customize some settings to serve your use case better. Available profiles are **[profile.dev]**, **[profile.release]**, **[profile. test]**, and **[profile.bench]** sections:

```
[profile.release]
opt-level = 3
debug = false
rpath = false
lto = false
debug-assertions = false
codegen-units = 16
panic = 'unwind'
incremental = false
overflow-checks = false
```

These values represent the default for the release target, and they can be changed to fit a specific use case. Typically that is only required in more advanced projects.

Targets are the output of a build. We have seen the defaults already with a lib.rs file for libraries and a main.rs file for the entry point of a binary. Here is what the docs (doc.rust-lang.org/cargo/reference/cargo-targets.html#configuring-a-target) show as an example:

```
[lib]
name = "foo"            # The name of the target.
path = "src/lib.rs"     # The source file of the target.
```

```
test = true              # Is tested by default.
doctest = true           # Documentation examples are tested by default.
bench = true             # Is benchmarked by default.
doc = true               # Is documented by default.
plugin = false           # Used as a compiler plugin (deprecated).
proc-macro = false       # Set to `true` for a proc-macro library.
harness = true           # Use libtest harness.
edition = "2015"         # The edition of the target.
crate-type = ["lib"]     # The crate types to generate.
required-features = []   # Features required to build this target (N/A for
lib).
```

Complex codebases sometimes have binaries and libraries in the same project, requiring them to configure either a [lib] or [bin] section. In fact, each project can have multiple of those, using the TOML (Tom's Obvious, Minimal Language: github.com/toml-lang/toml) array notation (for example, [[lib]]). Learn more at doc.rust-lang.org/cargo/reference/cargo-targets.html#configuring-a-target.

Over the course of the following chapters, we will occasionally introduce additional sections as required. In the next section, we are looking at what is probably the most important section: dependencies.

Adding third-party crates

The **dependencies** section provides references to crates outside of the current project, along with its sister section **dev-dependencies**, which only applies to test/bench builds. However, the declarations remain the same, which is why you can apply anything from this section to either **[dependencies]** or **[dev-dependencies]**.

Since each TOML section is essentially a JSON object, each key is unique and also represents the import name for your use statements. In its simplest form, the name is just what is used in the repository (crates.io is the official public repository). Here is an example of using the popular web request library **reqwest** (github.com/ seanmonstar/reqwest):

```
[dependencies]
reqwest = "0.11"
```

These key-value pairs can grow much more complex since the value can actually be a (JSON) object itself. This is very important when it comes to specifying a crate's features or using a Git repository directly (and a revision or tag with it):

```
[dependencies]
reqwest = { version = "0.11", features = ["json"] }
reqwest_gh = {
```

```
package = "request",
git = "https://github.com/seanmonstar/reqwest",
rev = "ab49de875ec2326abf25f52f54b249a28e43b69c",
features = ["json"]
}
```

In the preceding snippet, you will see **reqwest** imported twice, with different versions—one from Git with an exact revision reference (**rev**), the other with just what has been published on crates.io. Since we renamed the import to **reqwest_gh** (so now it is used **reqwest_gh::Client;** to import), the dependency resolution algorithm cannot know what package we want from the Git repository, so naming the package using the package key is a good idea.

Alternatively, you can also provide paths to crates as dependencies. Behind the scenes, the Git dependency is downloaded into a local directory anyways, so it really masks a local import. As an example, if you cloned the **reqwest** GitHub repository locally for your custom patches, you can use something like this to import it:

```
[dependencies]
reqwest = { version = "0.11", features = ["json"] }
reqwest_gh = {
  path = "../../projects/reqwest",
  version = "0.12",
  features = ["json"]
}
```

This alternative way relies on you updating your local copy and will not let others contribute. We will explore path imports more in the context of workspaces; until then, and we are sticking to the preceding Git example.

Importing multiple versions of the same crate will lead to trouble, so it makes sense to separate them for compilation by making one (or both) optional:

```
[dependencies]
reqwest = { version = "0.11", features = ["json"], optional = true }
reqwest_gh = {
  package = "request",
  git = "https://github.com/seanmonstar/reqwest",
  rev = "ab49de875ec2326abf25f52f54b249a28e43b69c",
  features = ["json"],
  optional = true
}
```

Optional dependencies are made mandatory when they are specified to be required for a feature. These features are simply compiler switches to include/exclude parts of the code—depending on **#[cfg(feature="featureName")]** declarations. To get into details, check out the **cargo** book's section about this conditional compilation at doc.rust-lang.org/cargo/reference/features.html.

Here is a quick example of how you make use of optional dependencies in your features:

```
[features]
default = [ "regular_edge" ]
cutting_edge = [ "request_gh" ]
regular_edge = [ "reqwest" ]

[dependencies]
reqwest = { version = "0.11", features = ["json"], optional = true }
reqwest_gh = {
  package = "request",
  git = "https://github.com/seanmonstar/reqwest",
  rev = "ab49de875ec2326abf25f52f54b249a28e43b69c",
  features = ["json"],
  optional = true
}
```

Note that all crates have default features that you can turn off to be more precise about what you compile and import. This is especially important for no-std (that is, without the standard library) crates, which we find a lot in the embedded space.

Versioning is another way of controlling what features (in the non-**cargo** sense) are included. In the preceding snippet, we only specified the major and minor versions but did not bother to add the patch part (the latest version is **0.11.6** at the time of this writing), which lets **cargo** upgrade to the latest version whenever we run cargo update. This is safe if the maintainer of the crate keeps with semantic versioning (see semver.org/ for more info) while it allows us to use the latest fixes.

This is a way of implicitly using a wildcard, and we will accept a version starting with **0.11**. **cargo** also has an explicit way of using wildcards:

- **Tilde (~)**: Allows only patch increases.
- **Caret (^)**: No major version increase (**0.11.0** or **0.99.28** are Ok, but **1.0.0** is not!).
- **Wildcard (*)**: Allows any version where it is used.

In the early stages of a project, you might replace the entire version with an asterisk (*****):

```
[dependencies]
```

```
hyper = "~0.14"
serde = "^1"
reqwest = "*"
```

In order to find out the actual version of a crate, the **Cargo.lock** file holds the dependency tree. In it, each dependency has its dependencies listed. The `cargo` Book FAQ specifies the lockfile's purpose as follows (doc.rust-lang.org/cargo/faq.html#why-do-binaries-have-cargolock-in-version-control-but-not-libraries):

"The purpose of a Cargo.lock lockfile is to describe the state of the world at the time of a successful build. Cargo uses the lockfile to provide deterministic builds on different times and different systems, by ensuring that the exact same dependencies and versions are used as when the Cargo.lockfile was originally generated."

This means that the file holds a serialized version of the dependency tree that it can modify as well as lookup existing versions. With the dependencies mentioned in the previous snippets, a blank `cargo` project ends up with a lock file of 900+ lines. Here is a small sample (shortened):

```
version = 3

[[package]]
name = "autocfg"
version = "1.0.1"
source = "registry+https://github.com/rust-lang/crates.io-index"
checksum =
"cdb031dd78e28731d87d56cc8ffef4a8f36ca26c38fe2de700543e627f8a464a"

[[package]]
name = "core-foundation"
version = "0.9.2"
source = "registry+https://github.com/rust-lang/crates.io-index"
checksum =
"6888e10551bb93e424d8df1d07f1a8b4fceb0001a3a4b048bfc47554946f47b3"
dependencies = [
 "core-foundation-sys",
 "libc",
]
```

The result is a dependency tree that you can check for duplicates, version differences, commit hashes, and so on since fewer dependencies are generally better. The changes have to go into **Cargo.toml**; however, since `cargo` manages the lock file independently. For example, running `cargo update` likely rewrites the lock file in considerable parts if there are crate updates available that fit the wildcards.

In case the regular cargo build process is not enough, though, let us dive a little deeper into customizing its behavior a bit more.

Going deeper into cargo

Projects that span multiple domains of software projects (for example, front- and back-end) make efficient builds more challenging since both "ends" often require different release cycles, technologies, and people. Rust's rise in WASM (Web Assembly—see webassembly.org/) also means that there is an additional compilation target to worry about, and not every dependency may be available for it.

To counter this, cargo provides several options to configure the build, so let us lay out some scenarios and what `cargo` has to offer for them:

- Integrating with other technologies.
- Targeting multiple platforms.
- Patching or replacing dependency sources.

The first one, integration with other technologies, will be covered in a later chapter (chapter 16 - Calling Unsafe And Foreign Functions). Since Rust compiles to native bytecode, it can integrate with anything that can work with these types of libraries (for example, `*.so`, `*.a`, or `*.dll`), but it requires either bindings and linking other dynamic libraries or adjusting the crate type. For a primer, you can read doc.rust-lang.org/reference/linkage.html.

When targeting multiple platforms (such as Windows, Linux, WASM, Android, Arm64, and so on), cargo can do several things for you. Primarily you can specify platform-specific dependencies (doc.rust-lang.org/cargo/reference/specifying-dependencies.html#platform-specific-dependencies) and use conditional compilation (doc.rust-lang.org/1.9.0/book/conditional-compilation.html) to solve these issues. In case there are linkers that are specific to the platform, you can use a target triple (doc.rust-lang.org/stable/rustc/platform-support.html) to specify a variety of options in `cargo`'s configuration or environment variables. Going deep on this topic can fill entire books, so if your use case requires such a specific configuration, start by reading the documentation at doc.rust-lang.org/cargo/reference/config.html. Just know that cargo supports a huge variety of use cases and can be configured to build almost anything.

The last point is especially interesting if your project encompasses dependencies that are specific to a technology or platform. Although it is very straightforward to add conditional compilation or other compilation targets to your own project, controlling what the included dependencies use is only possible if that maintainer is allowed to do so. Since this is not always the case (or even possible), the `cargo` manifest includes a patch section to simply replace entire crates based on their source URLs. Here is an example of how to replace the `reqwest` crate from crates.io (the default repository) in any dependency. Consequently, these lines will result in having the GitHub of **reqwest** everywhere:

```
[patch.crates-io]
reqwest = { git = "https://github.com/seanmonstar/reqwest" }
```

Since these definitions are exactly the same as other dependencies, the options for specifying a path or other repository to download them from still apply. Although this is a handy workaround for third-party crates that do not support what you require, it adds to the maintenance requirements of the overall project. For more information about what else is possible, check out doc.rust-lang.org/cargo/reference/overriding-dependencies.html.

We will now move on to fully customizing the actual build process.

Customizing the build

Next to the preceding configuration options that replace linkers, compilers, and other tooling, the Rust build can also use Rust code to build foreign code, to generate bindings, or types for database interaction. The convention is to use a file called build.rs, which is picked up and compiled automatically by cargo.

A typical example of including C code is by using Bingen, a program to generate Rust code wrappers for shared native libraries. Typically the Rust code uses the header files (**wrapper.h** in the following snippet) to generate the appropriate types as a Rust file (**bindings.rs** next). The file then communicates these outcomes to cargo via standard out, that is, the command line—hence, the **println!** statements in this snippet:

```
use std::env;
use std::path::PathBuf;

fn main() {
    println!("cargo:rustc-link-lib=bz2");

    let bindings = bindgen::Builder::default()
        .header("wrapper.h")
        .generate()
        .expect("Unable to generate bindings");

    let out_path = PathBuf::from(env::var("OUT_DIR").unwrap());
    bindings
        .write_to_file(out_path.join("bindings.rs"))
        .expect("Couldn't write bindings!");
}
```

Additionally, `cargo` provides a few environment variables that the build script can write to (for example, preceding **OUT_DIR**). From a technical level, these files can do anything and build entire projects before actually compiling the Rust code. We will use Bingen (rust-lang.github.io/rust-bindgen/introduction.html) in a later Chapter *16, Calling Unsafe and Foreign Functions*, when we call into native dependencies.

For more information on the build scripts and how to communicate with the parent `cargo` instance, check out doc.rust-lang.org/cargo/reference/build-scripts.html.

A build script provides a way to hook early into the build process and allows all kinds of changes. However, since this would mostly lead to a discussion of other languages and technologies, let us move on to more `cargo` stuff: workspaces.

Using workspaces for large projects

Workspaces are cargo's way of tying multiple projects together as one. There are three major upsides to this:

- Shared **Cargo.lock**.
- **cargo** commands apply to all projects.
- **patch** and other overrides apply throughout.

To create a workspace, simply put all projects in a common folder and add a **Cargo.toml** that has a workspace section instead of a package section:

```
[workspace]
members = [ "p1", "p2" ]
exclude = [ "p3" ]
```

The file in this snippet manages a workspace that features the following folder structure:

```
.
├── Cargo.lock
├── Cargo.toml
├── p1
│   ├── Cargo.toml
│   └── src
│       └── main.rs
├── p2
│   ├── Cargo.toml
│   └── src
│       └── lib.rs
└── p3
    ├── Cargo.toml
    └── src
        └── lib.rs

6 directories, 8 files
```

In this case, we have two projects **p1** and **p2,** that are part of the workspace and get called with each cargo command. The project **p3**, however, is somewhat unrelated, so it should not be part of the workspace - which is why it is explicitly excluded. Note also the lack of **Cargo.lock** files in **p1** and **p2**; since the workspace now manages the dependency tree, the file is also where the manifest lives.

References between projects do not change; however, they are still manual paths. In this case, if **p1** wanted to add **p2** as a dependency, the line would still be this:

```
[dependencies]
p2 = { path = "../p2" }
```

Considering that the workspace members also have to point to valid cargo projects, renaming folders and moving projects around is not recommended.

Running commands in the workspace will always result in all projects being called upon. This can generate considerable noise, like running 300 tests of a neighboring project while you wanted to run only one. For that, cargo has a **-p** flag to specify the project. Here is an example:

```
$ cargo run -p p1
    Finished dev [unoptimized + debuginfo] target(s) in 0.00s
     Running `target/debug/p1`
Hello, world!
```

cargo workspaces provide a great way to unify interdependent Rust projects cleanly. In fact, the workspace setup is helpful with also unifying dependencies since wildcards result now in a common version that is downloaded and included everywhere in the workspace. You can read more about that in the cargo book at doc.rust-lang.org/book/ch14-03-cargo-workspaces.html.

Conclusion

cargo is a tool to automate several aspects of Rust development. In particular, it looks up, compiles, and includes third-party dependencies within various stages and profiles. All of them are configurable using the manifest file **Cargo.toml** or, for more complex projects—a **config.toml**. Both will be picked up automatically if they reside within the folder hierarchy. These files use TOML as their language, and basically, all-important CLI commands for cargo interact with them in some way.

Under the hood, cargo orchestrates the rustc compiler and a platform-specific linker (or a custom one), as well as the required standard libraries for the target architecture and toolchain so they build the desired binary output. All of this is not only done for the project but also its dependencies, making cargo a very versatile and powerful tool. Its CLI is also comparatively easy. Let us recapitulate the most important subcommands:

- **run** runs the current project.
- **new** creates a new project in a subfolder of the current directory.
- **init** initializes a new project in the current directory.
- **build** builds the current project.
- **test** runs unit- and integration tests (see *Chapter 9. Testing What You Build.*)
- **clean** cleans the build directory (**target/**).
- **doc** generates the current project's documentation (see *Chapter 10, Documenting What You Build*) as HTML.

With these commands, a chain of instructions is run, and if a build script has been added, **cargo** will compile and run that first. Of course, if the current console is set within a workspace, the commands are run for all projects unless otherwise specified.

Challenge

In this chapter, you are—again—continuing with building out the **LinkedList** type from earlier chapters. Use the previous code, and instead of having this free-floating file, make it a library project using **cargo**. This means you have to create a new library project somewhere and add your code to the **lib.rs** file that was generated. On top of that, you can look into adding third-party crates if you want.

Install cargo and all required tools by following rustup.rs. **rustup** is a handy toolchain manager for all your Rust needs.

As a small primer on the next chapter, we are going to continue working with the library project to improve it more, so make sure the following commands work without error:

```
$ cargo build
$ cargo update
$ cargo clean
$ cargo test
```

Further reading

Learn more about configuring cargo and a project's manifest at their docs:

- doc.rust-lang.org/cargo/reference/config.html
- doc.rust-lang.org/cargo/reference/manifest.html

CHAPTER 9
Testing What you Build

So far, we have been avoiding one topic on the journey of writing great code: testing. There are different kinds of testing, which are typically distinguished by what they cover and how they view the code they test. However, since we focus on technology, these kinds of testing will be out of scope. Instead, we will explore Rust's built-in test framework, which is already quite powerful.

In addition to that, we will cover some benchmarking as well. There are many support crates out there for other topics, such as mocking, which this book will not cover in detail.

Structure

In this chapter, we will be covering the following topics:

- Testing Rust code
    - o   Testing units
    - o   Testing integration
- Benchmarking Rust code

Objectives

Once you read this chapter, you will be using unit tests, integration tests, and benchmark tests to produce high-quality code.

Testing Rust code

Tests are an important part of writing good software. Although we always know that our code is working, it is good to have proof whenever questions arise—and who knows, maybe sometimes we do make a mistake. In addition to that, tests are a great source of documentation for developers that show exactly how something is supposed to be used and what the expected outcome should be, including edge cases. Since Rust is a statically typed language without null, the compiler already takes away a good amount of type/null checks that are common in other languages.

The test framework built into the standard library allows to run the two kinds of tests: white box tests (for example, unit tests) and black-box tests (for example, integration tests). The former is able to access private functions since they have to be declared within the file they are testing, whereas the latter sit in an extra tests directory in the project and only see the module's public declarations. Rust's tests are configured via conditional compilation, which allows the build process to skip tests whenever a non-testing build runs—thereby saving compilation time.

The actual testing is simple: exit normally if the code works, else panic. However, there are a few ways to panic:

- **assert** macros (see doc.rust-lang.org/std/index.html#macros)
- **unwrap()** or **expect()** calls
- `panic!()`
- Returning an **Err()** variant

The most important macros are assert!, **assert_eq!** and **assert_ne!** all of which have a similar interface. assert! checks for a Boolean condition **(assert!(1 < 2))**, **assert_eq!** and **assert_ne!** test if both parameters are equal or not equal, respectively. panic! will explicitly fail the test for scenarios when assert macros do not work well, similarly to—the optional—returning of a Result<(), ...> where the returning of an **Err()** variant also triggers a failing of a test.

Unfortunately, the Rust testing framework does not support any hooks for running code before or after tests. As an additional note: All tests can use the [dev-dependencies] specified in **Cargo.toml**; those are also only downloaded and compiled with cargo test. Let us look at unit testing with Rust first.

Testing units

Unit tests are white-box tests, which means that they can access the internals of their test subject, and they should cover all possible execution paths. The testing code lives inside the same file as a conditionally compiled submodule:

```rust
#[cfg(test)]
mod tests {
  #[test]
  fn it_works() {
      let result = 2 + 2;
      assert_eq!(result, 4);
  }
}
```

The preceding snippet has all the required elements of a test: **assert_eq!** to crash if the result is not what is expected, a conditionally compiled tests module (**#[cfg(test)]** includes code only when running `cargo test`), and a declared **#[test]** function.

What is missing in the preceding snippet is actually testing a function that exists in its parent module. Since this requires importing them, let us add a test subject in the following snippet:

```rust
pub fn add(a: usize, b: usize) -> usize {
  a + b
}

#[cfg(test)]
mod tests {
  use super::*;

  #[test]
  fn test_add_valid_inputs() {
      let result = add(2, 2);
      assert_eq!(result, 4);
  }
}
```

Although naming test functions has a philosophy of its own, the names have to be unique (obviously) and conform to the same conventions (github.com/rust-dev-tools/fmt-rfcs/blob/master/guide/advice.md), so a test_**MyStruct_add__errors_ for_overflow** leads to a warning.

Rust's tests also allow for checking for expected panics, so we can test the limits of our code. All this requires is an attribute **#[should_panic]** on the test function, and the test will fail if no panic occurs (the expected message is optional but has to match the panic):

```rust
pub fn add(a: usize, b: usize) -> usize {
    a + b
}

#[cfg(test)]
mod tests {
    use super::*;

    #[test]
    fn test_add_valid_inputs() {
        let result = add(2, 2);
        assert_eq!(result, 4);
    }

    #[test]
    #[should_panic(expected = "attempt to add with overflow")]
    fn test_add_invalid_inputs() {
        let result = add(usize::MAX, 1 + 1);
    }
}
```

Finally, tests can also be ignored. This allows for quickly turning off tests or reserving them for running the tests individually:

```rust
pub fn add(a: usize, b: usize) -> usize {
    a + b
}

#[cfg(test)]
mod tests {
    use super::*;

    #[test]
    fn test_add_valid_inputs() {
        let result = add(2, 2);
        assert_eq!(result, 4);
    }

    #[test]
```

```
#[ignore]
fn test_add_ignored() {
  panic!("Not implemented")
}

#[test]
#[should_panic(expected = "attempt to add with overflow")]
fn test_add_invalid_inputs() {
  let result = add(usize::MAX, 1 + 1);
  assert_eq!(result, 4);
}
}
```

A typical way to run all tests is by issuing the **cargo test** command. However, there are several helpful options the command offers:

- **cargo test <name>** runs only tests containing **<name>**.

- **cargo test -- --test-threads=1** limits the number of concurrent threads that tests run in.

- **cargo test -- --nocapture** writes all the test's print statements to the command line.

The first option—the test filtering—is provided by the test subcommand itself, whereas both of the latter options (after the --) are passed into the test harness. All of these options can be combined, and there are many more (see doc.rust-lang.org/cargo/commands/cargo-test.html).

Rust's test harness also prints a nice overview and summary as to what has been run and the outcome. Here is what **cargo test** prints for the preceding snippet:

```
   Compiling p2 v0.1.0 (/private/tmp/playground/p2)
    Finished test [unoptimized + debuginfo] target(s) in 0.87s
     Running unittests (/private/tmp/playground/target/debug/deps/p2-53c232548530e733)

running 3 tests
test tests::test_add_ignored ... ignored
test tests::test_add_valid_inputs ... ok
test tests::test_add_invalid_inputs - should panic ... ok

test result: ok. 2 passed; 0 failed; 1 ignored; 0 measured; 0 filtered out; finished in 0.00s

   Doc-tests p2

running 0 tests

test result: ok. 0 passed; 0 failed; 0 ignored; 0 measured; 0 filtered out; finished in 0.00s
```

Figure 9.1: Output of "cargo test" with a test ignored

When removing the **#[ignore]** attribute from the preceding tests, we can run **cargo test test_add_ignored** with the following (expected) result:

```
   Compiling p2 v0.1.0 (/private/tmp/playground/p2)
    Finished test [unoptimized + debuginfo] target(s) in 0.99s
     Running unittests (/private/tmp/playground/target/debug/deps/p2-53c232548530e733)

running 1 test
test tests::test_add_ignored ... FAILED

failures:

---- tests::test_add_ignored stdout ----
thread 'tests::test_add_ignored' panicked at 'Not implemented', p2/src/lib.rs:17:5
note: run with `RUST_BACKTRACE=1` environment variable to display a backtrace


failures:
    tests::test_add_ignored

test result: FAILED. 0 passed; 1 failed; 0 ignored; 0 measured; 2 filtered out; finished in 0.00s
```

Figure 9.2: *Output of "cargo test" with a failing test*

As a last note for running these tests in an automated fashion: cargo sets the exit codes accordingly, so integrating with other programs, scripts, or the operating system is as easy as it should be.

Testing integration

The major difference between unit tests and integration tests is how the test subject is treated. Although in unit tests, the view is that of a white box, the integration test really only sees public interfaces without any implementation detail. These black-box tests are very useful to test component integrations or entire use journeys through the system.

Consequently, these tests require a different approach to instantiating the program, which can result in a large amount of code. This is why the integration test code lives inside a tests/folder by default, so they are picked up automatically. Alternatively, you can configure these tests in the cargo manifest by adding a section like this (**[[my_section]]** creates a list called **my_section**):

```
[[test]]
name = "integration"
path = "tests/integration_test.rs"
```

cargo treats each file in this folder as its own crate, so sharing code between them requires another module. However, since integration tests are also compiled in the test profile, you can use conditional compilation in your code to create the shared functions. Other than that, an integration test will remind you of a unit test:

```
use playground::add;

#[test]
fn test_add_valid_inputs() {
    let result = add(2, 2);
    assert_eq!(result, 4);
}
```

When running cargo test now, the output is probably also familiar by now:

```
Compiling playground v0.1.0 (/private/tmp/playground)
 Finished test [unoptimized + debuginfo] target(s) in 0.74s
  Running unittests (target/debug/deps/playground-67104622d239c6cd)

running 0 tests

test result: ok. 0 passed; 0 failed; 0 ignored; 0 measured; 0 filtered out; finished in 0.00s

   Running tests/integration_test.rs (target/debug/deps/integration_test-d1e8124ad37df0d4)

running 1 test
test test_add_valid_inputs ... ok

test result: ok. 1 passed; 0 failed; 0 ignored; 0 measured; 0 filtered out; finished in 0.00s

   Doc-tests playground

running 0 tests

test result: ok. 0 passed; 0 failed; 0 ignored; 0 measured; 0 filtered out; finished in 0.00s
```

Figure 9.3: Output of "cargo test" with an integration test

We will talk more about testing in the next chapter too, but this covers all the major test features included in the Rust standard library. However, there is another thing that is somewhat related to testing that we still have to explore: Benchmarking.

Benchmarking Rust code

The Rust testing framework has had an unstable benchmarking feature for a while now. It requires a nightly compiler (install via rustup.rs/, use with cargo + nightly)

Generally, this benchmarking allows to get an estimate of how quickly a function executes. However, comparing those numbers to others is very difficult since there are many factors that can influence the outcome, including hardware, how busy the system is, or compiler optimizations. Comparing to past runs to analyze how these changes influenced scalability or runtime complexity (remember the Big-O-Notation from before?) can make a lot of sense, though.

In previous chapters, we looked at a sorting algorithm called bubble sort; let us see how quickly it can reorder collections compared with the standard library's sorting:

```rust
#![feature(test)]

pub fn bubble_sort(collection: &mut [i32]) {
  for _ in 0..collection.len() {
    for i in 1..collection.len() {
      if collection[i - 1] > collection[i] {
        let tmp = collection[i];
        collection[i] = collection[i - 1];
        collection[i - 1] = tmp;
      }
    }
  }
}

pub fn std_sort(collection: &mut [i32]) {
  collection.sort_unstable();
}

#[cfg(test)]
mod tests {
  extern crate test;
  use super::*;
  use test::Bencher;

  #[bench]
  fn bench_bubble_sort_1k_desc(b: &mut Bencher) {
    let items: Vec<i32> = (0..1_000).rev().collect();
    b.iter(|| bubble_sort(&mut items.clone()));
  }

  #[bench]
  fn bench_bubble_sort_5k_desc(b: &mut Bencher) {
    let items: Vec<i32> = (0..5_000).rev().collect();
    b.iter(|| bubble_sort(&mut items.clone()));
  }

  #[bench]
  fn bench_bubble_sort_10k_desc(b: &mut Bencher) {
    let items: Vec<i32> = (0..10_000).rev().collect();
    b.iter(|| bubble_sort(&mut items.clone()));
  }
```

```
#[bench]
fn bench_stdlib_sort_1k_desc(b: &mut Bencher) {
  let items: Vec<i32> = (0..1_000).rev().collect();
  b.iter(|| std_sort(&mut items.clone()));
}

#[bench]
fn bench_stdlib_sort_5k_desc(b: &mut Bencher) {
  let items: Vec<i32> = (0..5_000).rev().collect();
  b.iter(|| std_sort(&mut items.clone()));
}

#[bench]
fn bench_stdlib_sort_10k_desc(b: &mut Bencher) {
  let items: Vec<i32> = (0..10_000).rev().collect();
  b.iter(|| std_sort(&mut items.clone()));
}
}
```

The two functions **bubble_sort()** and **std_sort()** require a mutable slice to perform their sorting on (in-place). This slice contains a number of **i32** values in descending order, which maximizes the work required for any sorting algorithm. As a technicality, each input slice has to be cloned since the bencher performs multiple iterations to calculate the nanoseconds per iteration (your numbers may look completely different):

```
   Compiling playground v0.1.0 (/private/tmp/playground)
    Finished bench [optimized] target(s) in 1.09s
     Running unittests (target/release/deps/playground-7932d69361696b14)

running 6 tests
test tests::bench_bubble_sort_10k_desc ... bench:  33,658,145 ns/iter (+/- 958,810)
test tests::bench_bubble_sort_1k_desc  ... bench:     351,506 ns/iter (+/- 9,079)
test tests::bench_bubble_sort_5k_desc  ... bench:   8,493,745 ns/iter (+/- 168,046)
test tests::bench_stdlib_sort_10k_desc ... bench:       5,303 ns/iter (+/- 276)
test tests::bench_stdlib_sort_1k_desc  ... bench:         555 ns/iter (+/- 24)
test tests::bench_stdlib_sort_5k_desc  ... bench:       3,076 ns/iter (+/- 158)

test result: ok. 0 passed; 0 failed; 0 ignored; 6 measured; 0 filtered out; finished in 18.70s
```

Figure 9.4: Output of "cargo bench" with a few benchmarks

By comparing the numbers between the algorithms, you can see how slow bubble sort actually is. In fact, you can plot the increase in collection length with the sorting times and see the exponential growth in runtime:

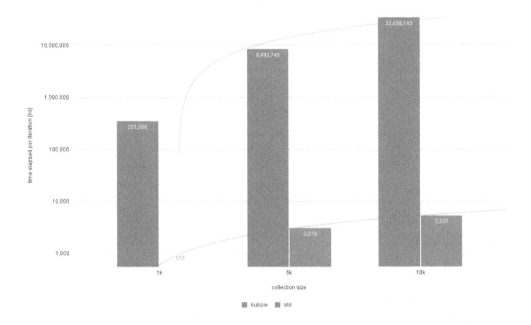

Figure 9.5*: Plotting the benchmark numbers shows the stark difference between sorting algorithms. Note that the Y-axis is logarithmically scaled, and the faint lines show the series' trend*

This sort of analysis allows us to see how some improvements impacted the overall performance of an algorithm so a decision to go for one or the other can be better supported. The limitation of having to use nightly Rust and a feature flag makes the benchmarks difficult to use, which is why a third-party crate called `Criterion` is typically recommended as a stable version of the preceding API. Read more at crates.io/crates/criterion.

Conclusion

Testing is an important tool and provides evidence of the quality of the code you wrote. Strictly speaking, a test verifies the claims developers make about fulfilling a particular requirement or use case.

Rust supports unit tests and integration tests in its standard testing framework built into `cargo`. Each test is a function with the **#[test]** attribute and a way to `panic!` via asserts or other control mechanisms to fail the test:

```
#[test]
```

```
fn test_add_valid_inputs() {
  let result = add(2, 2);
  assert_eq!(result, 4);
}
```

Benchmarks are special cases of tests where a function is repeatedly executed to measure its execution time. The Rust test framework provides a special feature to do these micro-benchmarks, and they live among unit tests sporting a #[bench] attribute with a parameter that does the iterations:

```
#[cfg(test)]
mod tests {
  extern crate test;
  use super::*;
  use test::Bencher;

  #[bench]
  fn bench_bubble_sort_1k_desc(b: &mut Bencher) {
      let items: Vec<i32> = (0..1_000).rev().collect();
      b.iter(|| bubble_sort(&mut items.clone()));
  }
  // ...
}
```

Since all tests are sub-modules or otherwise distinct from the production code, they have to import all functions they are testing. Integration tests can only access public interfaces; unit tests and benchmarks can also import private functions if they are part of a parent module.

Testing is an important topic, and this will not be the upcoming chapter that talks about it. In the next chapter, we will explore doc tests and documentation in general.

Challenge

Since the LinkedList is now a `cargo` project, let us add some tests! The previous main function already contained several test-like sections, and in this challenge, you should move them to individual tests, so each of them succeeds. This should also help you make future changes knowing that you did not break the data structure's behavior fundamentally.

Here is the previous test code. Feel free to add more:

```
fn main() {
  // Using the LinkedList in a for loop
  let mut list = LinkedList::new();
```

```rust
list.append(1);
list.append(2);
list.append(3);

assert_eq!(list.count(), 3);
// into_iter() takes ownership of the list
for elem in list {
  println!("> {}", elem);
}

// Using Iterators to manipulate
let mut list = LinkedList::new();
list.append(4)
list.append(5);
list.append(7);

let odd_squared_sum = list.into_iter()
  .filter(|(i, _)| *i % 2 == 1) // i has type &usize
  .map(|(i, _)| i * i)
  .fold(0, |prev, cur| prev + cur);

assert_eq!(odd_squared_sum, 5 * 5 + 7 * 7); // = 74

// Collect to HashSet
let mut list = LinkedList::new();
list.append(4)
list.append(4)
list.append(5);
list.append(7);

// Convert to a HashSet using Iterators
let a_set: std::collections::HashSet<_> = list.into_iter().collect();
let mut set_elems = a_set.into_iter().collect::<Vec<_>>();
set_elems.sort(); // HashSets are unsorted, so it's hard to compare
assert_eq!(set_elems, vec![4, 5, 6])

// Additional exercise: FromIterator
//let list: LinkedList = set_elems.into_iter().collect();

// Tests from the previous chapter
```

```
let mut list = LinkedList::new();
list.append(1);
list.append(2);
list.append(3);

assert_eq!(list.pop(), Some(3));
assert_eq!(list.pop(), Some(2));
assert_eq!(list.pop(), Some(1));
assert_eq!(list.pop(), None);
}
```

Instead of the preceding main function, use the tests submodule in the **lib.rs** file of your **LinkedList** cargo project just like that:

```
struct LinkedList {
  // ... your previous list
}

// other code and impls


##[cfg(test)]
mod tests {
  use super::*;

  #[test]
  fn test_LinkedList_append() {
    let mut list = LinkedList::new();
    list.append(1);
    list.append(2);
    list.append(3);
    // ... assert that it worked
  }
  // add more
}
```

CHAPTER 10
Documenting What You Build

Everyone dislikes writing documentation—in the beginning. Usually, this opinion changes quickly after you found out that nobody was able to use your code, and instead of what you anticipated as a simple code change, wrappers are being written, and support utils pop up.

The most important issue is commonly the lack of any documentation. The next big issue is the quality of the documentation itself and how accessible it is—or in other words: Can people find what they were looking for?

Like many modern languages, Rust ships with a documentation generator, and you are already familiar with its look and feel: it is what doc.rust-lang.org uses too.

Structure

In this chapter, we will be covering the following topics:

- Documenting Rust code
- Using sections, links, and others
- Writing documentation tests
- Publishing your documentation

Objectives

Once you have read this chapter, you are comfortable with writing documentation, testing your examples, and publishing the documentation as an HTML page.

Documenting Rust code

Writing well on technical topics is a sought-after skill and something that requires an understanding of what the code does, as well as how to explain its purpose and workings. Obviously, technical topics are not novels or have characters (although, why not?) and—as you probably noticed on yourself too—are often scanned to find the relevant parts.

All this implies three things:

1. Documentation has to have a structure.

2. Texts have to be concise.

3. Include short and clear examples (that work).

Rust has a built-in documentation generator that uses code comments and knowledge about types, modules, variables traits, enum variants, and so on to output a full HTML Web application that can be served for your users. In fact, even the third-party crates are included.

> **Note: Any crate that is published on crates.io has its documentation published on docs.rs.**

Let us look at the syntax:

```
mod MyModule {
  //!
  //! This is a **`rustdoc`** comment that allows [markdown](https://
commonmark.org/)
  //! This comment is attached to `MyModule`

  ///
  /// This function does _absolutely_ nothing.
  ///
  fn my_func() {}
}
```

Rust's regular code comments are // for single lines (or their remainder) or /* code comment */ for comment sections. Adding a third slash (///) tells rustdoc to use the provided text as documentation for the code that follows; however, if you add an exclamation mark instead (//!), the documentation goes to the containing code construct (for example, the module **MyModule** in the preceding snippet).

Within these /// or //! sections, you can use markdown (to be precise, the specification at commonmark.org) to format what you write. Here is a quick overview of the available syntax:

```
# Heading 1
## Heading 2
### Heading 3

*italic* or _italic_
**bold**

[link name](http://link-addr.com)

![Image Alt Text](http://path-to-image/myimg.png)

`single line code fence`

```
multi-line
code field
Those ` can also be replaced by ~
```

Header1	Header2
Row1H1	Row2H2
```

This allows these docstrings to have styling and emphasize the important parts, have code examples (more about that in a second), and even include images. One of the main features of documentation is also cross-linking. Just like in Wikipedia, anything that has its own page should be easily reachable via a link on the term of interest. However, do you always need to know the URL and apply any changes?

Let us take a closer look.

Using sections, links, and others

The link style in the preceding snippet (**[link name](http://link-addr.com)**) applies to external links (although you could make internal links work). For internal linking, `rustdoc` provides several variations of the link:

```
/// Some other type that does stuff.
pub struct AnotherType;

/// A struct to store data in called [`MyStruct`][m]
///
/// [m]: MyStruct
pub struct MyStruct {

    /// A collection ([`Vec<T>`]) of [`usize`]
    pub a_vec: Vec<usize>,

    /// Stores a [`AnotherType`] variable
    pub another_type: AnotherType,

    /// Stores a number of type [`usize`]
    pub a_number: usize,

    /// Stores a string [string](String)
    pub a_string: String,
}
```

After running cargo doc, the output looks something like the following:

Struct playground::MyStruct 📋

```
pub struct MyStruct {
    pub a_vec: Vec<usize>,
    pub another_type: AnotherType,
    pub a_number: usize,
    pub a_string: String,
}
```

[-] A struct to store data in called MyStruct

Fields

a_vec: Vec<usize>
    A collection (Vec<T>) of usize

another_type: AnotherType
    Stores a AnotherType variable

a_number: usize
    Stores a number of type usize

a_string: String
    Stores a string string

***Figure 10.1**: The generated HTML output of the previous snippet, showing documentation links*

If you compare the output in *figure 10.1* to doc.rust-lang.org, you will notice that the Rust standard library documentation of any language part uses sections to make reading easier.

In some instances, these link names may be ambiguous, like when you use the same name for functions and modules. Thus, links can include specifiers like **[MyStruct] (struct@MyStruct)** or **[MyFn](fn@MyFn)** to denote the namespace you are looking to link. Alternatively, **[`MyFn()`]** or **[`MyFn!`]** (if it's a macro) guide the rustdoc compiler as well (note the () and ! suffixes).

A section in a docstring—a **# Heading 1**—can be anything you deem necessary. However, the API guidelines recommend informing your users about three main aspects (rust-lang.github.io/api-guidelines/documentation.html#function-docs-include-error-panic-and-safety-considerations-c-failure):

1. Errors

2. Panics

3. Safety (if the function is unsafe—*Chapter 16, Calling Unsafe and Foreign Functions*)

Especially, **# Panics** is a great section to have since if one occurs, it will take the thread (or program) down with it.

In addition to that, it is a good idea to elevate certain aspects to the module level, and by using the appropriate structuring, a user can easily find their way around the documentation. A good example is the module page of std::collections (doc.rust-lang.org/std/collections), which features a full decision tree, links to all the available data structures, and a table detailing the runtime complexity of various operations.

The standard library docs provide excellent examples—and they actively encourage to include what every developer wants: code examples that work.

Writing documentation tests

Code examples that do not work are plentiful on the internet, especially with a fast-growing language like Rust. In many documentation frameworks, testing these examples can be difficult or too complex to automate.

The rustdoc program, however, provides the ability to compile and run Rust code in an Examples section:

```
/// A function to add two numbers
///
/// # Examples
```

```
///
/// ```rust
/// # use playground::add;
/// assert_eq!(add(2, 2), 4)
/// ```
pub fn add(a: usize, b: usize) -> usize {
  a + b
}
```

When running `cargo test` on the preceding example (or using **test** at play.rust-lang.org), the following is the output:

```
running 1 test
test src/lib.rs - add (line 5) ... ok

test result: ok. 1 passed; 0 failed; 0 ignored; 0 measured; 0
filtered out; finished in 0.22s
```

As we mentioned preceding, the section Examples produces a test that is actually run during cargo test. This is due to the code fence (the **rust** keyword provides syntax highlighting) nested in this *Examples* section; anywhere else, you may get syntax highlighting but no test.

This doctest is not regular Rust code—you cannot run a full program in these lines. What you can do, is hide lines by using a # in front and fail the test by panicking. Additionally, this only works for Rust's code, so using anything but Rust will also lead to errors.

The output documentation looks as follows:

Function playground::add 📋

```
pub fn add(a: usize, b: usize) -> usize
```

[-] A function to add two numbers

Examples

```
assert_eq!(add(2, 2), 4)
```

Figure 10.2: Output of a runnable example in the docs

Since creating useful and elegant examples is not always compatible, the code fence specifications include more options:

```
```no_run
loop {
    println!("Hello, Infinite Loop");
}
```


```should_panic
assert!(false);
```


```js,ignore
var not_rust = "This isn't actually Rust code";
```


```compile_fail
let x = 10;
x = 12; // <- compiler error
```
```

These options provide further customizations of the code snippets and their behavior. From top to bottom, the snippet shows:

- Compile but not run the example (**no_run**)
- A panic is expected (**should_panic**)
- Ignore the code entirely (**ignore**)
- Fail the compilation (**compile_fail**)

These modifiers help in providing instructive examples, complete with syntax highlighting and tests to show if your latest change did not break the docs and also behaves as it previously did.

> **Note: These tests are black-box tests and therefore have to import the functions they are testing. Consequently, doctests only work for public functions and structs.**

As an example of how great documentation looks like, check out the HashMap's docs at doc.rust-lang.org/stable/std/collections/hash_map/struct.HashMap.html#examples. Most functions sport examples, but also the struct features a full set of "how to use this" type examples at the top that are compiling and provide tests for future changes.

To see how they implemented this and which parts are hidden, check the source code at doc.rust-lang.org/stable/src/std/collections/hash/map.rs.html.

Now after writing great docs with examples, let us see how we can get them to the users so they can read them.

Publishing your documentation

There are many ways to publish the documentation effectively, but in 2021 the most common way is to use a website or HTML page. From there, many paths can be taken as to where the website lives: locally on your hard drive, in a shared drive, or somewhere on the Web using static hosting providers.

rustdoc outputs such HTML. In fact, it also provides the entire support structure around it, including interactive elements, adjustable styles, search, and keyboard shortcuts, and you can generate this using a simple cargo doc (learn more at doc. rust-lang.org/cargo/commands/cargo-doc.html). This command invokes rustdoc under the hood and places everything into the target/doc directory.

Although you can edit these files directly (for example, replace the logo), cargo doc will not care about those changes and overwrite them. Instead, you can use the **#[doc]** attribute to configure the output with these at the crate level (see also doc. rust-lang.org/rustdoc/the-doc-attribute.html#at-the-crate-level):

```rust
#![doc(html_logo_url = "https://my.project.rs/logo.pn",
       html_favicon_url = "https://my.project.rs/favicon.ico",
       html_root_url = "https://my.project.rs/")]

/// A function to add two numbers
///
/// # Examples
///
/// ```rust
/// # use playground::add;
/// assert_eq!(add(2, 2), 4)
/// ```
pub fn add(a: usize, b: usize) -> usize {
  a + b
}
```

Although *figures 10.1 and 10.2* show the outputs of the local crate from this book, docs.rs publishes all documentation generated by cargo doc if a package is available on crates.io.

Conclusion

Documenting code with `rustdoc`'s annotations is not complex and provides a large amount of flexibility with respect to formatting and configuration. The language it uses to format text is a flavor of markdown (commonmark.org), and it can be used extensively to describe what your code is doing.

The syntax consists of `///` (document what follows) or `//!` (document the containing element) and whenever a line starts like that, markdown can follow. This markdown should let the user reason about sections, use syntax highlighting, and contain runnable examples that actually work. The latter feature is called a doctest, and it augments the documentation as well as tests because every example that is not explicitly ignored or outside the *Examples* section will be run, and they will break the build if they do not work.

However, it is good practice to have tested documentation. Here is an overview of the most important features and configurations:

```rust
#![doc(html_logo_url = "https://my.project.rs/logo.pn",
       html_favicon_url = "https://my.project.rs/favicon.ico",
       html_root_url = "https://my.project.rs/")]


//! The main module

/// A function to add two numbers
///
/// # Examples
///
/// ```rust
/// # use playground::add;
/// assert_eq!(add(2, 2), 4)
/// ```
pub fn add(a: usize, b: usize) -> usize {
  a + b
}

/// Some other type that does stuff.
pub struct AnotherType;

/// A struct to store data in called [`MyStruct`][m]
///
/// [m]: MyStruct
pub struct MyStruct {
```

```
/// A collection ([`Vec<T>`]) of [`usize`]
pub a_vec: Vec<usize>,

/// Stores a [`AnotherType`] variable
pub another_type: AnotherType,

/// Stores a number of type [`usize`]
pub a_number: usize,

/// Stores a string [string](String)
pub a_string: String,
}
```

Once the docs are written, you can publish them online using a static file hoster. The required HTML pages are generated using cargo doc, which invokes all `rustdoc` commands and puts a full website into the **target/doc** directory. That is it! Documentation should not require a full book to read first; however, if you do want to get deeper into `rustdoc`, check out doc.rust-lang.org/rustdoc/what-is-rustdoc.html.

In the next chapter, you will learn how to create macros, such as assert! or `#[test]`. Maybe you can come up with your test framework one day?

Challenge

Most readers will already know the challenge ahead: document your **LinkedList**. Write at least one doctest in an example and generate some HTML output to start off. If you want to go deeper, look at the standard library (for example, the doc. rust-lang.org/stable/std/collections/struct.LinkedList.html or its module page `std::collections`) and see if you can reuse their examples to augment your code and adjust the output accordingly. If you want to use the online playground at play.rust-lang.org, be sure to run the test command to find out if your doctests are working.

To recall, here is a code scaffold from earlier chapters:

```
enum Link {
  Next(Box<Data>),
  Empty
}

struct Data {
  value: u128,
  next: Link
```

```rust
}

impl LinkedList {

  /// Document me
  /// # Examples
  /// ```rust
  /// # use myproject::LinkedList;
  /// let list = LinkedList::new();
  /// ```
  pub fn new() -> Self {
    LinkedList { head: None }
  }

  /// Document me
  pub fn append(&mut self, value: u128) {
    // your previous implementation
  }

  /// Document me
  pub fn count(&self) -> usize {
    // your previous implementation
    0
  }

  /// Document me
  pub fn pop(&mut self) -> Option<u128> {
    // your previous implementation
    Some(0)
  }
}

/// Document me
pub struct LinkedList {
  head: Option<Link>
}

/// Document me too
pub struct LinkedListIterator {
  // ...
}
```

CHAPTER 11
Generating Code with Macros

When writing code, you will often encounter situations where copy-pasting other code seems like the most efficient way to share behavior between two types. However, most developers also have experienced the situation where copy-pasting code led to more issues than it actually solved.

Rust features a mechanism to have the compiler do the heavy lifting of duplicating code for you, and the best part is that it is much more than simple text manipulation. In other words, it is programming programming—or metaprogramming.

Structure

In this chapter, we will be covering the following topics:

- Declarative macros
    - Using arguments with names and designators
    - Adding complexity to arguments
    - Exporting macros
- Procedural macros
    - Writing function-like macros

o Deriving stuff with macros

o Using attributes to extend code

Objectives

After this chapter, you will be great at using and implementing macros.

Declarative macros

We have used a range of macros already: `println!`, `assert!`, or panic! have all been part of previous chapters. Besides the curious syntax, this code has other features that make them stand out:

- When using `println!` without a literal, the compiler will complain.

- `println!` also knows that if a parameter is passed in, there has to be a placeholder in the string—at compile time.

- `assert_eq!` neatly wrap a panic, message, and the comparison of any type.

The reason for these powers is the fact that these are not functions that are executed at runtime. Rather these macros are resolved into the underlying code snippet after the source code has been transformed into an abstract syntax tree (AST—see also twilio.com/blog/abstract-syntax-trees). This allows to retain Rust's type system even in this text replacement scenario. Declarative macros can be thought of as more powerful versions of inline functions. One effect of this is that a macro can have syntax errors in one case but not another.

As appropriate, a macro is declared using a macro: `macro_rules!`. Let us see a simple macro that returns the result of a calculation: 1 + 1. Again, try out the following either on play.rust-lang.org or your local machine:

```
macro_rules! two {
    () => { 1 + 1 }
}

assert_eq!(2, two!());
```

In this snippet, you see the three parts any declarative macro has (note the new vocabulary):

1. A name (`two`).

2. A matcher (`()`)—empty in this case.

3. A transcriber, containing an expression (`{ 1 + 1 }`).

The matcher is the core part of a macro; it matches the parameters exactly (see following) and replaces those tokens with the transcriber. Matching the parameters exactly is important because macros can be overloaded—so one name can have many matches, each with its own transcriber:

```
macro_rules! calc {
  (two) => { 1 + 1 };
  (three) => { 1 + 2 }
}


assert_eq!(2, calc!(two));
assert_eq!(3, calc!(three));
```

In this example, two or three are literally words that match a pattern in the macro declaration. Any combination of characters can do the same, which makes macros great for creating a domain-specific language. However, you can also use the matcher for arguments.

Using arguments with names and designators

Arguments allow you to add some external input to your macro. Since the generation happens as a build step, their vocabulary as well as how you declare and pass arguments is a bit different:

```
macro_rules! repeat_n_times {
    ($n: expr, $text: expr) => {(0..$n).map(|_| format!("{}", $text)).
collect::<Vec<String>>()}
}


assert_eq!(vec!["Hello", "Hello", "Hello"], repeat_n_times!(3,
"Hello"));
```

Each argument has a name (**$name**) and a type (called designator) that matches the argument that is passed into the macro. The reference at doc.rust-lang.org/reference/macros-by-example.html#metavariables shows several designators to match. Check the reference link for specific documentation on each:

- **ident**: Identifier
- **block**: Block
- **stmt**: Statement
- **expr::** Expression
- **pat**: Pattern

- **ty**: Type

- **lifetime**: Lifetime

- **literal**: Literals

- **path**: Path

- **meta**: Meta items

Common macros use expressions, blocks, statements, and identifiers—so we will focus on those. Let us get more sophisticated and generate a hypothetical Web handler using a macro:

```rust
#[derive(PartialEq, Debug)]
struct Response(usize);

// Generate a function using a macro!
macro_rules! handler {
  ($i: ident, $body: block) => {
    fn $i () -> Response $body
  }
}

handler!(status_handler, { Response(200) });
assert_eq!(status_handler(), Response(200));
```

In this snippet, we used two arguments (officially called metavariables) to generate an entire function using an ident designator to name it and a block as its body. In order to refer to those arguments, a $name syntax is used—presumably to distinguish those easily from actual Rust code. Note that all arguments have to conform to the rules of each designator, so anything passed into an ident cannot be a String or other type—we are meta-programming; Strings do not exist yet.

Adding complexity to arguments

To get deeper into the arguments, let us look at repeating arguments. Compilers (parsers, actually) generate tokens from the code that you write so they can build a tree from those tokens. Since, at that point, tokens are valid, and in the right order, they may form a chain. A simple example is **1; 2; 3**, each of which is a literal expression.

Macros can match these repetitions without much prior knowledge. Consider the **vec!** a macro, which accepts any expressions that produce the same type and that are separated by a ","(comma). The syntax for this is a bit like a regular expression:

```rust
( $( $item:expr ),* ) => { ... }
```

This is part of a matcher of a macro (see next) that expects the repeated expression within its parentheses (`$( ... )`), each of which is an expr assigned to **$item**. The repetition pattern involves a comma as a separator and everything can appear zero or more times (*) in the order of **$item, $item,** .... Separators are limited to these characters:

- `=>` - a fat arrow

- `,` - a comma

- `;` - a semicolon

Let us put the preceding snippet into action by creating a **vec!** equivalent for the **BTreeSet**:

```
use std::collections::BTreeSet;

macro_rules! set {
  ( $( $item: expr ),* ) => {
     { // a nested scope to isolate the generated code
        let mut s = BTreeSet::new();
        $(s.insert($item);)*
        s
     }
  };
}


let actual = set!("a", "b", "c", "a");

// This is what the macro effectively generates:
let mut expected = BTreeSet::new();
expected.insert("a");
expected.insert("b");
expected.insert("c");
expected.insert("a"); // it's a set, so it de-duplicates

assert_eq!(actual, expected);
```

This **set!** macro matches on a repeated expression that it repeats internally **$(s.insert($item);)*** as many times as the incoming argument did. In this case, it generates the insert code for the **BTreeSet**, just like any programmer would write it. Consequently, a valid expr could also produce an invalid type (for example, a **usize**) that the macro then inserts, which will lead to an error that the compiler throws back to you.

> **Note: Calling a macro can be done with square brackets or parentheses**

The important part is the **$()*** syntax that repeats the statement. The ***** can also be + (one or more repetitions), and the separator follows between the repetition operator and the closing parenthesis, except for the "?" (zero or one) operator—where no separator is needed (and allowed). Here is another example to instantiate any key-value collection (that is, maps):

```rust
use std::collections::{BTreeSet, HashSet};

macro_rules! key_value {
  ( $cls: ty, $( $key: expr => $value: expr ),* ) => {
    {
        let mut s = <$cls>::new();
        $(s.insert($key, $value);)*
        s
    }
  };
}

let actual = key_value!(BTreeMap<&str, usize>, "hello" => 2, "world" =>
1);
let mut expected = BTreeMap::new();
expected.insert("hello", 2);
expected.insert("world", 1);
assert_eq!(actual, expected);

// or a different kind of map:
let actual = key_value!(HashMap<&str, usize>, "hello" => 2, "world" =>
1);
let mut expected = HashMap::new();
expected.insert("hello", 2);
expected.insert("world", 1);
assert_eq!(actual, expected);
```

Now that we have these great macros, how about we share them with the world?

Exporting macros

Just like any other type in Rust, macros obey scopes and have to be exported explicitly. Unlike a type, a simple pub in front is not sufficient. Instead, the language supports an attribute **#[macro_export]** that allows others to import this macro. If we place the key-value initializer from before in a mod, the difference is revealed:

```rust
mod helpers {
  #[macro_export] // remove this to see the error
```

```
macro_rules! key_value {
  ( $cls: ty, $( $key: expr => $value: expr ),* ) => {
    {
      let mut s = <$cls>::new();
      $(s.insert($key, $value);)*
      s
    }
  };
}
}
// Note the import is needed here, where the macro "expands"
use std::collections::{BTreeMap, HashMap};

let actual = key_value!(BTreeMap<&str, usize>, "hello" => 2, "world" =>
1);
let mut expected = BTreeMap::new();
expected.insert("hello", 2);
expected.insert("world", 1);
assert_eq!(actual, expected);

// or a different kind of map:
let actual = key_value!(HashMap<&str, usize>, "hello" => 2, "world" =>
1);
let mut expected = HashMap::new();
expected.insert("hello", 2);
expected.insert("world", 1);
assert_eq!(actual, expected);
```

Macros do not have a path-based scope, so they are always in the root scope and have to be imported from there. Additionally, macros are matched top to bottom, so if there are multiple variants, the compiler will use the first match—be aware of that when writing macros. Especially for more complex macros, check out the reference for any constraints, restrictions, and so on since they would be too complex to print them here: **doc.rust-lang.org/reference/macros-by-example.html**.

For complexity, we will instead look deeper into procedural macros.

Procedural macros

The second kind of macro Rust supports is called a procedural macro. Just like the first kind (declarative), the execution of the macro takes place during compilation, which allows to modify almost anything about the code it is associated with. Not only does that include extending the syntax but also auto-implementations using **#[derive()]** and general code generation. There are three general flavors of procedural macros:

1. Function-like macros

2. Derive macros

3. Attribute macros

The first flavor is very similar to what we used in the first section of this chapter, whereas we have already used **#[derive(Debug)]**, and we will see some more of the last kind in this section. What unites these kinds is the fact that they operate on a **TokenStream** type instead of individual parts of the AST (like in the previous section). Another commonality is that they have to live in a separate crate from where they are being used. In fact, the type of this crate has to be different in order for the compiler to accept **proc_macro** as an import. Here is what the **Cargo.toml** of a macro-exporting library has to look like (note the **[lib]** section):

```
[package]
name = "macros"
version = "0.1.0"
edition = "2021"


[lib]
proc-macro = true

[dependencies]
```

Even without any dependencies, this setup allows to import the compiler's **proc_ macro** crate, which contains the most important tools to create either of the three macro kinds. Let us look at them one by one.

Writing function-like macros

These are called like functions and declared like the following:

```
extern crate proc_macro;

#[proc_macro]
pub fn print_info(_item: TokenStream) -> TokenStream {
    "fn print_info() { println!(\"Hello!\"); }".parse().unwrap()
}
```

The extern crate declaration is a remainder of Rust 2015. In this edition, any import of an external crate required this extern crate **other_crate** statement before using **other_crate::myfunc**. Today, these are only required for specific—compiler-related—crates (such as the test crate for benchmarking and here).

In this case, it provides access to the **proc_macro** attribute, which does all the heavy lifting. The macro itself returns a **TokenStream** type, which is parsed Rust code—the AST. The quickest way to a **TokenStream** is via a regular &str (or String) that is fed into the parser. However, if you want to use the context where the macro was placed, use the input parameter **TokenStream**.

Using the macro is as simple as any declarative macro:

```
use macros::print_info;

print_info!();

fn main() {
    assert_eq!("Hello!", &print_info());
}
```

As implemented preceding, the macro creates a function that returns a String **"Hello!",** which the assert checks for. Consequently, running this (binary) project will simply show nothing. Passing anything into the macro will appear in the _item parameter, but those values will be exactly the same as in the other procedural macros.

Deriving stuff with macros

Derive macros are among the most useful macros since they allow to auto-implement a trait with minimal code changes. We have used that for implementing **#[derive(Display, Debug)]**. From a macro perspective, the difference is mainly that a derive macro receives the token stream of the struct, union, or enum it is placed on.

Any token stream that is returned from that function is placed after the type:

```
// macros/lib.rs
extern crate proc_macro;
use proc_macro::TokenStream;

#[proc_macro_derive(HelloFn)]
pub fn derive_hellofn(item: TokenStream) -> TokenStream {
    let parsed_input = item.to_string().replace("struct", "").
replace(";", "");
```

```
    let impl_ = format!(
        "impl {} {{
    pub fn hello(&self) -> String {{ \"Hello\".to_string() }}
  }}",
        parsed_input
    );
    impl_.parse().unwrap()
}
```

Just like the function-like macro, the derive macro is actually just a function that takes in and returns a **TokenStream**. The input is the item the derive macro is placed on (see following), and it can be parsed using more sophisticated crates like syn (docs. rs/syn/syn/index.html). For the preceding example, we contend with a few **String** operations to extract the type name. Once extracted, the type name is inserted as part of its **impl** declaration since the goal of this derive macro is to add a function that we can call without having to copy-paste it into every type. Here is what using the derive macro looks like:

```
// importer/main.rs
use macros::HelloFn;

#[derive(HelloFn)]
struct Greeter;

fn main() {
  let b = Greeter {};
  assert_eq!("Hello", &b.hello())
}
```

The reason these works is simply because the macros are compiled and executed before finalizing the binary's compilation process. Consequently, when parsing and compiling the macro's output fails, the error messages can be somewhat cryptic. Let us add a syntax error to the preceding example by generating a function hello without a return type:

```
// macros/lib.rs
extern crate proc_macro;
use proc_macro::TokenStream;

#[proc_macro_derive(HelloFn)]
pub fn derive_hellofn(item: TokenStream) -> TokenStream {
    let parsed_input = item.to_string().replace("struct", "").
replace(";", "");
```

```
    let impl_ = format!(
        "impl {} {{
    pub fn hello(&self) -> {{ \"Hello\".to_string() }}
}}",
        parsed_input
    );
    impl_.parse().unwrap()
}
```

With this faulty code, the compilation of the macro looks like that:

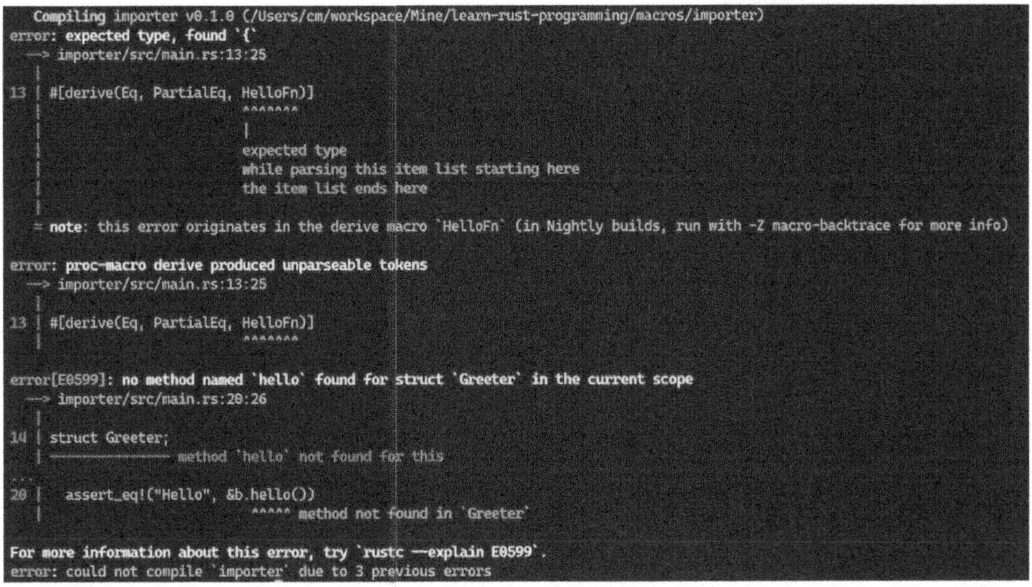

Figure 11.1: Macros can introduce errors

For more complex macros, it is highly recommended to use crates that simplify the parsing process and not just put some Rust code into a string. However, this goes beyond the scope of this book.

Using attributes to extend code

The last kind of procedural macro is the attribute macro. Attributes can be attached to several item types, such as extern blocks, trait implementations, and definitions. You will encounter those types of macros in the async world a lot, as we will discuss in *Chapter 14, Writing Async Code*. These attributes typically add a runtime or allow traits to declare async functions, with some attributes also allowing for some customization.

Attributes also allow for arguments to be passed into the macro alongside the item they are placed on, so the resulting **TokenStream** can be much more complex and have configurability. Examples include tracing via a crate like tokio-trace (docs.rs/ tracing/tracing/attr.instrument.html) or the **#[async_trait]** attribute that enables traits to have async functions. Here is how you define such an attribute:

```
extern crate proc_macro;

use proc_macro::TokenStream;

#[proc_macro_attribute]
pub fn inspect(arguments: TokenStream, item: TokenStream) -> TokenStream
{
    println!("arguments: \"{}\"", arguments.to_string());
    println!("item: \"{}\"", item.to_string());
    item
}
```

Using the attribute is straightfoward as well:

```
use macros::inspect;

#[inspect]
use std::collections::HashMap;

#[inspect(stdout)]
fn abc() -> usize {
    let a = 10;
    100 + 10
}
```

The **inspect** attribute covers both calls, with and without the argument. When issuing a cargo run, the result allows us to see how the macro is actually compiled and executed before the main compilation finishes:

```
   Compiling importer v0.1.0 (/Users/cm/workspace/Mine/learn-rust-programming/macros/importer)
arguments: ""
item: "use std :: collections :: HashMap ;"
arguments: "stdout"
item: "fn abc() -> usize { let a = 10 ; 100 + 10 }"
    Finished dev [unoptimized + debuginfo] target(s) in 0.30s
     Running `target/debug/importer`
```

Figure 11.2: Macros are executed at build time

Additionally, the preceding **cargo run** command shows how different items and arguments are actually passed into the stream. Inside the attribute macro, we could then make decisions as to what to do with the code. However, let us conclude this chapter now—we will be using attributes a lot more in other contexts as well.

Conclusion

Macros—or metaprogramming—allow a programmer to be lazy without compromising on code quality with the compiler's help. Macros also facilitate the **Don't Repeat Yourself (DRY)** rule that has become standard practice among many programmers, and it reduces general boilerplate code to a minimum when done correctly.

Rust features two general groups of macros, declarative and procedural macros. The former is easier to use and operates on specific leaves of the parsed abstract syntax tree. Procedural macros, however, are more complicated but also more powerful since they operate on entire branches of the syntax tree.

Consequently, macros are compiled and executed before the rest of the code is, which also means that they can introduce syntax errors and other oddities for the compiler. Creating good macros is not always easy and requires some practice—a practice that you can get with the preceding challenge! First, let us quickly recap the syntax of declarative macros (this is the example from before that creates a **BTreeSet** in **vec!** style):

```
macro_rules! set {
  ( $( $item: expr ),* ) => {
    { // a nested scope to isolate the generated code
      let mut s = BTreeSet::new();
      $(s.insert($item);)*
      s
    }
  };
}

let btreeset = set!("a", "b", "c", "a");
```

Procedural macros come in three flavors: attributes, function-like, and derive:

```
extern crate proc_macro;

use proc_macro::TokenStream;
```

```
#[proc_macro_attribute]
pub fn inspect(arguments: TokenStream, item: TokenStream) -> TokenStream
{
  println!("arguments: \"{}\"", arguments.to_string());
  println!("item: \"{}\"", item.to_string());
  item
}


#[proc_macro]
pub fn print_info(_item: TokenStream) -> TokenStream {
  "fn print_info() -> String { \"Hello!\".to_string() }"
      .parse()
      .unwrap()
}


#[proc_macro_derive(HelloFn)]
pub fn derive_hellofn(item: TokenStream) -> TokenStream {
    let parsed_input = item.to_string().replace("struct", "").
replace(";", "");
    let impl_ = format!(
        "impl {} {{
    pub fn hello(&self) -> String {{ \"Hello\".to_string() }}
  }}",
        parsed_input
    );
    impl_.parse().unwrap()
}
```

Procedural macros live in their own crates and are somewhat special, which makes them much more powerful than declarative macros. How about you try building one (declarative or procedural, your choice!) for the challenge?

Challenge

By now, your LinkedList project already looks pretty formidable. To recap, the past challenges require you to:

- Implement basic operations

- Implement a trait or two for display

- Convert it to a cargo project

- Add tests

- Add documentation

Although we are going to continue building out the example, this chapter would like you to add an initialization macro that can be used like the **vec!** macro. Here is a test that you can use to check whether it works:

```
#[test]
fn test_new_list_macro() {
  let my_list = llist![];
  assert_eq!(my_list.len(), 0);

  let my_list = llist![1, 2, 3];
  let actual = my_list.into_iter().collect::<Vec<u128>>()
  assert_eq!(actual, vec![1, 2, 3]);
}
```

Pick a name that you like and that speaks to your users (the test uses **llist!** for **LinkedList**). With successful tests, you can move on to the upcoming chapter!

CHAPTER 12
Using Heap Memory Effectively

One of Rust's strengths is the fine control of where memory is coming from without sacrificing memory safety or much convenience. However, the terms, methods, and patterns for using heap memory well are somewhat obscure compared to other languages and technologies. As a consequence, it can be a daunting task to write optimized software and only use the—slower—heap memory when required, but to it is the fullest extent.

Structure

In this chapter, we will be covering the following topics:

- Putting things in boxes
- Boxing data
- Boxing behavior
- Counting references
- Counting references with multi-threading
- Creating mutability as required
- Using locks for global mutability

Objectives

In this chapter, you will learn about heap allocation structures and patterns and how to use them well.

Putting things in boxes

A Box is a struct in Rust that acts as a container for anything to be put onto the heap memory. As we have previously discussed (in *Chapter 5, Borrowing Ownership with Scopes*), heap memory is an unstructured, large portion of the random access memory (RAM) that the operating system assigns to a process. This is where all the large stuff should be stored; for example, **Vec<T>** puts all elements on the heap.

We have also learned that the default is stack allocation for most types, which means it lives in a much smaller space that is bound to threads and functions. While the stack is a lot faster to allocate and access, as the size of such a variable grows, moving it will become slower and eventually stop working since the stack is limited and cannot increase easily (in fact, that happens during compilation).

This is where the Box type helps out. What remains on the stack is a pointer that can be used to read and write to the contents (on the heap) just as any other variable— with the caveat that anything on the heap is somewhat slower than on the stack. These trade-offs are an essential part of creating software.

As of this writing, this is how the Rust source code defines the Box struct (doc.rust-lang.org/src/alloc/boxed.rs.html#172-175):

```
/// A pointer type for heap allocation.
///
/// See the [module-level documentation](../../std/boxed/index.html) for
more.
#[lang = "owned_box"]
#[fundamental]
#[stable(feature = "rust1", since = "1.0.0")]
pub struct Box<
    T: ?Sized,
    #[unstable(feature = "allocator_api", issue = "32838")] A: Allocator
= Global,
>(Unique<T>, A);
```

Leaving the allocator bits aside (Rust allows custom allocators for more exotic hardware), a Box is essentially a wrapper around a pointer to a type. We will explore generics more in *Chapter 15, Working with Generics*, so in brief, here is what this <T: ?Sized> means:

As with the Vec<T>, the T is a placeholder for the actual type, and the <T> syntax lets the compiler know about it. Box<T> will come with a lot of issues since it can literally have any type that goes into the struct—so what should the compiler plan for? How can it provide type safety if T turns out to be an invalid pointer?

Sized is a marker trait that marks when a type has size at compile-time, which is implicitly required (doc.rust-lang.org/std/marker/trait.Sized.html). ?Sized allows to remove this requirement, which makes sense since a **Box<T>** only holds a pointer to the T value on the heap, and pointers have a known, constant size. The notation with <T: MyTrait> allows the compiler to check for this type boundary, so whichever actual type T is going to be, the compiler knows that it will implement **MyTrait**.

For using a type in a Box, no trait implementation is required.

Boxing data

You can use a Box like any other type (for example, **Box<usize>** as a type definition for a parameter), and all attached functions of the underlying type are available seamlessly. The main difference is that instead of a direct read of a **usize**, a read of the value results in a read from the heap, which introduces indirections.

These indirections (that is, pointers) are trivial and small to move around, and via a simple dereference (*) you can get the original value back. Here is an example:

```
fn print_hex(data: Box<u128>) {
  println!("Your data in hex: 0x{:x}", *data);
}

fn main() {
  print_hex(Box::new(1535));
}
```

The prints resulting from running the snippet (play.rust-lang.org or locally, as usual) are as follows:

```
Your data in hex: 0x5ff
```

The data in this Box is an unsigned 128-bit integer (u128) which lives directly where the Box allocates its memory. The thing with pointers is—they pile up. Consider using a String, which is already a heap-allocated type, and you will get a pointer to another pointer. Therefore, a Box does not make a lot of sense from a data perspective. In fact, you will use Box a lot more with behavior.

Boxing behavior

A Box is great for these two things:

1. Trait objects

2. Boxed functions

A trait object is a more versatile form of the new(ish) **impl** Trait syntax—it tells the recipient to expect a type to implement said trait. Although **impl Trait** uses compiler magic to figure out the memory required, function addresses, and so on. a trait object uses dynamic dispatch (read more about that in the *further reading section*). Dynamic dispatch is a fancy name for a lookup routine that searches for the expected trait functions in the provided type, which results in considerable overhead. Intuitively, the call address for a function can only be known if the entire type is known, which is called static dispatch.

> Note: In any case, if performance is highly critical to your application, dynamic dispatch may not be what you are looking for. Be sure to benchmark if your trait object is getting you in trouble.

Let us see how we can use those trait objects:

```rust
trait Greeter {
  fn hello(&self) {
      println!("Hello!");
  }
}


struct Person;


impl Greeter for Person {}


fn say_hello(who: Box<dyn Greeter>) {
  who.hello();
}


fn main() {
  let p = Box::new(Person {});
  say_hello(p);
}
```

In **say_hello()**'s signature, we do not find a reference to the **Person** type, which is a typical way to create decoupled APIs. In many cases, using generics with trait bounds is an easier way to achieve the same thing.

However, sometimes a **Box** is absolutely necessary—for example when you want to store a closure:

```
use std::io::Result;
type ConnectionFactoryFn<T> = Box<dyn Fn(host: String) -> Result<T> +
Send>;
```

```
fn connect_and_read<T>(hosts: &[&str], factory: ConnectionFactoryFn<T>)
-> Result<Vec<String>> {
  let contents = vec![];
  for host in hosts {
    let conn = factory(*host)?;
    let content = conn.read_to_string()?;
    contents.push(content);
  }
  Ok(contents)
}
```

```
fn main() {
  let test_factory = Box::new(move |host: String|
Ok(SimpleStream::connect(host)));
  let hosts = vec!["localhost", "1.1.1.1", "blog.x5ff.xyz"];
  let all_content = connect_and_read(&hosts, test_factory)?;
}
```

In this manner, you can pass and store a function as soon as the trait boundary requirements are met, which is an easy way of creating factories. These factories typically create data in a decoupled way, allowing for different behaviors to be encapsulated dynamically. This is a great tool for testing since these boxed traits are easy to implement and replace (called mocking). However, a Box is just a way of storing something on the heap, but there is still only a single owner. Reference counting is one way to change that.

Counting references

Surprisingly, Rust's memory management allows for multi-ownership of a memory segment as well. Although indirectly and without mutability (see the next section for that) only.

Since ownership answers the question of when can I free this memory segment with "when there is no more owner", counting these owners is a logical next step. Therefore if the number of owners of a memory segment reaches zero, it can be freed.

This is exactly what the **Rc<T>** type in the Rust standard library provides; it counts references and drops the value as that number hits zero. Just like the **Box** type, T is heap-allocated with the **Rc** providing access. Cloning the **Rc** variable will not clone the underlying value, just the pointer, which is a great way to manage access to shared data. Note that **Rc**s generally do not allow mutable access to the underlying data.

Let us see how the standard library implements reference counting (from doc.rust-lang.org/src/alloc/rc.rs.html):

```
struct RcBox<T: ?Sized> {
    strong: Cell<usize>,
    weak: Cell<usize>,
    value: T,
}

// [...]

pub struct Rc<T: ?Sized> {
    ptr: NonNull<RcBox<T>>,
    phantom: PhantomData<RcBox<T>>,
}
```

The **Rc** struct relies on the **RcBox** struct, which has two counters: how many weak and how many strong references there are left (we will cover Cells in the next section). Strong references keep the data alive, and weak references do not. The reason for this difference is the fact that Rcs can be cyclical, creating a memory leak. In such a case, a Weak type can avoid this issue entirely with some other consequences (read more at doc.rust-lang.org/std/rc/struct.Weak.html).

The concept is straightforward: each clone increments the strong property of the underlying data container, and each **drop()** call decrements it. As it reaches zero, the value is dropped together with the last reference. Let us look at an example:

```
use std::rc::Rc;
use std::fmt;

#[derive(Debug)]
struct SharedData(Vec<u8>);

impl fmt::Display for SharedData {
  fn fmt(&self, f: &mut fmt::Formatter<'_>) -> fmt::Result {
    write!(f, "SharedData: {}", String::from_utf8_lossy(&self.0))
  }
```

```rust
}

struct ApplicationData {
  cache: Rc<SharedData>
}

fn main() {
  let cache = Rc::new(SharedData(b"DATADATADATA".to_vec()));
  let app_data_1 = ApplicationData { cache: cache.clone() };
  let app_data_2 = ApplicationData { cache: cache.clone() };

  drop(cache);

  println!("App data 1: {}", app_data_1.cache);
  println!("App data 2: {}", app_data_2.cache);
}
```

In this example, we want to share some **SharedData** with a byte cache between **ApplicationData** instances. Since holding a borrow could be tricky in terms of lifetimes, the **Rc** is a great way of providing each **ApplicationData** instance with an owned version of **SharedData**. Once created and wrapped into an **Rc**, we can clone the cache variable without cloning the content and even drop the original without also dropping the shared data.

Counting references with multi-threading

One drawback of a regular **Rc** is its lack of support for concurrency, which is due to Rust's data race safety. Since these situations still exist in a concurrent environment as well *Chapter 13, Running Concurrent Code,* the Rust standard library provides an Arc ("Atomic Reference Counting") as a solution.

When introducing a thread to print **app_data_2** from the example earlier, the compiler is telling us something:

```
error[E0277]: `Rc<SharedData>` cannot be sent between threads safely
  --> src/main.rs:27:3
   |
27 |       thread::spawn(move ||{
   |       ^^^^^^^^^^^^^ -
   |  _____|_____|
   | |     |
   | |     `Rc<SharedData>` cannot be sent between threads safely
28 | |       thread::sleep(Duration::from_secs(1));
29 | |       println!("App data 2: {}", app_data_2.cache);
30 | |     }).join().unwrap();
   | |_____- within this `[closure@src/main.rs:27:17: 30:4]`
   |
   = help: within `[closure@src/main.rs:27:17: 30:4]`, the trait `Send` is not implemented for `Rc<SharedData>`
   = note: required because it appears within the type `[closure@src/main.rs:27:17: 30:4]`
note: required by a bound in `spawn`

For more information about this error, try `rustc --explain E0277`.
error: could not compile `arcs` due to previous error
```

Figure 12.1: Rc<T> is not Send.

Arcs implement the Send marker-trait—and they are basically a drop-in replacement. According to the docs, the main difference is the fact that using Atomic variables (variables that can be modified in a single CPU instruction) have worse expected performance. From a code perspective, Arcs can be used as a drop-in replacement:

```rust
use std::sync::Arc;
use std::fmt;
use std::thread;

#[derive(Debug)]
struct SharedData(Vec<u8>);

impl fmt::Display for SharedData {
  fn fmt(&self, f: &mut fmt::Formatter<'_>) -> fmt::Result {
    write!(f, "SharedData: {}", String::from_utf8_lossy(&self.0))
  }
}

struct ApplicationData {
  cache: Arc<SharedData>
}

fn main() {
  let cache = Arc::new(SharedData(b"DATADATADATA".to_vec()));
  let app_data_1 = ApplicationData { cache: cache.clone() };
  let app_data_2 = ApplicationData { cache: cache.clone() };
```

```
  drop(cache);

  println!("App data 1: {}", app_data_1.cache);
  thread::spawn(move ||{
    println!("App data 2: {}", app_data_2.cache);
  }).join().unwrap();
}
```

Contrary to Rcs, Arcs have the Send marker-trait, which tells the compiler that it is safe to send the value across threads. We will talk more about that in the upcoming chapter. Here is the output of the preceding snippet:

```
App data 1: SharedData: DATADATADATA
App data 2: SharedData: DATADATADATA
```

Let us see how we can make immutable values mutable using interior mutability.

Creating mutability as required

In most use cases, you will have to declare a variable mut in order to mutate the data that it manages. However, we have seen that Rcs and Arcs only provide a read-only view of their data, so what if there was a struct to control mutability at run time?

These structures are called Cells and come in two variants:

- RefCell handing out references (doc.rust-lang.org/std/cell/struct.RefCell. html).

- Cell handing out the owned data (doc.rust-lang.org/std/cell/struct.Cell. html).

Both variants are gatekeeper structures that provide the required functions to obtain their mutable inners—while staying safe. If you recall, safety is primarily concerned with avoiding data races and data anomalies (that is, reading and changing outdated data)—which means that a Cell effectively has to check for safety guarantees at runtime. This is exactly what it does: panic! when there are read references (RefCell only) while you are trying to make the data mutable.

Since neither Cell is safe for multi-threading, this does not require any locking (more on that in the next section), but the calls look very similar to obtaining a lock. However, placing a variable into a Cell or RefCell and making it mutable at runtime is not what you typically would do. Instead, Rust promotes a pattern called the "interior mutability pattern" (read also doc.rust-lang.org/book/ch15-05-interior-mutability.html). There, the power of "ad-hoc mutability" is combined with an **Rc** to create multiple owners of that RefCell (a regular Cell makes limited sense in this scenario).

For the pattern to work, the Rc controls the RefCell's lifecycle by providing access to the functions of the RefCell. You can then call **borrow_mut()** (or **replace()**) to get a mutable reference, mutate away, and return the data. Each owner of an **Rc** copy can then access the data (**borrow()**), whereas it will not be possible to read invalid or stale data—all of them are referring back to the same RefCell after all. Let us look at an example:

```rust
use std::rc::Rc;
use std::cell::RefCell;
use std::fmt;

#[derive(Debug)]
struct SharedData(Vec<u8>);

impl fmt::Display for SharedData {
  fn fmt(&self, f: &mut fmt::Formatter<'_>) -> fmt::Result {
    write!(f, "SharedData: {}", String::from_utf8_lossy(&self.0))
  }
}

struct ApplicationData {
  cache: Rc<RefCell<SharedData>>
}

fn main() {
  let cache = Rc::new(RefCell::new(SharedData(b"DATADATADATA".to_
vec())));
  let app_data_1 = ApplicationData { cache: cache.clone() };
  let app_data_2 = ApplicationData { cache: cache.clone() };

  cache.replace(SharedData(b"NODATA :(".to_vec()));

  drop(cache);

  println!("App data 1: {}", app_data_1.cache.borrow());
  println!("App data 2: {}", app_data_2.cache.borrow());
}
```

In this snippet, we used the interior mutability pattern to change what is stored in the cache after providing the **ApplicationData** instances with their own owned copies. The result of running the preceding snippet is as follows:

```
      Finished dev [unoptimized + debuginfo] target(s) in 0.00s
        Running `target/debug/cells`
App data 1: SharedData: NODATA :(
App data 2: SharedData: NODATA :(
```

Figure 12.2: Sharing data with interior mutability

Comparing the bytes with the previous outputs shows that the data was indeed replaced—as expected. Note that we never had to declare a variable mut—instead, access was managed through the RefCell, which was owned by the **Rc**. In this manner, sharing common data is indeed easy, and it can be changed safely.

The interior mutability pattern breaks down, however, when we want to use threads in the mix. Just like the **Rc**, a RefCell does not implement the fundamental marker-trait required for many multi-threaded operations: Sync.

Using locks for global mutability

In a multi-threaded environment, it becomes a lot harder to avoid those data race conditions: read and write access may be obtained at any time from anywhere in the code. One good way to solve this issue is by using a program-wide locking mechanism like a Mutex (doc.rust-lang.org/std/sync/struct.Mutex.html). Functionally, the Mutex is similar to the RefCell in that it lets you create references with the call of a function, although this time, the thread calling that function is exclusively locking the Mutex. Other callers queue up, blocking their own threads from continuing.

In order to use the interior mutability pattern in multi-threaded environments, we now have all the ingredients: A Mutex to control the type of access to data and an Arc to control access to the Mutex. Let us transform the previous example into something multi-threaded:

```rust
use std::fmt;
use std::sync::{Arc, Mutex};
use std::thread;

#[derive(Debug)]
struct SharedData(Vec<u8>);

impl fmt::Display for SharedData {
  fn fmt(&self, f: &mut fmt::Formatter<'_>) -> fmt::Result {
    write!(f, "SharedData: {}", String::from_utf8_lossy(&self.0))
  }
}

struct ApplicationData {
```

```rust
  cache: Arc<Mutex<SharedData>>,
}

fn main() {
  let cache = Arc::new(Mutex::new(SharedData(b"DATADATADATA".to_
vec())));
  let app_data_1 = ApplicationData {
    cache: cache.clone(),
  };
  let app_data_2 = ApplicationData {
    cache: cache.clone(),
  };

  let _ = thread::spawn(move || {
    *cache.lock().unwrap() = SharedData(b"NODATA :(".to_vec());
    drop(cache);
  })
  .join();

  let t1 = thread::spawn(move || {
    println!(
      "{:?} App data 1: {}",
      thread::current().id(),
      app_data_1.cache.lock().unwrap()
    );
  });
  let t2 = thread::spawn(move || {
    println!(
      "{:?} App data 2: {}",
      thread::current().id(),
      app_data_2.cache.lock().unwrap()
    );
  });
  let _ = t1.join();
  let _ = t2.join();
}
```

As expected, the output remains the same as preceding:

```
Compiling mutex v0.1.0 (/Users/cm/workspace/Mine/learn-rust-programming/ch12/mutex)
 Finished dev [unoptimized + debuginfo] target(s) in 0.72s
  Running `target/debug/mutex`
ThreadId(4) App data 2: SharedData: NODATA :(
ThreadId(3) App data 1: SharedData: NODATA :(
```

Figure 12.3: *Multi-threaded interior mutability*

As before, we used **ApplicationData** to hold a **SharedData** instance, which we then replaced from a different thread. Later, each of the **ApplicationData** instances is moved to their own threads and printed from there, which also requires locking the **SharedData** Mutex. Less strict forms of a Mutex like the RWLock do not need a full lock to read the data. Read more about the various forms available at doc.rust-lang.org/std/sync/index.html.

> **Note: Multi-threaded programming is hard and requires a good amount of experience to get right. Typical issues involve dead-locks where a thread is waiting for a Mutex that it already holds or when a thread that holds a lock panics—thereby blocking access indefinitely (poisoning). In the upcoming chapter, we will explore strategies to mitigate some of these issues.**

With interior mutability in multi- and single-threaded environments discussed, we can now conclude this chapter and look towards fearless concurrency!

Conclusion

Explicit heap memory allocation comes in various flavors in Rust, and the most important ones are as follows:

- **Box**, which allows you to simply put types on the heap.
- **Rc** to enable multiple owners through reference counting.
- **Cell**/**RefCell** for storing and mutating data.

Here is an illustration of these types:

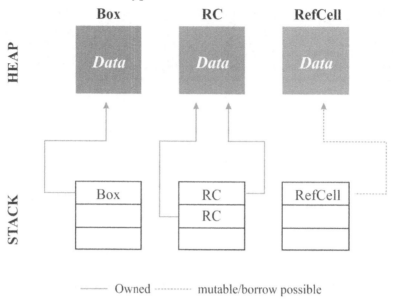

Figure 12.4: Types for allocating heap memory

Combining these types provides a great way to share data by simply sharing a pointer—and with the interior mutability pattern—including options to change the data.

These options also extend to multi-threaded scenarios where a `Mutex` replaces the `RefCell` and an `Arc` the regular **Rc**. However, the upcoming chapter is going deeper into concurrency as a whole, so we will touch on these types a lot.

Let us see if you can solve this chapter's challenge.

Challenge

Once again, it is time to improve the LinkedList from earlier chapters and this time, we had a love for you to tie in the first algorithm we explored in this book: bubble sort!

Here is the unoptimized version from *Chapter 9, Testing What You Build*:

```
pub fn bubble_sort(collection: &mut [i32]) {
  for _ in 0..collection.len() {
    for i in 1..collection.len() {
      if collection[i - 1] > collection[i] {
        let tmp = collection[i];
        collection[i] = collection[i - 1];
```

```
      collection[i - 1] = tmp;
    }
  }
}
}
```

Ideally, you can attach the function to the **LinkedList** like so:

```
// ...
impl LinkedList {
  pub fn sort_unstable(&mut self) {
    // .. implement me
  }
}
```

```
##[cfg(test)]
mod tests {
  use super::*;

  #[test]
  fn test_LinkedList_sort_unstable() {
    let mut list = LinkedList::new();
    list.append(3);
    list.append(2);
    list.append(1);

    list.sort_unstable();
    let actual = list.into_iter().collect::<Vec<_>>();
    assert_eq!(actual, vec![1, 2, 3])
  }
  // add more
}
```

Since the current node implementation has a Box to hold the data, is this still the best choice? Could your **LinkedList** also become thread-safe with an easy swap?

Find out in the upcoming chapter!

Further reading

- Dynamic dispatch is a concept used by trait objects: doc.rust-lang.org/book/trait-objects.html.

CHAPTER 13

Running Concurrent Code

Up to now, we have only seen sequential code execution. That means that the code is running from top to bottom, starting with the function **main()**—without any concurrency. However, real-world software cannot execute only a single command at a time. Not only are modern CPUs built with parallel operations in mind but also the problems we are solving with computer programs also require concurrency to accomplish their goals in a reasonable amount of time. The mechanism to execute any code in parallel is threading, where each thread has private and shared memory managed by the operating system.

A few years ago, the Rust project had the slogan Fearless Concurrency. Although not entirely serious, the slogan aimed to dispel a general fear (or caution) against concurrent programming, which has always been dominated by race condition bugs that are incredibly hard to test and debug. However, thanks to the nature of data ownership, the Rust compiler catches part of those data race conditions early, and it will seem like it just works. Thus you can venture fearlessly into the world of threads and concurrency!

The key aspect is not only ownership but also Rust's strong focus on immutable data. Like in many functional languages, the explicit mut declaration and the constraints that come with it encourage creating and replacing data instead of mutating. Without these "mutations", operations are a lot more transactional, and data anomalies will happen less.

Structure

In this chapter, we will be covering the following topics:

- Threading with Rust
- Using send and sync
    - o   Using alternatives
- Bridging threads with channels

Objectives

After completing this chapter, you will be able to engage in concurrent programming fearlessly.

Threading with Rust

Threads are separate execution paths provided by the operating system that allows a program to run code concurrently. In fact, all code is executed on a thread with the default being the main thread, of which a process has exactly one. Each thread has a dedicated stack, and only heap memory is shared across all threads of a process.

Rust's standard library provides a threading interface for both Windows and POSIX (that is, Linux, Unix, and MacOS), and except for a few details, they work the same. Here is a very simple example of how you can use threads in Rust:

```rust
use std::thread;

fn main() {
  println!("main: {:?}", thread::current().id());

  let handle = thread::spawn(|| {
    println!("spawned: {:?}", thread::current().id());
  });
  // Wait for the thread to finish
  handle.join().unwrap();
}
```

In the preceding snippet, the closure runs on a new thread, printing out the thread's id. The spawn function also returns a handle to interact with the thread, for example, waiting for the thread to finish (**join()**). There are a few noteworthy functions for threads:

- **handle.join()**, which blocks the calling thread until the joining thread is finished.

- **thread::current()**, which retrieves a handle for the thread that function is called from.

- **thread_local!()**, a macro for creating static storage that is created for each thread individually (read more at doc.rust-lang.org/std/macro.thread_local.html).

- **thread::spawn()**, which is a shorthand for creating a new thread using a closure.

Threads in Rust (see also doc.rust-lang.org/std/thread/) are closures without a parameter—so any variables that you use from the closure's parent are borrowed. What makes this complicated is the fact that a thread might actually outlive its parent scope, making any borrows invalid. Here it becomes even more important to move the variables into the scope via the move keyword since the compiler will not be able to infer the appropriate lifetimes.

> **Note: Instead of using thread::spawn() you can use the thread::Builder type to create a thread and configure it to your needs. Options are—as of this writing—a name and the thread's stack size. Read more at doc.rust-lang.org/std/thread/struct.Builder.html**

Here is a snippet where we do not move the variable message:

```rust
use std::thread;

fn main() {
    println!("main: {:?}", thread::current().id());
    let message = "A message from the main thread".to_string();
    let handle = thread::spawn(|| {
        println!("spawned: {:?}, with message: {}",
            thread::current().id(),
            message
        );
    });
    // Wait for the thread to finish
    handle.join().unwrap();
}
```

Predictably, the compiler notices the conflict and complains:

```
   Compiling threads v0.1.0 (/Users/cm/workspace/Mine/learn-rust-programming/ch13/threads)
error[E0373]: closure may outlive the current function, but it borrows `message`, which is owned by the current function
 --> src/main.rs:6:30
  |
6 |    let handle = thread::spawn(|| {
  |                               ^^ may outlive borrowed value `message`
7 |      println!("spawned: {:?}, with message: {}", thread::current().id(), message);
  |                                                                          ------- `message` is borrowed here
  |
note: function requires argument type to outlive `'static`
 --> src/main.rs:6:16
  |
6 |    let handle = thread::spawn(|| {
  |  _____^
7 | |      println!("spawned: {:?}, with message: {}", thread::current().id(), message);
8 | |    });
  | |_____^
help: to force the closure to take ownership of `message` (and any other referenced variables), use the `move` keyword
  |
6 |    let handle = thread::spawn(move || {
  |                               ++++

For more information about this error, try `rustc --explain E0373`.
error: could not compile `threads` due to previous error
```

Figure 13.1: Threading and lifetimes

As the compiler suggests, we could use the move keyword and move the variable into the scope, thereby losing access to it from the main thread:

```rust
use std::thread;

fn main() {
    println!("main: {:?}", thread::current().id());
    let message = "A message from the main thread".to_string();
    let handle = thread::spawn(move || {
        println!("spawned: {:?}, with message: {}",
            thread::current().id(),
            message
        );
    });
    // Wait for the thread to finish
    handle.join().unwrap();
}
```

With the expected output:

```
main: ThreadId(1)
spawned: ThreadId(2), with message: A message from the main thread
```

However, the previous chapter explained another way of accessing data from multiple locations and threads by using an **Arc**. The **Arc** can be cloned cheaply and moved into the scope:

```rust
use std::thread;
use std::sync::Arc;

fn main() {
    println!("main: {:?}", thread::current().id());
    let message = Arc::new("A message from the main thread".to_string());
    let message_ = Arc::clone(&message);
    let handle = thread::spawn(move || {
        println!("spawned: {:?}, with message: {}",
            thread::current().id(),
            message_
        );
    });
    println!("{}", message);
    // Wait for the thread to finish
    handle.join().unwrap();
}
```

The output looks something like this (the order could change, depending on which **println!** is executed first):

```
main: ThreadId(1)
A message from the main thread
spawned: ThreadId(2), with message: A message from the main thread
```

To enforce the boundaries of the scope, the compiler uses two special marker traits: Send and Sync. Let us see what those are about.

Using Send and Sync

Send and Sync are two marker traits that show the compiler at type is as follows:

- Safe to send between threads (Send—doc.rust-lang.org/std/marker/trait. Send.html)

- Safe to access from multiple threads (Sync—doc.rust-lang.org/std/marker/trait.Sync.html)

As a consequence, these traits form the core of Rust's type strategy around concurrency.

Note: Note that implementing Send or Sync is unsafe since the compiler has no way of checking whether the implementation is actually valid. If such an issue comes up, having to implement either trait is very unlikely; maybe there is something else you can change?

Like—for example—the thread::spawn function has this signature (from doc.rust-lang.org/src/std/thread/mod.rs.html):

```
pub fn spawn<F, T>(f: F) -> JoinHandle<T>
where
    F: FnOnce() -> T,
    F: Send + 'static,
    T: Send + 'static,
// ...
```

The input function has the generic closure type **F** with boundaries that it implements **Send** (and has a **static** lifetime since the thread might be alive as long as the entire program). Since a type can only be **Send** if all sub-types are Send, it means that anything moving into the closure needs to be Send as well (most standard library types are). Similarly, custom types are automatically **Send** if all their properties are, too.

An **Arc** will not add this trait either since it too only implements **Send** for types that also implement **Send** (from doc.rust-lang.org/src/alloc/sync.rs.html#235-241):

```
pub struct Arc<T: ?Sized> {
    ptr: NonNull<ArcInner<T>>,
    phantom: PhantomData<ArcInner<T>>,
}

// ...
unsafe impl<T: ?Sized + Sync + Send> Send for Arc<T> {}
```

As we will explore in *Chapter 15, Working with Generics*, the unsafe **impl<T: ?Sized + Sync + Send> Send for Arc<T>** part means that **Send** is only implemented when T conforms to the type constraints **?Sized**, **Sync**, and **Send**. Since most types are automatically Send, you will have few issues moving variables across threads.

Similarly, **Sync** requires that a reference produced by the type implements **Send**. This means that the reference can be sent across threads in order to access the owned type (which is **Sync**). One such construct is the multi-threaded interior mutability pattern with an **Arc<Mutex<MyType>>**.

To simplify:

- Almost all types are Send by default, so moving between threads is not an issue.
- Accessing a complex type from multiple threads is best done using a Mutex/RwLock.

For less complex types, there are alternative solutions as well, just like for more complex synchronization needs.

Using alternatives

While Mutex is great, it also locks the entire object and forces every other **lock()** call to block. Consequently, reads and writes are treated equally even though reads are thread-safe. This is why there are different synchronization types that the Rust standard library provides, like the RwLock, which differentiates between reading and writing. Using the appropriate locking mechanism for your use case can significantly improve performance, so read up on what is available for higher-level synchronization types at doc.rust-lang.org/std/sync/#higher-level-synchronization-objects

Another great way of synchronizing data across threads with minimal locking are atomic types. They cover all numeric types up to 64 bits, including bool and the generic pointer type. The docs provide a great overview at doc.rust-lang.org/std/sync/atomic/. Wrap them into an **Arc** for shared ownership and use the provided methods to load or mutate the data it contains. Let us look at a quick example where we increment a counter 10 times in different threads, no locking required:

```rust
use std::thread;
use std::sync::Arc;
use std::sync::atomic::{AtomicUsize, Ordering};

fn inc_ten_times(counter: Arc<AtomicUsize>) -> thread::JoinHandle<()> {
  thread::spawn(move || {
    for _ in 0..10 {
        counter.fetch_add(1, Ordering::SeqCst);
    }
  })
}

fn main() {
  let counter = Arc::new(AtomicUsize::new(0));
  let handle1 = inc_ten_times(counter.clone());
  let handle2 = inc_ten_times(counter.clone());
  // Wait for the thread to finish
  handle1.join().unwrap();
  handle2.join().unwrap();
  assert_eq!(counter.load(Ordering::SeqCst), 20);
}
```

Note that these atomic types are highly platform-dependent and may not be available for all CPU architecture—the documentation will tell you more about this topic. These atomic types are also what the **Arc** uses internally to count the number of active clones across threads.

However, they only cover a small range of available types. A better way to send data across threads is the use of Rust channels.

Bridging threads with channels

Many use cases involve sending data from one thread to the other for processing in a **First-In-First-Out** (**FIFO**) manner. In particular, most popular big-data processing systems work in a similar manner on a higher level since it lets developers decouple the individual components.

In Rust, this works in a similar way. However, there are no external components; instead, the standard library provides a type that acts just like an external queue, the **std::sync::mpsc::channel**. Although there are more sophisticated versions developed by third parties, this function creates a typed sender/receiver pair with functions to send and receive custom data types. The shorthand MPSC in the module path stands for multi-producer single-consumer, which means that the data can be sent from many threads but consumed only from a single thread.

As a consequence, the two types **Sender<T>** and **Receiver<T>**, differ not only in function but also in their Clone implementation: **Receiver<T>** does not implement clone. The channel itself is unbound, so it has an unlimited capacity (that is, it is limited by the available heap memory), which means that it also blocks on **send()** calls. On the receiving side, **recv()** is always blocking the calling thread.

A channel is also only valid as long as there are senders, so if all senders have been dropped, the **recv()** call will return an **Err()** variant: **RecvError** (doc.rust-lang. org/std/sync/mpsc/struct.RecvError.html).

As a simple example, let us create a worker thread that sums up all numbers that it receives via a channel:

```rust
use std::thread;
use std::sync::mpsc;

fn main() {
  let (number_tx, number_rx) = mpsc::channel();
  let worker_thread = thread::spawn(move || {
    let mut total = 0;
    while let Ok(number) = number_rx.recv() {
      total += number;
      println!("Received new number {}, the new total is {}", number,
total);
    }
    println!("Channel closed, exiting.");
```

```
  });

  for i in 0..20 {
    let tx = number_tx.clone();
    thread::spawn(move || {
      tx.send(i).unwrap()
    });
  }
  // close channel
  drop(number_tx);
  let _ = worker_thread.join();
}
```

When running the code, it outputs the following:

Figure 13.2: Channels can send data across threads

In essence, the worker thread calls the (blocking) **recv()** function to wait for anything that comes down the channel. Each of the 20 threads created in the for loop then sends its number to the channel before we drop the last remaining sender and close the channel.

Each message has a type, and **send()** transfers the ownership of that message to the channel, from where the **recv()** call takes it to the receiving scope. By having these non-overlapping scopes, it is impossible to, for example, send data and then change it while it is underway (at least not in safe Rust).

Channels in Rust come in variations: Bounded and unbounded, broadcast, oneshot, and whatever other third-party crates can think of. Bounded channels simply have a limited number of messages they can store, protecting them against overflowing; broadcast channels clone messages for multiple recipients, and oneshot channels close after a single message. Crates such as crossbeam (github.com/crossbeam-rs/crossbeam]), tokio, or async-std provide tools for many use cases.

A more exotic use of messages between threads is an actor system which treats entire components as actors that can send and receive messages in a very similar fashion. Actix-web (actix.rs) is a famous Web framework for Rust that is built on the actix actor system (docs.rs/actix/latest/actix/).

Most modern Rust applications that requires concurrency and messaging; however, do it asynchronously using the async/await syntax.

Conclusion

Let us put everything into one picture:

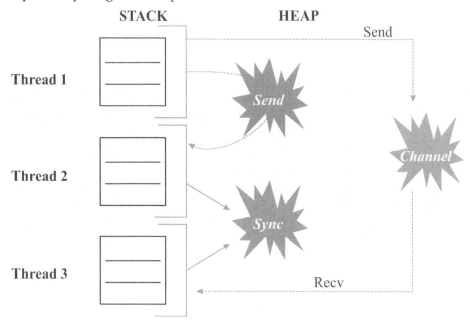

Figure 13.3: *Each thread has its own stack but can share data via heap memory. The required marker traits Send and Sync qualify data structures for multi-threaded programming, whereas a channel provides the means to send data from one (or more) channel(s) to the other*

As *figure 13.3* shows, there are essentially three ways to share data between threads:

- Moving data types that implement Send between threads.

- Accessing data types that implement Sync from multiple threads.

- Moving data between threads via a channel data structure.

Most data types implement Send automatically; however, Sync is available to add via locking structures such as a Mutex—or atomic variants of numeric types.

Safe Rust's primary approach is to use scopes and ownership to avoid data race conditions. Unlike with threads, async programming will show us how these clear boundaries can easily blur—in the upcoming chapter.

Challenge

In this challenge, we are going to take a break from **LinkedList**. Instead, let us implement a game—not a game for humans, though, a game that the computer plays with itself, kind of. With your newly acquired threading knowledge, make a ping-pong game with at least two threads (players)—but a single ball!

Think of the following questions:

- How can you send the ball from one player to the next?

- How does a player know about its turn?

- How can you make the entire game CPU efficient (that is, avoid frequent polling)?

If that is easy for you, why not try different patterns like a ring or even a team game?

Here is some code to get you started:

```rust
use std::thread;

struct Ball {}

fn player(/* Share the ball here? */) -> thread::JoinHandle<()> {
  thread::spawn(move || {
    // move the ball when it's this player's turn
  })
}

fn main() {
  let ball = Ball {};
  // add players!
  let p1 = player(/* ... */);
  let p2 = player(/* ... */);

  p1.join();
  p2.join();
}
```

CHAPTER 14
Writing Async Code

Threading is a great form of concurrency, and it provides fine-grained control over how many threads there are and their dedicated tasks. However, many people will find that past a certain number of threads, it is hard to keep track of them and whether they use their resources efficiently. For example, a download is mostly waiting, waiting for the server, and then waiting for the disk to write a chunk. Given that this rarely uses 100% of bandwidth or disk speed—cannot we do more things in this thread?

The answer is, obviously, yes—by using an I/O scheduler (also called event loop). Since these things are highly complex to handle, the Rust project (after many debates) settled on using async and await in the syntax directly as keywords to signal to the compiler that whatever they are attached to requires this I/O scheduler to run. To further complicate matters, I/O schedulers can run across different threads, so the Send and Sync are constant companions! Let us see how we can use that.

Structure

In this chapter, we will be covering the following topics:

- Scheduling tasks in a loop
    - o Polling futures

- Using futures-rs
- Using async-std
  - o Working asynchronously
  - o Running blocking code

Objectives

After completing this chapter, you will be able to enjoy concurrent programming using async.

Scheduling tasks in a loop

In 2018, the Rust project teams decided to implement async/await as keywords (as opposed to macros) and thereby extend the language. This paved the way for Rust to adopt futures (as those async blocks are called) as a core part of the language. Despite that, the Rust standard library does not come with a futures executor or other operations on these async constructs in an effort to keep the library small and portable.

Consequently, several projects took it upon them to implement their version of an event loop and associated non-blocking wrappers for various common tasks (for example, reading files, mutexes, and so on) in addition to the Rust project's futures-rs (github.com/rust-lang/futures-rs). Incredibly, many implementations remain compatible with each other!

As for the syntax, there are two ways of making something async:

1. Use the **async** keyword to declare a function: `async fn my_func()`.

2. Make a block async: `async { /* this is a regular block */ }`.

Either of the two ways returns a `std::future::Future`, which is Rust's base trait for asynchronous programming (more on that later). As soon as you declare something async the compiler adds the return type `impl Future<Output=TheReturnTypeYouUsed>`, so a `async fn my_func()` is syntactic sugar for `fn my_func() -> impl Future<Output=()>` and the error messages will reflect that.

To avoid having to deal with polling the **Future** (more on that later), we have the await keyword, which is used somewhat akin to a function call (**my_func()**.await). This allows treating async functions just like regular functions since only calling await results in a continuation after finishing the async function call. In Rust, **Future** execution is lazy, so the code will not even execute until you call await or spawn the future as a task.

Note: Asynchronous code and synchronous code should not be freely used together. Typical assumptions about blocking a thread (for example, `thread::sleep()`) pause all async executions on the current thread, leading to anomalies and crashes. Use async versions of a function where possible, or wrap them in blocking tasks.

An async framework consists of three parts:

1. A task is a wrapped **Future** that runs to completion.

2. The executor, which runs tasks.

3. The spawner that schedules what task to run next.

In essence, whenever the compiler encounters an `async` keyword, it wraps the block into a task that returns a **Future**. When you call `await` on that task, the spawner places the task in a queue for the executor to run. As soon as execution hits another `.await`, the executor switches to whichever task is next in the queue, sending the now awaiting task back to the spawner. This loop continues until the **Future** is complete. Here is a code example to illustrate this point:

```
fn main() {
  let my_future = async {
    let x = 10;
    let double_task = async move {
      x * x
    };
    assert_eq!(double_task.await, 20);
  }
  executor::block_on(my_future); // poll the future until finished
}
```

This snippet shows no concurrency, but it pauses executing the outer task in order to finish the inner task first—at the `await` call. If there were many more `await`s, how would the previously mentioned spawner know which task should run and which task should sleep?

Polling futures

Simply put, a future implements the trait **Future**, which—in its simplest form— looks like this (from rust-lang.github.io/async-book/02_execution/02_future.html):

```
trait SimpleFuture {
    type Output;
    fn poll(&mut self, wake: fn()) -> Poll<Self::Output>;
}
```

```
enum Poll<T> {
    Ready(T),
    Pending,
}
```

The trait's poll function is essential because it tells the spawner whether the future can run or has to wait using the Poll enum. In order to avoid constantly calling the **poll()** function, the spawner reverses the process and provides a waker (the wake parameter), which tells the spawner to call **poll()**.

Over the course of an async execution, the spawner can send a future to the executor several times to make progress, saving the state of execution for each one when pausing. These executions are not thread-bound, so a multi-threaded executor can run steps on different threads seamlessly.

To make matters even more complex, there are multiple definitions of what a future is (that is, the **Future** trait). You can find the core definition in the Rust standard library at **std::future::Future**. doc.rust-lang.org/std/future/trait.Future.html shows the actual definition:

```
pub trait Future {
    type Output;
    fn poll(self: Pin<&mut Self>, cx: &mut Context<'_>) ->
Poll<Self::Output>;
}
```

This trait makes sure that the **async/await** syntax is available in the language but lacks anything complex such as async streams, executors, or async wrappers.

Note: A Pin<T> is a stable memory reference that allows borrowing even in an async context. Check out the chapter in the Rust Asynchronous Programming book for details: rust-lang.github.io/async-book/04_pinning/01_chapter.html. In essence, the compiler guarantees that the underlying data will be accessible through a reference regardless of where it lives and whether it moves.

Consequently, a Future is only a lazy type that can be polled in a loop to yield data. A loop that resolves these lazy types is called an executor, and it typically handles many such futures, which are scheduled—or spawned—by a different component: The spawner. There is an excellent example to deepen your knowledge about all these components in the async book at rust-lang.github.io/async-book/02_execution/04_executor.html.

In your typical project, there is no need to implement the **Future** trait yourself; instead, you can use crates by the Rust team and others to build your project. One such crate is **futures-rs**.

Using futures-rs

futures-rs (rust-lang.github.io/futures-rs/) provides the necessary additions to the standard library's futures so you can build actual software around them. The crate contains definitions for streams, sinks, executors, channels, and other useful things which should unify any downstream crate that runs async code. Without going into much detail about what is in the crate, let us dive straight into their code example.

First, let us add the **futures-rs** dependency to **Cargo.toml**:

```
[dependencies]
futures = {version = "0.3.19", features = ["executor", "thread-pool"]}
```

This crate allows us to use a simple executor and spawner—most frameworks have a similar API for creating and running futures. Let us look at a slightly modified version of their primary example on **docs.rs/futures/0.3.19/futures/**:

```
use futures::executor;
use futures::executor::ThreadPool;
use futures::channel::mpsc;
use futures::StreamExt;

fn main() {
    let pool = ThreadPool::new().expect("Failed to build pool");
    let (tx, rx) = mpsc::unbounded::<i32>();

    let fut_values = async {
        let fut_tx_result = async move {
            (0..10).for_each(|v| {
                tx.unbounded_send(v).expect("Failed to send");
            })
        };
        pool.spawn_ok(fut_tx_result);

        let fut_values = rx
            .map(|v| v * 2)
            .collect();
        fut_values.await
    };

    let values: Vec<i32> = executor::block_on(fut_values);
    println!("Values={:?}", values);
}
```

The modifications were to reduce the number of integers sent (from 100 to 10) and to remove all comments. Check the website for the original (docs.rs/futures/0.3.19/futures/). However, the same thing is happening: first, we create a thread pool for spawning and executing futures (**pool**) and an unbounded channel to send futures from one task to the other ((**tx, rx**)).

Using an async scope, **fut_values** is a future that the executor can run (**executor::block_on()** runs a future to completion in the current thread). Inside that future, we can use other async tasks (like **fut_tx_result**) but spawn them in our thread pool. Once this future is running, it starts sending data into the channel—and since it is an unbounded channel, the sending is blocked until the recipient starts receiving as well. This is what happens with **rx.map()**, which iterates over the incoming stream of messages at the point of the await.

Once the loop in the **fut_tx_result** task finishes, the sender goes out of scope and is dropped, thus closing the channel. This causes the **fut_values** iteration to finish as well, finishing the entire **async** scope. Since a stream is the async version of an iterator, the **collect()** function does what you know from *Chapters 4, Interfacing with Code* and *Chapter 6, Working with Collections*, and produces a **Vec<i32>** from the stream of values on return.

Here is the output for the preceding snippet:

```
Finished dev [unoptimized + debuginfo] target(s) in 0.01s
  Running `target/debug/futures`
Values=[0, 2, 4, 6, 8, 10, 12, 14, 16, 18]
```

Figure 14.1: Async multiplication

However, **futures-rs** provides limited async wrappers for daily tasks, but it provides async versions of common traits for others to create concrete implementations. One such implementation is the framework **async-std**, which is what we will discuss next.

Using async-std

Like the regular standard library, its async counterpart allows for interacting with the operating system, network, and file system—but in an asynchronous manner. The maintainers wrote an in-depth book at book.async.rs/ and have a website (async.rs/) to explain their motivations and provide other insights.

The framework is compatible with several executors in addition to providing its own variant. For many tasks, **async-std** can replace the standard library in async as the foundation, which is also why it largely mirrors its module structure.

The main reason for adopting such a crate and not simply using the standard library version of a struct is that many—unexpected—functions are blocking the executing thread for a long time. One such example is resolving DNS (domain name system) queries, which is innocently wrapped in a function called **to_socket_addrs** in the standard library (doc.rust-lang.org/std/net/trait.ToSocketAddrs.html#tymethod. to_socket_addrs). The `str` implementation of **ToSocketAddrs** uses a system call (on Linux/Unix) that can take tens or hundreds (or more) milliseconds to complete. This pause causes the `async` runtime to be unable to poll other futures on this thread, leading to an effective halt on all tasks that were supposed to be executed. The result is unexpected and weird behavior on other functions.

For this reason, `async-std` provides an async version (docs.rs/async-std/1.10.0/ async_std/net/trait.ToSocketAddrs.html), which is aware of the runtime and uses the event loop accordingly. However, let us look at how the example from before changes:

```
async fn double(x: usize) -> usize {
  x * x
}

async fn my_future() -> usize {
  let x = 10;
  double(x).await
}

#[async_std::main]
async fn main() {
    my_future().await;
}
```

One thing that typically stands out is the use of an attribute to spawn the runtime. This allows **main()** to be `async` too and removes the (boilerplate) code to create runtime and **block_on** the first future. The attribute is feature-gated, and you can enable it by adding this to your **Cargo.toml**:

```
[dependencies]
async_std = {version = "1.10", features = ["attributes"]}
```

This attribute essentially wraps your async main into a regular **main** function, blocking on your async version. This is from the async-std source code for the **async_std::main** attribute:

```
// ...
    let result = quote! {
        #vis fn main() #ret {
            #(#attrs)*
            async fn main(#inputs) #ret {
```

```
        #body
    }


    async_std::task::block_on(async {
        main().await
    })
}

};
// ...
```

As we explored in *Chapter 11, Generating Code with Macros*, this attribute rewrites your function to run inside a **block_on** function call, executing your async function to completion. This is also a great way to run async code in a sync environment—take a handle to your runtime and call **block_on** on the future you want to execute, and it behaves like any other function call with minimal overhead.

> Note: Although async-std provides its own runtime, it can also serve as an abstraction layer for the tokio runtime. Check the crate's features to enable tokio support: docs.rs/async-std/1.10.0/async_std/index.html#features. In case you need to be able to switch between runtimes more frequently, check out the Agnostik crate (docs.rs/agnostik/latest/agnostik/).

Testing **async** code works in a similar fashion. Use the provided attribute **#[async_std::test]** instead of your regular **#[test]** attribute:

```
#[cfg(test)]
mod tests {
  #[async_std::test]
  async fn test_one_plus_one_is_two() {
      assert_eq!(1 + 1, 2);
  }
}
```

This should get you started in the land of **async-std**. Let us see how you can use some of the structs and tasks to get some work done.

Working asynchronously

Networking is probably the primary domain for async programming. This is due to network communication being relatively slow and not using a lot of CPU resources. Therefore most async frameworks have TCP server examples like the following, which was taken from the **async-std** examples (github.com/async-rs/async-std/blob/1d875836a2302681a395ee44512a518f0222da4a/examples/tcp-echo.rs):

```rust
use async_std::io;
use async_std::net::{TcpListener, TcpStream};
use async_std::prelude::*;
use async_std::task;

async fn process(stream: TcpStream) -> io::Result<()> {
    println!("Accepted from: {}", stream.peer_addr()?);

    let mut reader = stream.clone();
    let mut writer = stream;
    io::copy(&mut reader, &mut writer).await?;

    Ok(())
}

fn main() -> io::Result<()> {
    task::block_on(async {
        let listener = TcpListener::bind("127.0.0.1:8080").await?;
        println!("Listening on {}", listener.local_addr()?);

        let mut incoming = listener.incoming();

        while let Some(stream) = incoming.next().await {
            let stream = stream?;
            task::spawn(async {
                process(stream).await.unwrap();
            });
        }
        Ok(())
    })
}
```

Running the example binds a server to port **8080** on your localhost interface and simply echoes the input you are providing in your TCP package. After binding to this port and interface, the code starts iterating over incoming connections asynchronously, extracting the stream, and spawning a new task into the runtime that processes the `TcpStream` (docs.rs/async-std/latest/async_std/net/struct.TcpStream.html).

Since a `TcpStream` implements the traits `Read` and `Write` (docs.rs/async-std/latest/async_std/io/index.html#read-and-write), the process function can copy from one to the other direction.

The `await` calls in this code allow the runtime to pause the tasks where synchronous implementations would be blocking the thread from doing anything else like waiting for a connection or copying from one stream to the other.

Let us extend the preceding example with a client that runs inside the same thread. Knowing that networking is mostly a lot of waiting for data, we should be able to run both client and server in the same thread as well. Let us start by modifying the dependency as follows (unstable features are required for the **interval()** call):

```
[dependencies]
async_std = {version = "1.10", features = ["unstable"]}
```

This is the modified Rust code:

```
use async_std::io;
use async_std::net::{TcpListener, TcpStream};
use async_std::prelude::*;
use async_std::stream;
use async_std::task;
use std::thread;
use std::time::Duration;


async fn process(stream: TcpStream) -> io::Result<()> {
  println!(
    "[Server] {:?} Accepted from: {}",
    thread::current().id(),
    stream.peer_addr()?
  );
  let mut reader = stream.clone();
  let mut writer = stream;
  io::copy(&mut reader, &mut writer).await?;

  Ok(())
}

async fn client() -> io::Result<()> {
  let mut interval = stream::interval(Duration::from_secs(1));
  while let Some(_) = interval.next().await {
    let mut connection = TcpStream::connect("localhost:8080").await?;
```

```
        connection.write(b"Hello World").await?;
        let mut buf = vec![0; 20];
        let n = connection.read(&mut buf).await?;
        println!(
            "[Client] {:?} Read {:?}",
            thread::current().id(),
            String::from_utf8_lossy(&buf[..n])
        );
    }
    Ok(())
}

async fn server(addr: &str) -> io::Result<()> {
    let listener = TcpListener::bind(addr).await?;
    println!("Listening on {}", listener.local_addr()?);
    let mut incoming = listener.incoming();
    while let Some(stream) = incoming.next().await {
        let stream = stream?;
        task::spawn(async {
            process(stream).await.unwrap();
        });
    }
    Ok(())
}

fn main() -> io::Result<()> {
    std::env::set_var("ASYNC_STD_THREAD_COUNT", "1");
    task::block_on(async {
        let server_task = task::spawn(server("127.0.0.1:8080"));
        task::spawn(client());
        server_task.await?;
        Ok(())
    })
}
```

async-std lets you configure the thread count for the runtime using an environment variable **ASYNC_STD_THREAD_COUNT** so we can make sure it is only running on a single thread. As confirmation, we added the thread ID to the output, and here is the result:

```
    Finished dev [unoptimized + debuginfo] target(s) in 0.02s
     Running `target/debug/async-std-network`
Listening on 127.0.0.1:8080
[Server] ThreadId(2) Accepted from: 127.0.0.1:63135
[Client] ThreadId(2) Read "Hello World"
[Server] ThreadId(2) Accepted from: 127.0.0.1:63143
[Client] ThreadId(2) Read "Hello World"
[Server] ThreadId(2) Accepted from: 127.0.0.1:63161
[Client] ThreadId(2) Read "Hello World"
[Server] ThreadId(2) Accepted from: 127.0.0.1:63180
[Client] ThreadId(2) Read "Hello World"
[Server] ThreadId(2) Accepted from: 127.0.0.1:63193
[Client] ThreadId(2) Read "Hello World"
[Server] ThreadId(2) Accepted from: 127.0.0.1:63198
[Client] ThreadId(2) Read "Hello World"
[Server] ThreadId(2) Accepted from: 127.0.0.1:63206
[Client] ThreadId(2) Read "Hello World"
^C
```

Figure 14.2: A server client application in a single thread

To conform to Rust's lifetime requirements, the server and client code has been moved into their own async functions, which are both effectively infinite loops. We spawn the futures of these functions as tasks, awaiting the server task. Just like before, the server's job is to simply echo what the client sends, so the client uses the **connect()** function to obtain a client stream (the connection variable), sends **"Hello World"** (a byte literal), and then immediately awaits reading into a 20-byte buffer. Since the read function returns the actual number of bytes read, we can create a String from the buffer and print the output—**[Client] ThreadId(2) Read "Hello World"** in the preceding snippet.

Since both the server and client show the same thread id, it is clear that the runtime uses only a single thread to switch between executing client and server code. We have achieved what looks like concurrency through scheduling async tasks efficiently. Yet not all use cases can support an async implementation, which is why we are looking at running sync code within an executor's context.

Running blocking code

Generally, blocking code is not an issue—it is the long-running blocking code that not only stops the code execution but the executor entirely. What is long-running? Hard to say exactly, a second is definitely too long, but an execution time in the 100s of milliseconds may also disrupt the executor sufficiently. Usually, a good indicator that code should be considered blocking is whether the execution time is sync and unpredictable; that is, it is possible to grow indefinitely. In this case, think of either a different way to work on the task at hand—or, if this is not possible—spawn a blocking task.

Blocking tasks in async frameworks are basically threads where the handles are managed by the executor—so you can await the result. These blocking tasks should finish eventually as well and not run indefinitely. If you need an indefinite thread, you can always spawn a regular thread.

Let us see how **async-std** spawns and handles blocking tasks:

```
use async_std::task;
use std::net::TcpStream;
use std::io::{Read, Write};

#[async_std::main]
async fn main() {
  let data = task::spawn_blocking(|| -> String{
    let mut connection = TcpStream::connect("httpbin.org:80").unwrap();
    connection.set_nonblocking(false).unwrap();
    connection.write(b"GET /get?book=learnrustprogramming HTTP/1.1\r\
nHost: httpbin.org\r\n\r\n").unwrap();
    let mut buf = vec![0; 1000];
    let n = connection.read(&mut buf).unwrap();
    String::from_utf8_lossy(&buf[..n]).to_string()
  }).await;
  println!("HTTP DATA: {}", data);
}
```

In this snippet, we used a standard TCP stream to connect to the HTTP test site httpbin.org which echoes whatever you send to it. Here is the result:

```
    Finished dev [unoptimized + debuginfo] target(s) in 0.05s
     Running `target/debug/async-std-web`
HTTP DATA: HTTP/1.1 200 OK
Date: Sun, 02 Jan 2022 20:58:17 GMT
Content-Type: application/json
Content-Length: 263
Connection: keep-alive
Server: gunicorn/19.9.0
Access-Control-Allow-Origin: *
Access-Control-Allow-Credentials: true

{
  "args": {
    "book": "learnrustprogramming"
  },
  "headers": {
    "Host": "httpbin.org",
    "X-Amzn-Trace-Id": "Root=1-61d211e9-0d98a6e327b713b162e08adf"
  },
  "origin": "...",
  "url": "http://httpbin.org/get?book=learnrustprogramming"
}
```

Figure 14.3: Working synchronously within an asynchronous context

spawn_blocking   (docs.rs/async-std/latest/async_std/task/fn.spawn_blocking.html) creates a new thread that allows the blocking TcpStream to write a raw HTTP request right before waiting to read up to 1,000 bytes into buf. The resulting string can then be printed after awaiting the future that the **spawn_blocking** function returns. The network read just serves as an easy example, but it is only one of many that have turned out disrupting blocking in the past:

- DNS queries (with a slow DNS server) since they involve networking.

- FFI and system calls (*Chapter 16, Calling Unsafe and Foreign Functions*).

- Waiting for **std::sync::Mutex** or similar locks (use the async versions).

Additionally, CPU-heavy work does not benefit from async since both the executor and the task require compute cycles; thereby, they are cannibalizing each other's resources. So, if a single-threaded CPU intense workload is part of your application, give it its own thread and let the operating system do the scheduling. If your entire application is very CPU-heavy, async programming may not be the right choice, and you should stick with a more traditional approach with thread pools.

This also concludes our async journey, and we will explore generics next.

Conclusion

Asynchronous programming is great for I/O heavy applications that do a lot of waiting. This waiting time can be spent doing other things—which is exactly what these event loops do. In this environment, the paradigm should be async first since a long-running, blocking operation prohibits the executor from running anything else—including its own management tasks.

The Rust standard library, however, only provides a minimalistic Future trait to offer the async/await syntax. This syntax is effectively a convenience wrapper:

- **async** functions and scopes implicitly return a **Future**.

- **await** implicitly polls a **Future** to completion before continuing.

Since both of these operations require additional code to actually execute, third-party crates are encouraged to implement these. These provide executor and spawner components and sometimes wrappers for other daily operations for accessing the network and file streams, as well as channels and data streams. The most official ones are **futures-rs** and **async-std**, although tokio (tokio.rs) is popular and greatly influenced how async programming works in Rust today.

All in all, async programming provides a layer of abstraction and lets an algorithm decide on more efficient scheduling and execution of work on the available resources. This allows you to minimize paused threads and, when done properly, allows you to stop thinking of thread management as a whole. Spawning threads and async runtimes are not mutually exclusive, however, so use each approach when they fit best. Here is an idea of how to differentiate:

- **Threads**/`task::spawn_blocking`: Long-running CPU-bound work, blocking work without a wrapper.

- **Tasks**/`task::spawn`: Concurrency, network/file-system IO, streams, intervals, and timer-based work.

Use the challenge to get some practice with Rust async!

Challenge

For this challenge, we are going to build on the last challenge, and since only one player is active at one time, you can build the entire game on a single thread!

Use your previous code as a basis, together with the example from the networking section of this chapter. **async-std** should have everything that you need to translate your thread-based code into an async version—so make sure to explore the documentation (docs.rs/async-std/latest/).

In the upcoming chapter, we will return to the **LinkedList** challenge with generics.

CHAPTER 15
Working with Generics

In many previous chapters, we have come across the idea of Generics. There was always a mysterious T that was meant to represent several possible types instead of a concrete type with many sub-types. However, the Rust project is very keen on minimizing overhead and producing a reliable and fast language, which means having a global super-type would result in unnecessary lookups of where a function is actually located on the concrete type.

Instead, Rust uses a process called monomorphization—it replaces the generic type with the concrete type—to generate zero overhead at runtime. Consequently, you can call Rust's Generics more of a syntactic addition that provides the compiler with information on when to fail while it replaces your generic type with what actually is spelled out in the code.

Yet even this replacement strategy can lead to sufficient headaches if the mechanisms are not understood properly. In this chapter, we want to explore the mechanism and thereby, hopefully reduce such headache moments.

Structure

In this chapter, we will be covering the following topics:

- Using Generics

  o Parameterizing functions

  o Parameterizing structs, traits, and enums

- Going deeper

  o Using const Generics

  o Working with lifetimes

Objectives

Once read, this chapter sheds light on declaring and using generic types and lifetimes in structs, functions, traits, and enums.

Using Generics

The Rust language does not have a feature called method overloading, which would allow functions (methods) to be identified by their parameters and return values along in addition to their names. Consequently, if your function dealt with the same operation on a different data type, you had to come up with a different name and sometimes also copy/paste the code. This has a range of downsides:

- Duplication increases the chances of errors.

- Duplicated functions need duplicated tests which also might contain errors.

- Forced naming choices (for example, **find_largest_usize**).

So this is clearly not a great way to manage a large codebase. Sure, you can write a macro and automate the code generation, but there is a more elegant and proven way to get to a shared codebase for overlapping functions, descriptive names, and even improved testability: Generics.

Since we covered some Generics in previous chapters already, let us recap what we know:

Using a notation of **<T>** after the identifier, we can declare a generic type. This acts as a placeholder for the real type, and the compiler replaces it with whatever you actually use it with. **<T>** can also have added constraints like the traits it is required to implement, so the compiler knows which functions are available. These traits can be specified either:

- With the type parameter, that is, **<T: MyTrait>**.

- As a **where** clause, that is, **<T> ... where T: MyTrait**.

Note: You can use any identifier for T; T is a convention.

Additionally, explicit lifetimes are specified right before the generic type parameter: `<'a, T>` means we are naming some lifetime `'a`. Recall the **run_app** example function where the trait `Configuration` was required (in *Chapter 4, Interfacing with Code and Errors*). Since this is a borrow, we can make sure the borrow conforms to a specified lifetime **'a**:

```
pub fn run_app<'a, T: Configuration>(config: &'a T) {
  //...
}
```

The same function can also use the **where** clause for the type constraint:

```
pub fn run_app<'a, T>(config: &'a T) where T: Configuration {
  //...
}
```

Many times the lifetime is automatically filled in by the compiler (lifetime elision, read more doc.rust-lang.org/nomicon/lifetime-elision.html), but there are cases where being explicit about them is important.

However, let us look at some concrete examples using the **Configuration** trait from *Chapter 4, Interfacing with Code and Errors*. Here is the trait again:

```
/// A simple trait with getters
trait Configuration {
  /// Returns the number of threads
  fn no_threads(&self) -> usize;

  /// Returns verbosity settings 0 = none, >3 = high
  fn verbosity(&self) -> u8;
}
```

Let us see how we can use this trait in functions, structs, and other traits.

Parameterizing functions

We already had some examples of how a function can have type parameters constrained by the **Configuration** trait. Since the compiler elides the lifetime, the named lifetime **'a** does not change how the compiler sees the borrow in this first example:

```
pub fn run_app<'a, T: Configuration>(config: &'a T) {
  start_threads(config.no_threads());
}
```

Sometimes additional traits are required as well, so we can just chain them together with **+**:

```rust
pub fn run_app<'a, T: Configuration + Clone>(config: &'a T) {
  spawn_subprocesses(config.clone());
  set_verbosity(config.verbosity());
}
```

Alternatively, the **where** clause looks like this:

```rust
pub fn run_app<'a, T>(config: &'a T) where T: Configuration + Clone {
  // ...
}
```

You can use the generic parameter anywhere inside the function, just like you would any other type:

```rust
fn find_smallest<T: PartialOrd>(coll: &[T]) -> &T {
  let mut smallest: &T = &coll[0]; // panics if coll.len() is 0
  for i in  coll {
    if i < smallest {
      smallest = i;
    }
  }
  smallest
}
```

Parameterizing functions in that way allows you to create more flexible functions that can handle various types, which makes testing them significantly easier. For example, here is the useful **Into<T>** trait:

```rust
fn print<S: Into<String>>(s: S) {
  println!("{}", s.into());
}

fn main() {
  print("Hello");
  print(String::from("Hello"));
  print(&String::from("Hello"));
}
```

Since we have encountered these examples during the book already, let us move on to something a little more challenging: parameterizing structs and enums.

Parameterizing structs, traits, and enums

Structures and enums can have properties that have a generic type by declaring them together with the struct and preparing an **impl** block for this (constrained) generic type as well. Here is a quick example:

```
pub struct App<C> where C: Configuration {
  config: C
}

impl<C> App<C> where C: Configuration {
  pub fn new(config: C) -> Self {
    App {
      config
    }
  }
}
```

Previously we also created a **SimpleConfiguration** implementation of the **Configuration** trait, which works as an input parameter for the **App** struct we just defined. Here is the **SimpleConfiguration** again:

```
struct SimpleConfiguration {
  no_threads: usize,
  verbosity: u8,
}

impl Configuration for SimpleConfiguration {
  fn no_threads(&self) -> usize { self.no_threads }
  fn verbosity(&self) -> u8 { self.verbosity }
}
```

Let us create another **Configuration** instance based on an enum too:

```
enum LazyConfiguration {
  FromFile(String),
  FromEnv,
}

impl Configuration for LazyConfiguration {

  fn no_threads(&self) -> usize {
    match self {
      LazyConfiguration::FromFile(path) => { ... }
```

```
        LazyConfiguration::FromEnv =>
          std::env::var("no_threads").unwrap_or_default()
    }
  }

  fn verbosity(&self) -> u8 {
    match self {
      LazyConfiguration::FromFile(path) => { ... }
      LazyConfiguration::FromEnv =>
        std::env::var("verbosity").unwrap_or_default()
    }
  }
}
```

Methods (functions attached to structs) can have individual generic parameters too:

```
impl LazyConfiguration {
  pub fn new_from_file<S: Into<String>>(path: S) -> Self {
    LazyConfiguration::FromFile(s.into())
  }
}
```

Since this enum-based type may lead to a different choice, we can dedicate a specialized **impl** block of the **App** struct for it:

```
impl App<LazyConfiguration> {
  pub fn new(config: LazyConfiguration) -> Self {
    App { config }
  }
}
```

Enums are very similar to structs (since they are a union of multiple structs), which makes using them with Generics the same as structs. However, any generic parameter applies to all variants. Consider the **Option<T>** where **None** has no value for **T**, which trips up the compiler. This function makes it impossible for the compiler to infer the type of **T** if it is not explicitly provided:

```
fn my_func<T>() -> Option<T> {
  None
}
```

There are a few ways to do that, like calling with an explicit type: **my_funct::<usize>()**. Sometimes the **None** return value has to be typed, which leads to a **None::<usize>** construct. Consequently, even an enum variant without a type may have to provide a type so the compiler knows what the other variant would look like.

Similarly, an enum to capture all your application errors can look like that:

```
pub enum AppError<E: std::error::Error> {
  InputError { location: usize, error: E }
  GeneralError(E),
  UserCancel,
}
```

In this preceding snippet, you also may have to provide a type for **E** in cases where the compiler does not have the ability to infer it automatically. In more realistic use cases, crates like `quick-error` (docs.rs/quick-error/latest/quick_error/) provide additional features for a more complete error type.

Traits use the same notation as structs too:

```
pub trait ConfigSync<C: Configuration> {
  fn reload(&mut self) -> C;
}
```

However, this leads to a situation where we have to know which **Configuration** type we want to sync as a caller. In fact, the combination of **ConfigSync** implementor and **Configuration** that we need could even be non-existent, giving us another headache. For that reason, associated types exist:

```
pub trait ConfigSync {
  type Config: Configuration;
  fn reload(&mut self) -> Self::Configuration;
}
```

These types are specified by the implementor, allowing the caller to just call use a **ConfigSync** implementation. Although there could still be no implementation for the **Configuration** instance we are looking for; we do not have to guess by using type parameters. Instead, we can just have a **JsonFileConfigSync** implement **ConfigSync**, and therefore, we can anticipate what this struct is going to do: reload a file from the disk.

For additional information, check out the chapter in the Rust book at doc.rust-lang. org/book/ch19-03-advanced-traits.html#specifying-placeholder-types-in-trait-definitions-with-associated-types.

Going deeper

Generics allow you to create great and easy-to-use APIs within your applications. However, you will notice that sometimes elegant solutions are tricky to get right.

Whether it is an enterprise application using the factory pattern (Design Patterns, '94 by the Gang of Four) or software that has to limit its memory allocations, there will be specific situations that we cannot cover in this book, especially with Generics.

What we can do is to provide a few ideas on what else there is in Rust's world of Generics. Although not as powerful as, for example, C++'s templates, the Rust team has done great work on covering a lot of use cases. Let us start with const Generics.

Using const Generics

For a long time, the Rust standard library had array functions that only worked up to a certain size of 32 elements (see rust-lang.github.io/rfcs/2000-const-generics. html). This was due to the fact that arrays have to be created using a literal, and since nobody wanted to write an unlimited number of array functions, it was automated—up to a size of 32 elements. With the introduction of const Generics, this issue could be solved much more elegantly and for unlimited sizes by providing the value via the same mechanism as type parameters. For more background, check out the document on the preceding GitHub link.

The syntax looks very similar to regular type parameters:

```rust
const TWO: usize = 2;

fn print_n<const N: usize>() {
  println!("n={}", N);
}

fn main() {
  print_n::<42>();
  print_n::<0x5ff>();
  print_n::<{2 * 2}>();
  print_n::<TWO>();
  print_n::<{ TWO * TWO }>();
}
```

Running the example results in the following prints:

```
n=42
n=1535
n=4
n=2
n=4
```

Note the const expression {2 * 2} which works just as if we were to write **4**. We can also recreate the same functions using a struct instead of a function:

```rust
const TWO: usize = 2;

struct Printer<const N: usize>;

impl<const N: usize> Printer<N> {
  fn print_n() {
    println!("n={}", N);
  }
}

fn main() {
  Printer::<42>::print_n();
  Printer::<0x5ff>::print_n();
  Printer::<{2 * 2}>::print_n();
  Printer::<TWO>::print_n();
  Printer::<{ TWO * TWO }>::print_n();
}
```

There are also several exceptions and things you cannot do, and it is expected that this is a list that will shrink over time. Check the docs at doc.rust-lang.org/reference/items/generics.html#const-generics to find out more.

Working with lifetimes

There are a few situations where lifetimes are different with Generics from without. Whereas most situations can also be worked around with Arc/Rc constructs, sometimes it is not possible to gain ownership over a type, and therefore, you have to make sure the lifetimes are known—if the compiler cannot figure them out.

Typically, this depends on the situation; usually through, threads and async present challenges with respect to borrowing across these scopes since one may outlive the other easily. Additionally, when implementing a data structure, the associated borrows are a source of errors. Check out doc.rust-lang.org/rust-by-example/scope/lifetime.html for examples.

Another situation is the use of borrows within function pointers that use generic parameters and borrows. In such a case, a value passed in when executing the function pointer has to outlive this execution. The issue with the current syntax is that there is only a static naming scheme, which does not allow for accounting into the future. In other words, if you declare a lifetime 'a, any caller of that function has to provide this 'a lifetime—it cannot just be 'b. This is why there is something called **higher-ranked trait bounds** that use a for declaration to anticipate such a lifetime (doc.rust-lang.org/reference/trait-bounds.html#higher-ranked-trait-bounds).

Let us look at an example:

```
struct LoggedFunctionCall<T, F, U>
where
  for<'a> F: Fn(&'a T) -> &'a U,
  T: std::fmt::Debug
{
  pub name: String,
  pub data: T,
  pub func: F,
}


impl<T, F, U> LoggedFunctionCall<T, F, U>
where
  for<'a> F: Fn(&'a T) -> &'a U,
  T: std::fmt::Debug
{
  fn call<'a>(&'a self) -> &'a U {
      println!("Called '{}' with '{:?}'", self.name, self.data);
      (self.func)(&self.data)
  }
}


fn do_something<'b>(data: &'b (usize, u8)) -> &'b usize {
  &data.0
}


fn main() {
  let logged = LoggedFunctionCall {
      name: "do_something".into(),
      data: (0x5ff, 42),
      func: do_something,
  };
  println!("Result {}", logged.call());
}
```

Running this example yields the following:

```
Called 'do_something' with '(1535, 42)'
Result 1535
```

The snippet contains a lot of things, but the code's goal is to log a call to a function together with the arguments that are passed in. This can be useful for recording runtimes of functions or trace calls. What is important is that we would not be able to write this for every possible combination of lifetimes and argument types—and this is where the higher-ranked trait bounds come in.

The **for<'a> F: Fn(&'a T) -> &'a U** declaration specifies that the lifetime 'a at the time of calling the **Fn** (a function pointer) has to apply. The name of this lifetime does not have to match, so 'a in the declaration could be named anything. Find more examples at doc.rust-lang.org/nomicon/hrtb.html.

The remainder of the snippet is what we already saw in previous examples and includes three type parameters, one for the function and one for the function's input parameters and its outcome. The input parameters have to be **Debug** printable in order for the logging to include it. As for the function pointer, this could also be a closure instead of a declared fn.

One special case is also the type **PhantomData**. In some cases, especially with unsafe programming, the compiler will not be able to verify whether your struct owns the data it points to (via the pointer type ***const T**) or whether a lifetime you declared is being used (see next example). Here, **std::marker::PhantomData** allows you to mark that you either own an instance of **T** or that your type actually needs the lifetime it declared to function properly. This becomes much clearer in an example from the Rust standard library (**IntoIter** is the **Vec<T>** iterator type, see doc.rust-lang.org/src/alloc/vec/into_iter.rs.html):

```rust
// [...]
pub struct IntoIter<
    T,
    #[unstable(feature = "allocator_api", issue = "32838")] A: Allocator
= Global,
> {
    pub(super) buf: NonNull<T>,
    pub(super) phantom: PhantomData<T>,
    pub(super) cap: usize,
    pub(super) alloc: A,
    pub(super) ptr: *const T,
    pub(super) end: *const T,
}
// [...]
```

Here, we see the **IntoIter<T>** struct that a **Vec<T>** uses for a consuming iterator. These are the properties:

- **buf** holds a pointer to the first item.
- **phantom** provides the **PhantomData** so the compiler does not assume **T** can be dropped; thus, **buf, ptr,** and **end** always point to valid memory).

- **cap** is buf's capacity.
- **ptr** is a pointer to the current **item. next()** will move it forward toward the end.
- **end** is the end of items in **buf**, so as soon as **ptr == end**, the iteration stops.

All of this is relevant with unsafe code since operating with pointers and such is not necessarily safe Rust. In fact, it is the compiler trying to make things safe that would drop the data immediately if it were not for the **PhantomData** marker.

For more explanations and examples, check the Rust nomicon page (doc.rust-lang. org/nomicon/phantom-data.html) and docs for **PhantomData** (doc.rust-lang.org/ std/marker/struct.PhantomData.html).

Conclusion

Generics are tricky: many times, they turn out to be surprisingly simple to implement, but when elegant architecture demands more flexibility, those Generics become very complex very quickly. The reason for this sudden increase is typically found in various lifetime requirements and type constraints that surface downstream. Especially in an async context, Send together with a static lifetime is often frustrating.

Generics, in general, are placeholder type names that the compiler replaces with the concrete type when compiling. This allows for checking whether the constraints are met and if there is a specialized implementation for this specific type (**impl App<LazyConfiguration> { ... }**).

A recent addition to the Generics is const Generics, which add the ability to use concrete values for types as if they were literals. This is especially important for arrays that used to require an integer literal to instantiate, whereas now the const Generic parameter will do. For example, in **my_func<const N: usize>()**, you can use the parameter to create an array with length **N**.

Finally, managing explicit lifetimes and **PhantomData** both provide ways for advanced use cases to instruct the compiler about when and how to drop associated data. You will know when you need them.

Let us now turn to the conclusion of the **LinkedList** challenge!

Challenge

This is the second to last challenge, which means that you can almost consider yourself an expert Rust programmer! As such, you should not have any problems in upgrading your linked list one last time using Generics.

Currently, your **LinkedList** looks somewhat like this:

```
enum Link {
  Next(Box<Data>),
  Empty
}


struct Data {
  value: u128,
  next: Link
}


pub struct LinkedList {
  head: Option<Link>
}
```

The data type is **u128**, which is great but will not let us store anything other than unsigned numbers! To finish the implementation of the list, you should replace it with an appropriate type parameter and adjust all the functions you have built over the course of the book. Luckily, your tests and benchmarks should still be working fine, giving you something to double-check your efforts! Here is a skeleton of new the **LinkedList** struct:

```
enum Link<T> {
  Next(Box<Data>),
  Empty
}

struct Data<T> {
  value: T,
  next: Link<T>
}
impl<T> LinkedList<T> {

  pub fn new() -> Self {
    LinkedList { head: None }
  }

  pub fn append(&mut self, value: T) {
    // ...
  }
  pub fn count(&self) -> usize {
    // ...
```

```rust
    }

  pub fn pop(&mut self) -> Option<T> {
      // ...
  }
}

pub struct LinkedList<T> {
  head: Option<Link<T>>
}

##[cfg(test)]
mod tests {
  use super::*;

  #[test]
  fn test_LinkedList_append() {
    let mut list = LinkedList::new();
    list.append(1);
    list.append(2);
    list.append(3);

    assert_eq!(list.count(), 3);
    assert_eq!(list.pop(), Some(3));
    assert_eq!(list.pop(), Some(2));
    assert_eq!(list.pop(), Some(1));
    assert_eq!(list.pop(), None);

    let mut list = LinkedList::new();
    list.append("1");
    list.append("2");
    list.append("3");

    assert_eq!(list.count(), 3);
    assert_eq!(list.pop(), Some("3"));
    assert_eq!(list.pop(), Some("2"));
    assert_eq!(list.pop(), Some("1"));
    assert_eq!(list.pop(), None);
  }
}
```

If you are in the mood, you can also implement a generic iterator and make the sorting work by requiring a trait bound for **std::cmp::PartialOrd**.

CHAPTER 16

Calling Unsafe and Foreign Functions

O ver the course of this book, we explored a lot of concepts and aspects of the safe Rust programming language. In this last chapter, we will expand a bit on the "dark side" of Rust: unsafe. As we discussed earlier in the book, safety is an aspect of memory management that allows the Rust compiler to allocate and free memory on your behalf. unsafe lets you take care of that.

This allows Rust to interact with other native code and interoperate with other programming languages, the LINUX kernel, or even hardware. The drawback of this power is the lack of safeguards, so writing robust and safe software should now be much more on your radar. As a good defensive programmer, you should, therefore, use these powers only when necessary and even then, with caution.

For the last chapter, let us take the seatbelts off.

Structure

In this chapter, we will be covering the following topics:

- Working with unsafe
- Sharing native Rust code
- Importing a shared library

- Binding Rust code

- Exporting as a shared library

Objectives

After finishing this chapter, you will be confidently writing unsafe Rust code and interoperating with external Linux libraries.

Working with unsafe

Rust's unsafe keyword tells the compiler that what follows (for example, a scope or function) will not conform to the usual rules about borrowing and ownership (or, in other words: undefined behavior is now allowed). In these sections, you can work with pointers, read from any memory that the operating system allows you to, but also leak memory, overrun buffers, and do pointer math. The idea behind this unsafe code is that other shared binaries cannot be (borrow-)checked by the compiler, and therefore, you need the tools to work with them.

Additionally, when working with hardware, it is impossible to check for memory safety. Some sensors require you to write to one memory address (that is, leak memory from a compiler's point of view) and then read from a different memory address (technically a buffer overrun) since the device's registers are memory-mapped and look like regular RAM.

Consequently, unsafe code is necessary for advanced use cases—although it is generally better to stick to safe code as much as possible. The Rust team also provides a book called "The Rustnomicon" (a play on the Necronomicon—the book of the dead in H.P. Lovecraft horror novels) with all kinds of unsafe additions at doc.rust-lang.org/nomicon/.

Let us recap, and those are the unsafe powers in Rust:

- Calling unsafe functions.

- Implementing unsafe traits.

- Dereferencing raw pointers.

- Write to memory locations.

- Read from memory locations (for example, fields of unions).

The syntax is straightforward:

```
unsafe fn do_crazy_stuff() {
  // only unsafe code here
}
```

```rust
fn main() {
  unsafe {
    do_crazy_stuff();
    // do more unsafe stuff here
  }
}
```

Within the unsafe section, we can now do all the things that we mentioned, like dereferencing and then writing to memory locations without the Rust compiler complaining (the operating system might, though). Let us see what kind of code we can now produce.

> **Note: As with many things in life, there is a rabbit hole about soundness, trust, and type safety. You will find great discussions that go deep on the language's type system, but this book cannot prepare you for these. Ask the community for resources on the topics you do not understand; rustaceans are known to be helpful and accepting!**

One example is to cast types and use them as their new type:

```rust
use std::sync::mpsc::{Sender, channel};
use std::slice;

unsafe fn unsafe_casting(
    sender_ptr: *mut Sender<u8>,
    data_ptr: *const u8,
    data_len: usize,
) {
  let data: &[u8] = slice::from_raw_parts(data_ptr, data_len);
  let sender: Box<Sender<u8>> = Box::from_raw(sender_ptr);
  for d in data {
    let _ = sender.send(*d);
  }
  std::mem::drop(sender);
}

fn main() {
  let (tx, rx) = channel::<u8>();
  let data = vec![1, 2, 3, 4];
  unsafe {
    let tx_ptr = Box::into_raw(Box::new(tx));
    let data_ptr = data.as_ptr();
```

```
    unsafe_casting(tx_ptr, data_ptr, data.len());
  }
  while let Ok(n) = rx.recv() {
    println!("Received: {}", n);
  }
}
```

The output of this snippet is as follows:

```
Received: 1
Received: 2
Received: 3
Received: 4
```

The snippet shows two core aspects: the `unsafe` scope (wrapper) in the main function and the fully unsafe function that we are calling to mess around with pointers. In this case, the goal is simple: Use a channel to send data from inside the unsafe parts to the safe parts. The example was taken from a real-world problem—sending data from inside an encrypted enclave across threads.

The **unsafe_casting** function uses three parameters:

1. A mutable pointer to Sender<u8>, the sending end of the channel.

2. A const pointer to a u8 which is actually a slice.

3. The length of the data slice in a number of elements.

unsafe casts do not care about the actual data type that much, but it is nice to use the compiler's type checking. Since all pointers are of **usize** length, using it would eliminate all types of information and make unsafe even less safe. Many heap-based types in Rust already feature a raw parts type function that allows a somewhat safe cast into the desired type. Once created, the type instances can be used like any other instance of that type. Therefore, we allocate the sender to the heap, so we can—unsafely—get the heap pointer back and use the inner Sender<u8> type to transfer data to the Receiver waiting outside of the unsafe scope. Dropping the sender instance after the sending is finished also leads to the channel closing and the **recv()** loop to end.

In the excellent book *Learning Rust With Entirely Too Many Linked Lists* (rust-unofficial. github.io/too-many-lists/), there is one implementation of a LinkedList that uses unsafe pointers to improve efficiency. Clearly, pointer swaps are much simpler too when compared to numerous **unwrap()** calls and *if* let statements when working with Options, Arcs, Boxes, and so on. However, using pointers over safe Rust also means not using the benefits of Rust. This is a decision that you have to make for your own specific use case if unsafe gains outweigh the costs of not having a compiler check your code. Check out the unsafe chapter in the book mentioned earlier: rust-unofficial.github.io/too-many-lists/fifth.html.

Let us see how we can use unsafe code to share with libraries from other languages.

Sharing native Rust code

Implementing (UNIX/LINUX) kernel modules, drivers, or using legacy software requires Rust to interact with other native code at a compiled level. Since this is far beyond the compiler's reach for safety checks, we have to resort to raw pointers and fairly unsafe casting to interact with these interfaces.

The same goes for the reverse—if your Rust code is supposed to work together with other software on a binary level, you will have to provide interfaces at the unsafe level as well. There is no way for the Rust compiler to enforce any kind of safety if outside data is in the mix.

The good news is that interacting with the software on a binary level was built into the Rust tools from the start, and the required changes for building a library native to a specific platform are only a matter of configuration (when running on that platform). Rust's compiler uses the **Low-Level Virtual Machine (now called just LLVM)** compiler toolkit as a base to generate byte code. In short, the toolkit consists of two parts, a frontend, and a backend. This decoupling allows an aspiring language to implement only the frontend and get all backends as an inherent benefit. The details of the LLVM project and its components go beyond this book, so let us just look at it from a high level.

A compiler frontend is generally responsible for syntax checking and analysis so it can extract all semantic information for generating the abstract syntax tree and, ultimately, a binary intermediate representation of the program. This happens in a multi-stage process (from rustc-dev-guide.rust-lang.org/overview.html) during compilation:

1. Configure the compiler (flags, command-line arguments, and so on).

2. Lexical analysis that creates tokens:

   • This stage preserves tokens for the language server and IDE.

   • After this stage, it is various forms of bytecode, no more text.

3. Token parsing into an **Abstract Syntax Tree (AST)**.

4. AST validation and macro expansion.

5. **High-Level Intermediate Representation (HIR)** generation.

   • Type inference happens here.

- Loop expansion and other desugaring are done in this stage.

6. Generate the **Mid-Level Intermediate Representation (MIR)**:
   - This stage does borrow checking.
   - Optimize the bytecode.
   - Monomorphize generics.

7. Pass the MIR into the LLVM codegen.

Once the MIR bytecode reaches the LLVM codegen, it is transformed into the LLVM-IR (LLVM intermediate representation), optimized once again, and forwarded to the last stages of compilation and linking. Since these are mostly maintained by the LLVM project, any programming language that compiles to the LLVM-IR can immediately have a range of binary output targets (CPU architectures) and platforms available. Rust (and other languages on the LLVM); therefore, can cross-compile and interoperate with a broad range of available CPU architectures and platform configurations (learn more at rust-lang.github.io/rustup/cross-compilation.html), including WASM (WebAssembly), iPhoneOS, Android, and others. This means you can use Rust to build even web frontends that run in a browser (check rustwasm. github.io/ to learn more).

From a syntax perspective, Rust uses the extern keyword to declare externally linked (or linkable) functions. Thus a function with a body will be exported, whereas a function without a body will be imported. The specific case of extern C specifies to export via the C (the programming language) application binary interface, which is the de-facto standard (read more doc.rust-lang.org/book/ch19-01-unsafe-rust. html#using-extern-functions-to-call-external-code). Here is an example of an exported function. Note that sometimes a **#[no_mangle]** attribute is required so other technology can actually find the function by name:

```
#[no_mangle]
pub extern "C" fn absinput: i32) -> i32 {
  // ...
}
```

Similarly, if a function is coming from external code, the interface just lacks a body. Here, we also see a different way of declaring one or more functions that ought to be imported:

```
extern "C" {
    fn abs(input: i32) -> i32;
}
```

An extern declaration also implies that the function is unsafe, so calling any of the preceding functions needs to be within an `unsafe` context. Let us see how this works in practice.

Importing a shared library

Only a few large projects have the luxury of starting from scratch—most software has to build on some pre-existing code. This is why many libraries offer bindings for a core binary they maintain, which is typically also natively compiled. Unlike Rust, however, many higher-level abstractions require significant work to maintain (for example, to add required type metadata). With Rust, these bindings are very close to what C/C++ has as header files. In those, the developer specifies function headers and types, so when the compiler links the native binary, all function calls line up.

Let us look at the usual steps required to import a shared library:

1. Compile the library's source code or have a precompiled library with headers.

2. Generate Rust bindings.

3. Use from your Rust code.

Steps 1 and 2 can also be included in your build scripts to compile the code and generate bindings on the fly (read more on that doc.rust-lang.org/cargo/reference/build-scripts.html).

Let us look at how you can use bindgen to generate Rust code.

Binding Rust code

Writing bindings by hand is usually not a feasible option, so the Rust team provides a tool called `bindgen` to automate the process. Like most other projects in Rust, it comes with its own book at rust-lang.github.io/rust-bindgen/, and we will cover some of the contents here.

The `bindgen` project has two primary modes of operation, as an API and as a binary. The API mode lets you add the code generation to the build script and generate Rust files on a build that you can dynamically import.

Alternatively, you can use the binary directly, which is as simple as cargo install bindgen and then using **bindgen input-header.h -o output-rust.rs** on the command line to read input-**header.h** to generate **output-rust.rs**. Whichever way you choose, the result is the same; you have to include the resulting Rust source file in your project to get the data structures, functions, and tests to work with your code. Since the file might end up somewhere hidden in a dependency directory, the easiest way to get the code into your project is to use the `include!` macro which includes a file before compilation:

```
include!(concat!(env!("OUT_DIR"), "/bindings.rs"));
```

```
pub fn my_func() {
  use_some_function_from_bindings();
}
```

Let us consider a short C header (**wmath.h**) file that we are going to create bindings from:

```
#ifndef WMATH_H_
#define WMATH_H_

void add(int a, int b);

void multiply(int a, int b);

#endif // WMATH_H_
```

A corresponding source file (**wmath.c**) looks like that:

```
void add(int a, int b)
{
    printf("%d + %d = %d\n", a, b, a + b);
}

void multiply(int a, int b)
{
    printf("%d * %d = %d\n", a, b, a * b);
}
```

Using a C compiler, the **wmath.c** file will be compiled to a shared static (or dynamic) library that we can link to the Rust code. The header file is usually distributed as plaintext alongside the (compiled) sources, so this is bindgen's input for generating our Rust file. Note that we will not cover compiling C code in this book—just assume that the binary output of **wmath.c** can be linked to the Rust code. Alternatively, take a close look at the bindgen book mentioned earlier.

Once we have this header file, you can run bindgen on it to get a Rust file that allows you to include and just use the functions and structs in a header file. By running **bindgen wmath.h -o bindings.rs**, you get the following code:

```
/* automatically generated by rust-bindgen 0.59.2 */
```

```
extern "C" {
    pub fn add(a: ::std::os::raw::c_int, b: ::std::os::raw::c_int);
}
extern "C" {
    pub fn multiply(a: ::std::os::raw::c_int, b: ::std::os::raw::c_int);
}
```

You then can include this file in your **main.rs** file as mentioned preceding using the include! macro (CARGO_MANIFEST_DIR is a variable populated by cargo doc.rust-lang.org/cargo/reference/environment-variables.html#configuration-environment-variables). Note that the functions are not explicitly marked unsafe either, extern does that implicitly (see also doc.rust-lang.org/std/keyword.extern.html).

```
include!(concat!(env!("CARGO_MANIFEST_DIR"), "/bindings.rs"));

fn main() {
  unsafe {
    add(1, 2);
    multiply(2, 2);
  }
}
```

Finally, the linker needs to know about the C library so it can include the binary properly, so there is a **build.rs** file that informs the build process via **stdout** (see also doc.rust-lang.org/cargo/reference/build-scripts.html):

```
use std::env::var;

fn main() {
  let project_dir = var("CARGO_MANIFEST_DIR").unwrap();
  println!("cargo:rustc-link-search={}/../wmath/target", project_dir);
  println!("cargo:rustc-link-lib=static=wmath");
}
```

With **cargo** run, we finally get this output:

```
    Finished dev [unoptimized + debuginfo] target(s) in 0.00s
     Running `target/debug/wmath-rust`
1 + 2 = 3
2 * 2 = 4
```

Figure 16.1: *Unsafe math with generated C bindings*

This is to provide a glimpse into how Rust is interoperable at a binary level and how you can use this to do things like replacing legacy code module by module or simply use software packages from other vendors (like 3D engines). Transitioning legacy software can also happen the other way around, so let us look at how you can create native libraries using `cargo` and Rust.

Exporting as shared library

Using Rust from any language that supports interoperating with native shared libraries (**.dll** on Windows, **.dynlib** on MacOS, **.so** on LINUX/UNIX) is a matter of only two major aspects:

- Making function names discoverable (no name mangling and exporting them).

- Change the binary output format to a shared library.

After that, you can use the resulting library from any language that supports this kind of interoperability. Examples are C/C++, Python, C#, or Java—so most major languages have an easy-to-use wrapper for these imports.

Internally, however, Rust code has to produce usable types for the other languages to interpret the data correctly. This is important for complex data beyond numerics or Booleans since a wrong interpretation can result in array overruns or other invalid memory reads on the consumer's side—Rust's safety system does not apply there. Let us look at an example where we produce a SHA256 digest of an incoming message. This library should be consumed from a simple C program.

> **Note: These examples are a lot easier on UNIX/LINUX systems. If you want to try out this code on Windows, use the Linux Subsystem For Windows—WSL. Read more at docs.microsoft.com/en-us/windows/wsl/install.**

Let us start off with some Rust code:

```rust
use std::ffi::{CStr, CString};
use std::os::raw::{c_char, c_void};

use ring::digest;

#[no_mangle]
pub extern "C" fn sha256_digest(data: *mut c_char) -> *mut c_char {
  unsafe {
    let data = CStr::from_ptr(data);
    let signature = digest::digest(&digest::SHA256, data.to_bytes());
    let hex_digest = signature
```

```
        .as_ref()
        .iter()
        .map(|b| format!("{:X}", b))
        .collect::<String>();

    CString::new(hex_digest).unwrap().into_raw()
  }
}
```

The snippet includes `ring`, an external crate for all kinds of encryption tasks. This library is fully written in Rust and can therefore be embedded into the resulting binary—other native dependencies would have been dynamically linked to the program giving us a bigger headache. Similarly, we are going to build a static shared library (as opposed to a dynamic one) to simplify the linking process. Here is the **Cargo.toml** file where we specify the output (different types of outputs can be found at doc.rust-lang.org/reference/linkage.html or doc.rust-lang.org/cargo/reference/cargo-targets.html#the-crate-type-field):

```toml
[package]
name = "sha256-digest"
version = "0.1.0"
edition = "2021"

[lib]
name = "sha256digest"
crate-type = ["staticlib"]

[dependencies]
ring = "0.16"
```

The recipient or user of that **sha256-digest** library (on Linux, **libsha256digest.a**) is a simple C program with an extern declaration for the function coming from the Rust library. The linker throws an error if no function with a matching signature can be found, even though we are using C native types here. Since C has had a major influence on the Rust programming language, here is the code to import a function from Rust into C. After all the Rust code, you will certainly see the similarities:

```c
#include <stdio.h>

// This Rust function is linked to the project
extern char* sha256_digest(char *str);

int main() {
```

```
char *result = sha256_digest("Learn Rust Programming");
printf("SHA256 digest of \"Learn Rust Programming\": %s", result);
return 0;
}
```

The last thing to note is the Makefile to compile the C code and link the files together. Since Make is an automation tool that has volumes written about it, we will not cover the linking here. You can read more at gnu.org/software/make/. After compiling and linking it to the Rust output, here is what the code prints:

```
$ ./main
SHA256 digest of "Learn Rust Programming":
1CE88A88ECCC9C7E5B5A1B8BC957BFD74B5C04C8E786BD8C9274151E9
```

What we will cover is Rust's output—if you initialize a crate with the Rust code and **Cargo.toml** preceding, the compilation process creates a target/debug directory as follows:

```
$ ls target/debug
build    deps    examples    incremental    libsha256digest.a
libsha256digest.d
```

There we see the output file **libsha256digest.a**, which can be used by anything that can use static libraries (on Linux). Let us recap: In Rust, we can export functions using the extern C declaration with a function body attached to it. The types that are being used in such a function internally do not matter as long as the interfaces conform to the expectations of the importing language, which will almost always be C-like. Consequently, parameter types and return types are expected to be in this format, or the recipient will complain. Their collections are unlikely to look like Rust's **Vec<T>**.

The other major factor is the binary output configuration in the **Cargo.toml** file. Other values in crate-type than the default (**rlib**) will also result in different outputs, **staticlib** or **cdylib**/**dylib** are typically used for native code sharing. Note that for dynamic linking, you can use bindgen to generate the header files required to import in C/C++ and other languages.

Rust's binary output is—since it is a natively compiled language—compatible with the operating system's standard for libraries, so anything that can work with these can work with Rust.

Conclusion

Over the course of this book, we have taken a deep dive into the Rust programming language, and while it is a very popular language, it is far from the only one. If you want to become a great engineer, you will have to go beyond a single language—even if Rust really is a great tool.

Part of what makes it great is also the ability to interoperate with existing technologies, something that provides a powerful lever for using Rust in large and small projects. People are writing operating systems, kernel modules, Web servers, and web frontends—all of which need some kind of interoperability.

The basis for Rust's interoperability is the LLVM backend that can produce a range of binary outputs. The most common one is the platform's native application binary interface, but there is also WebAssembly (WASM) to run in the browser. Regardless of the actual output, Rust uses an `extern "C"` declaration to import and export functions.

Once declared, the function has to be linked to its consumer, which often requires bindings in the target language. Although those can be generated (along with required data structures), the Rust compiler cannot ensure safety around these parts, so extern declarations are always unsafe to call. The last step is linking the binaries together, which is something the build script (when linking to Rust) or the **Cargo. toml** (when linking from somewhere else) have to configure.

Since this is the last chapter in this book, we will not have a specific challenge for you. Instead, you should go out and find a project to work on—be it your own or a contribution to someone else's. In the following section, we have some interesting (and challenging) suggestions. Have fun!

Further reading

Rust has a very active community that is busy porting libraries and tools, re-implementing common software, and just having fun.

- For a biased list of projects, check out this awesome-Rust list: github.com/ rust-unofficial/awesome-rust.

- Furthermore, the Rust community has events (online, offline, local, and global), a very well-written code of conduct, and a range of places for daily chats. You can find links to the most recent ones at rust-lang.org/community as well as reddit.com/r/rust.

- Finally, the author has a blog for working through the occasional Rust project at blog.x5ff.xyz. See you there.

Index

A

Abstract Syntax Tree (AST) 235
alternatives
  using 195
async code
  writing 201
async-std
  blocking code, running 212-214
  using 206-208
  working asynchronously 208-212
attribute macros
  code, extending with 167, 168

B

balanced binary tree data structure 88
benchmarking 137
blocking code 212-214
Boolean algebra 15
borrowing 64, 68

example 69
Box 174, 175
  behavior 176, 177
  data, boxing 175
  trait object 176
  type, using in 175
BTreeMap 89
BTreeSet 89
bubble sort algorithm 22, 23
build manifest
  writing 119-121

C

cargo 115
  build, customizing 126, 127
  build manifest, writing 119-121
  crates, creating with 116-119
  exploring 125, 126
  third-party crates, adding 121-124

workspaces, for large projects 127, 128

cargo test command 135

clones 75

  implementing 76

collect() function 94

collection

  iterating over 92, 93

command-line arguments 111

  using 112

compilation 2, 3

concurrent code

  running 189

conditions

  using 14-16

configuration options, for
    programs 111

  command-line arguments,
    using 111, 112

  environment variables,
    using 112, 113

count references, heap
    memory 177-179

  with multi-threading 179, 180

Criterion 140

D

declarative macros 158, 159

  arguments, using with names
    and designators 159, 160

  complexity, adding to
    arguments 160-162

  exporting 162, 163

dependencies section 121

derive macros 165-167

documentation, Rust code

  generating 146, 147

  links, using 147-149

  publishing 152

section, using 147-149

  tests, writing 149-151

dynamic dispatch 176

dynamic typing

  versus, static typing 5

E

enumerate() function 93

enums 52

  errors handling with 54, 55

  pattern matching, for extracting
    data 56-59

  variations, creating with 52, 53

environment variables 112

  using 112, 113

expressions 17

F

filter() function 93

First-In-First-Out (FIFO) 196

fold() function 93

for loop 21

  using 22, 23

formatting 108, 109

  custom types, printing 110, 111

  options 109

function-like macros

  writing 164, 165

functions 28

  behavior, encapsulating with 28, 29

  combining, with structs 32-34

  parameterizing 30

futures

  polling 203, 204

futures-rs

  using 205, 206

G

Generics 217
  const Generics, using 224, 225
  enums, parameterizing 221-223
  exploring 223, 224
  functions, parameterizing 219, 220
  lifetimes, working with 225-228
  structs, parameterizing 221-223
  traits, parameterizing 221-223
  using 218, 219

H

HashMap 90
HashSet 90
heap memory
  Box 174
  counting references 177-179
  mutability, creating 181-183
  working with 66-68

I

if condition
  evaluation, to false 16, 17
if/else expression
  using 17, 18
if expression 14
impl block 33
impl trait 50
integer literal 11
integration tests 136
interior mutability, using 181
interior mutability pattern 183
IntoIterator trait 47, 49
I/O streams
  console 103, 108
  file systems 103
  formatting print, using 108, 109

  networking 103-107
  reading from 102, 103
  writing to 102, 103
iteration 21
  performing, over collection 92, 93
  results, collecting 94, 95
iterators
  chaining 93, 94
Iterator trait 47, 93

K

keys
  deriving from values,
    with sets and maps 87
  sorting 88-90

L

Last In, First Out (LIFO) 66
literals 11
LLVM
  URL 3
locks
  for global mutability 183, 185
loop 19
  breaking, with values 19-21
  continuing, with values 19-21
  for loop 21
  while loop 23, 24

M

map() function 93
maps 90
  using 90, 91
match expression 56
memory
  borrowing 68, 69
  heap memory 66

owning 64, 65

stack memory 66

memory management 4

dynamic, versus static typing 4, 5

modules

aliases, using 41, 42

exporting 37-40

importing 37-40

types, accessing 41, 42

multi-threaded interior
mutability 183, 185

mutability

controlling 72-75

mutable variables 74

N

native Rust code

shared library, exporting 240-242

shared library, importing 237

sharing 235, 236

networking streams 102

O

ownership 64

memory, owning 64, 65

rules 64

P

pattern matching 45

for data extraction 56-59

procedural macros 163, 164

attribute macros 167, 168

derive macros 165-167

function-like macros 164, 165

programming, in Rust 6

literals 11

memory management 6, 7

Rust code, writing 7, 8

variable types, working with 8-11

R

Random Access Memory (RAM) 6

read() function 102

reuse 27

Rust 2

programming 6

threading, with 190-193

Rust code

benchmarking 137-140

binding 237-240

compiling 2, 3

documenting 146, 147

executing 5, 6

integration testing 136, 137

testing 132

unit testing 133-136

S

scopes 69

working 70-72

Send marker trait

using 193, 194

sequential collections

slice 82

using 82

Vec<T> 82

sets 87

using 90, 91

shadowing 73

simple echo server implementation 104

slice 82

stack memory 66

working with 67, 68

static dispatch 176

String 36
String literal 11
structs
  adding, in Rust 35-37
  behavior, encapsulating with 30, 31
  combining, with functions 32-34
  exploring 34
Sync marker trait
  using 193, 194

T
tasks
  scheduling in loop 202, 203
tests 132
  integration tests 136
  unit tests 133
third-party crates
  adding 121-123
threading
  with Rust 190-193
threads
  bridging, with channels 196-198
trait object 50, 176
traits 45
  implementing 48, 49
  using 46, 47
  using, in functions 49-51
type alias
  using 42

U
unit tests 133
unsafe
  working with 232-234
unsafe_casting function
  parameters 234

V
variable shadowing 73
variations
  creating, with enums 52, 53
Vec<T> 82
  borrowing 85, 86
  elements, accessing 85
  elements, adding 84
  elements, removing 84
  initialization 83
  operating 83
versioning 123

W
while loop 23, 24
workspace, cargo
  creating 127, 128
  using, for large projects 127
write() function 103

Made in United States
North Haven, CT
16 November 2022

26818205R00148